D0207465

Understanding Peasant China

Daniel Little

Understanding Peasant China

Case Studies in the Philosophy of
Social Science

YALE UNIVERSITY PRESS   New Haven and London

305.563
L77u

Published with assistance from the Louis Stern Memorial Fund.

Copyright © 1989 by Yale University.

All rights reserved.

This book may not be reproduced, in whole or in part, including illustrations, in any form (beyond that copying permitted by Sections 107 and 108 of the U.S. Copyright Law and except by reviewers for the public press), without written permission from the publishers.

Set in Trump Roman type by The Composing Room of Michigan.

Printed in the United States of America by BookCrafters, Inc., Chelsea, Michigan.

Library of Congress Cataloging-in-Publication Data

Little, Daniel.

  Understanding peasant China : case studies in the philosophy of social science / Daniel Little.

    p. cm.

  Bibliography: p.

  Includes index.

  ISBN 0–300–04399–6

  1. Peasantry—China.   2. Marketing—China.   3. Transportation—China.   4. Regionalism—China.   5. Agriculture—Economic aspects—China.   6. Peasant uprisings—China—History.   7. Social sciences—China.   I. Title.

HD1537.C5L58 1989

305.5′63—dc19

88–37233

CIP

MB

The paper in this book meets the guidelines for permanence and durability of the Committee on Production Guidelines for Book Longevity of the Council on Library Resources.

10 9 8 7 6 5 4 3 2 1

For Ronnie, Joshua, and Rebecca

UNIVERSITY LIBRARIES
CARNEGIE-MELLON UNIVERSITY
PITTSBURGH, PENNSYLVANIA 15213

Contents

Figures, Tables, and Maps

Acknowledgments

This book could not have reached completion without generous support, advice, and comments from scholars within the Asian studies disciplines discussed here. I am particularly grateful to Paul Cohen, Prasenjit Duara, Lloyd Eastman, Joseph Esherick, Philip Huang, David Hunt, Bill Joseph, Sucheta Mazumdar, Ramon Myers, Peter Perdue, Dwight Perkins, Samuel Popkin, James Scott, Vivienne Shue, Tam Tai, and David Washbrook for their comments and advice at various stages of this project. I have also received welcome comments and criticisms from other philosophers, including Josh Cohen, Owen Flanagan, Russell Hardin, Jeff Poland, Michael Taylor, and Ken Winkler. I am grateful to my Colgate colleagues Gloria Bien for her help in correcting the pinyinization of Chinese place names throughout the manuscript and Tom Fogarty for extensive comments on chapter 3. Meticulous copyediting was provided by Laura Jones Dooley.

The bulk of this book was written during my two-and-a-half-year stay at Wellesley College. I warmly thank colleagues in the Philosophy Department there for the friendship and stimulation they provided. I am grateful for institutional support provided by Colgate University and Wellesley College, and for the research time provided for me by Colgate University's sabbatical program. The final six months of composition were supported by a generous research grant from the National Science Foundation within the History and Philosophy of Science program.

Portions of chapters 2 and 3 have appeared in the *Journal of Agricultural Ethics* and the *Journal of Asian Studies*. Versions of chapters 3, 4, and 5 were presented to the Fairbank China Seminar series, the New England Association for Asian Studies, and the New England Historical Association, respectively. Comments received on these occasions have strengthened the arguments in these chapters.

Chapter 1
Preliminaries

This is a philosophical book, and one about agrarian change within Asian peasant societies. This combination is unusual enough to need preliminary stage-setting. Why is a philosopher writing about peasant collective action, marketing hierarchies, and the stagnation of traditional Chinese farming? The most direct answer is that I am a philosopher of social science, which means that I am interested in foundational questions about the logic of the social sciences: What is a good explanation of social phenomena? How are theoretical models used in the social sciences? What are the main features of empirical reasoning in social science? What role does quantitative reasoning play in social science? And so on. These are traditional questions in the philosophy of science. But I am convinced that it is desirable to pose these questions not in the abstract but in the context of current social science practice. So I have selected a handful of current social science debates and have subjected them to a full-scale examination in light of these sorts of foundational questions. I hope the results will constitute a useful contribution to our understanding of the logic of social inquiry.

This answers part of the above question. But it does not explain why I have selected these *particular* debates; my goals as a philosopher of social science could be served through studying any collection of rich controversies in the social sciences. So again, why peasants and agrarian change as opposed to countless other areas of social science research today? And why Asian rather than European peasant societies? My focus on agrarian change stems from the intrinsic interest of the subject. First, I am interested in assessing the power and scope of rational choice models of social explanation. In general, the program for rational choice theory is this: to explain a variety of social phenomena as the aggregate outcome of the rational decision making and action of the individuals who constitute those phenomena. This model has been used to explain many phenomena within modern industrialized society: voter behavior, strikes and boycotts, contribution levels to providers of public goods (for example, public television), and the like. But agrarian societies have not often been analyzed from this point of view, although agrarian change would appear a valuable test case. Peasants are presented with readily discernible choices in their economic and political lives: what crops to plant, what techniques to use, whether to provide labor for a village work project, whether to join in a rent strike, whether to support a call for rebellion. To what extent can we understand peasant behavior as a rational effort to fulfill their goals through their choices? And to what extent can we understand agrarian phenomena as the aggregate result of such rational decisions?

A second concern that drew me to the topic of agrarian change is my previous work on Marxism and historical materialism (*The Scientific Marx*, 1986). Marx offered a basis for understanding historical change in terms of objective factors—technology, class conflict, modes of production, and the economic structure of society. This model has been applied extensively to the emergence and development of European capitalism. But classical Marxist theory has a distinctly urban, industrial slant; the constructs of historical materialism have been less fully applied to agrarian societies. (Recall Marx's dismissal of the French peasantry as a "sack of potatoes.") And yet agrarian societies would seem to represent a particularly interesting test case for historical materialism. Economic relations in peasant society are simple, the class system transparent, and the technologies—cultivation techniques and craft skills—have obvious effects on the everyday lives of participants. It would seem that if the categories of historical materialism are useful anywhere, they should be in the analysis of agrarian society. Is it possible to explain agrarian change as the result of class conflict? Do agrarian societies embody "modes of production" that develop through a dynamic of conflict between forces and relations of production? It seemed plausible that a study of agrarian change would shed light on the value of historical materialism as a program of research for social science.

By focusing on agrarian societies, then, I hoped to be able to test two general frameworks of social explanation—rational-choice theory and historical materialism. It emerges from these cases that both frameworks survive but require substantial elaboration. Classical Marxism suffers the most in application to agrarian society; it emerges that a wider range of causal variables are at work in agrarian change than this framework predicts. And in some cases, social factors that, according to the theory, ought to be secondary—such as lineage and kinship relations—emerge as primary. The world of agrarian change is more complex and diverse than classical Marxism predicts. Rational-choice theory, too, confronts a more complex world: peasant economic and political behavior is influenced by norms and values in unexpected ways, and the social effects of rational deliberation are more sensitive to the institutional context of deliberation. At the same time, both materialism and rational-choice theory emerge as fruitful research frameworks to analyze and explain agrarian change.

A final pair of concerns has led me to focus on *Asian* peasant societies. First is an interest in cultural relativism and social generalization. Are there social processes at work in societies that transcend cultural boundaries? Or, must each culture and its social phenomena be understood sui generis? My assumption has been that patterned regularities may be identified across cultures—for example, the importance of land tenure arrangements to explain rural unrest. But the best way to consider such questions, it has seemed to me, has been to focus on non-Western societies, because the central theories that have been offered to explain social change have been based largely on the European historical experience. If it emerges that through these theories we can identify comparable processes of change in Asian societies, this is a blow for some degree of crosscultural regularities.

Second is the intrinsic interest and importance of China—the main Asian culture considered here. An empire whose longevity dwarfed the Roman Empire, an economy that towered over the medieval European system, a scientific culture that predated the European Renaissance, a rebellion (the Taiping) whose social costs greatly exceeded its North American contemporary, the terrible American Civil War, and a revolution that culminated in the first conquest of power by a party representing a militant peasantry—China represents something akin to a laboratory for social science. By focusing on China, it is possible to raise and discuss virtually any problem of social inquiry and to discover extensive empirical data on the basis of which to evaluate hypotheses.

I hope that several groups will read this book. First among these are scholars within empirical Asian studies—historians and economists of China, political scientists, and anthropologists. The study of agrarian societies is inherently interdisciplinary, encompassing theories and research from a range of empirical social sciences. Investigators in these areas may find it useful to see a philosopher's analysis of the logic and presuppositions of important theoretical contributions in their fields.

Philosophers should also benefit from a selective but detailed look at some of the most interesting and fruitful work being done today in social science. Philosophers have a professional interest in many topics I discuss: the theory of rationality, effectiveness of norms and values in regulating behavior, logic of explanation, role of empirical data in social science, and nature of generalization in the human sciences. And since I believe that philosophy is at its best when its abstract, spare analysis is complemented by knowledge of appropriate bits of the world, I hope that philosophers will take an interest in the empirical phenomena presented here.

Finally, this book should interest scholars concerned with agrarian change in the premodern world. The questions that underlie the research I discuss are intrinsically interesting and important: Why is it difficult to modernize traditional agriculture rapidly? What leads to rural unrest and rebellion? How effective are the institutions of community in premodern societies? How do the constraints of commercialization structure social development and culture? How important are religious and moral values in explaining individual behavior?

At the core of this book are four case studies: examinations of the empirical and theoretical arguments contained in controversies in current social science to analyze the logic of explanation and empirical analysis of each. I then discuss general topics in the philosophy of social science: the character of generalizations in social science, the logical character of social explanation, and the nature of empirical reasoning in social science.

The Cases

The Moral Economy Debate

What relative weights do (1) moral values and group solidarity and (2) individual rationality and competition have in explaining important features of agrarian societies in Southeast Asia? James Scott holds that peasant communities are integrated by a shared subsistence ethic (a moral economy) that protects the subsistence needs of all villagers. Samuel Popkin holds instead that Vietnamese peasants are rational decision makers concerned primarily with family security and welfare and that free-rider problems and competition soon undermine group solidarity.

The Macroregions Debate

How did economic constraints (such as transport cost) affect social, political, and cultural developments in traditional agrarian China? G. William Skinner argues that the villages, market towns, and cities of traditional China were knit into separate urban-rural systems (macroregions) with specific spatial features. He further holds that the structure of these macroregions imposes both constraints and impetus on the development of noneconomic features of traditional Chinese society—for example, the diffusion of heterodox religions, the spread of rebellion, and the administrative capacities of the traditional state. Against Skinner, Barbara Sands and Ramon Myers argue that available economic data do not support the macroregions analysis.

The Breakthrough Debate

What impeded technical innovation in traditional Chinese agriculture? Why did the Chinese rural economy not break through into a process of modern economic growth? Kang Chao argues that rural China was caught in a demographic trap that pushed poor farmers into inefficient, labor-absorbing techniques of agriculture. Victor Lippit holds that the rural economy was capable of creating a significant surplus that could have funded agricultural innovation but that a rentier class that had no material interest in innovation appropriated this surplus. The Chinese rural economy thus stagnated because no rural class had both the incentive and the political capacity to reorganize property rights for the capitalist farm to emerge.

The Peasant Rebellion Debate

What led peasants into violent collective action and rebellion in traditional rural China? And what facilitated or impeded the spread of rebellion? Susan Naquin analyzes the Eight Trigrams rebellion as a manifestation of the millenarian worldview of the White Lotus sect. Elizabeth Perry explains the Nian rebellion as the unintended consequence of local strategies of survival based on local collective action (banditry and village militias). Robert Marks analyzes peasant support for the Nationalist Revolution in Haifeng county as a consequence of local class conflict and the shared interests of tenants against landlords.

I have selected these cases around the theme of agrarian change, a topic that cuts across disciplinary boundaries. This subject is of intrinsic interest, since most of the world's population, past and present, has lived within agrarian societies. Whether one is interested in economic development, rebellion and revolution, or the survival of traditional ways, problems of agrarian change are of central importance. A unifying set of concerns thus weaves through the cases considered here and makes it likely that the cases will interact usefully.

Each case is central to current studies of Asian peasant societies. The authors provide paradigms and theories that other researchers have applied to new contexts. Skinner's analysis of marketing hierarchies has reshaped the landscape that historians of China now confront; researchers have adopted the terms of the moral economy debate in a range of area studies; Perry's analysis of peasant rebellion as the unintended outcome of local survival strategies has altered the way that other investigators conceive of rural collective action; and so forth. These theories have shaped the debate within current empirical Asian studies.

The cases also illuminate problems about the logic of social science. The moral economy debate raises issues concerning the role of rational decision-making models in applied social science and problems about how social science should analyze norms and values. Skinner's treatment of the market structure of traditional China is an important example of the use of formal mathematical models in social science. Kang Chao's analysis of the land–man ratio in China illustrates the role of economic reasoning in historical explanation. Competing theories of peasant rebellion illustrate problems of causal reasoning in cases of large-scale social phenomena and raise questions related to collective action theory. These cases also span many disciplines: history, economic history, anthropology, and political science. Finally, they display first-rate research, analysis, and theory formation, amply repaying scrutiny by a philosopher of social science.

Although each case derives from a different disciplinary matrix, range of empirical data and cases, and explanatory models, the cases interact substantially. All concern aspects of traditional agrarian societies; all involve China or Southeast Asia; most seek to explain peasant behavior (economic, political, or symbolic). Finally, the theories are intertwined with cross-references. Naquin, Marks, and Perry use Skinner's marketing-hierarchy models; Marks employs the moral economy framework to analyze nineteenth-century rural violence in South China; Perry's work has suggestive parallels to Popkin's; and so forth.

What questions will elicit information from the cases relevant to the philosophy of science? The central purpose of the case-study method is to allow examination of the practice of science to suggest the right questions to pose within the philosophy of science, rather than forcing the cases into predetermined categories. This requires an open-minded stance concerning the issues that turn up. Nonetheless, a core set of topics has proved useful in examining these controversies. (Not all these questions, of course, are applied fully to each case.)

Scope of Research

How does the investigator define the scope of research goals? How general or specific are the phenomena under study? A range of levels of generality is possible in social research; in the case of rebellion, for example, the investigator may consider peasant rebellion in general, Chinese peasant rebellion, millenarian Chinese peasant rebellion, or the Eight Trigrams rebellion in its unique particularity. Some investigators (chiefly historians and anthropologists) limit their inquiries narrowly and are suspicious of generalizations beyond the phenomena in question, whereas others (often political scientists and sociologists) study concrete phenomena to understand more general social processes (often across cultures and times).

Theoretical Models

What theoretical models and paradigms does the investigator bring to the subject? Each investigator approaches concrete phenomena—explicitly or tacitly—with theoretical tools to analyze and explain the phenomena. Popkin brings collective action theory to bear on traditional Vietnamese village life; Naquin applies Hobsbawm's construct of the millenarian rebellion to the White Lotus uprisings; Marks employs the premises of classical Marxism to explain Chinese peasant political behavior; Skinner applies the models of central place theory to the economic geography of China; and so forth.

Explanatory Models

What types of explanation does the investigator advance? Two questions follow: What factors (for example, economic, religious, ecological, structural) does the investigator identify in explanations? And what are the logical and pragmatic features of the explanations the investigator puts forward? Popkin, for example, offers abstract deductive explanations within the framework of rational choice theory. Naquin regards a detailed narrative of events and motives as an adequate explanation of the occurrence of a social event. Scott explains details of the subsistence ethic by showing its functional relation to the circumstances of marginal peasant cultivation. My discussion of the cases makes explicit significant differences among these explanation-schemata.

Assumptions about Individual Motivation

What assumptions does the investigator make about the motivations and process of decision making of those whose actions constitute the social phenomena in question? In particular, how does the investigator weigh individual rationality, traditional norms and values, symbolic behavior, and other springs of action? Popkin emphasizes individual rationality, whereas Naquin selects religious worldview and values as primary factors to explain rebellion. Such differences give rise to substantial contrasts in focus of research, explanatory strategies, and expectations about collective behavior.

Assumptions about Collective Behavior

How does the investigator analyze problems of collective action and the relation between individual and group? Some authors (for example, Popkin and Perry) raise problems of collective rationality and emphasize the political difficulties of securing collective action; others (for example, Scott and Naquin) assume that norms and values coordinate collective action effectively, so that collective action is relatively easy to achieve.

Empirical Practice

What is the investigator's empirical method? What data sources are emphasized—archival narrative material, economic statistics, interviews and fieldwork, secondary sources, or other data? How does the investigator employ empirical data to support a position, to criticize or evaluate competing positions, and so on? And what critical problems appear in the investigator's data? The way an investigator approaches and selects empirical data differs substantially between disciplines (such as history and political science).

Critical Assessment of Arguments

Finally, in each case close attention is needed to the logic of the investigator's arguments and analyses. Problems differ from case to case: a sensitive study must be alert to the possibility of an argument going wrong, a theoretical model being applied in a formally invalid way, or an inference being made from data that do not support the conclusion. My critique of Skinner's urbanization argument is such a case; I argue that his construction contains logical problems concerning the measurement and aggregation of causal factors.

A progressive order emerges from the four cases. I study peasant mentality and village institutions in chapter 2 and the structures inherent in village, market, and city relations in chapter 3. In chapter 4 I move to the level of the agrarian economy as a whole and examine relations among systems of land tenure, population increase, and economic and technological development. And in chapter 5 I return to the peasant and village and ask what provokes peasant political activity and rebellion.

The Philosophy of Social Science

The philosophy of social science sets itself varied tasks: to describe the chief logical features of social explanations, to analyze the relation between evidence and theory in social science, to consider the relation between social science and natural science, and to account for some of the distinctive constructs in use in social explanation (for example, rationality, social laws, moral values, or social structures). Most generally, philosophers aim to produce an account of the logic of the social sciences: the form of knowledge and explanation to be found in the social sciences, nature of empirical reasoning, logical character of concepts in the social sciences, and so forth.[1]

This description contains several ambiguities, however. First, it requires that we address the distinction between descriptive and normative philosophy of science. Is the aim of the philosophy of science to describe accurately the practices, institutions, and norms that actually guide social scientists? In this case, the task of the philosopher of science is similar to that of the linguist who attempts to determine the grammatical rules that underlie speech. (This analogy tacitly assumes that science is a rule-governed practice.) Or, is the aim to provide an epistemologically satisfactory account of how science *should* be practiced—whether or not working scientists actually do their work in this manner? If we take this approach, then the task of the philosopher of science is more like that of the logician who attempts to account for all the rules of valid deductive inference (whether or not human reasoners actually observe these rules fully).

I take the view that the philosophy of science requires *both* descriptive and normative elements. Science is not a pursuit whose methods can be determined a priori; rather, it is a set of practices that have developed within a particular historical tradition and institutions, with the aim of discovering truths about nature and society on the basis of empirical investigation. Consequently, the subject matter of the philosophy of science is a contingent set of practices and institutions that the philosopher of science must consider in detail. At the same time, the aims of these practices are epistemic. Scientists attempt to arrive at *true* beliefs about the world, and these beliefs are thought to be *justified* on the basis of the empirical methods of scientific research and evaluation embodied in scientific practices. Consequently, it is essential that the philosophy of science assess the methods and practices of science. Are there good reasons to believe that the methods of a particular area of science are truth enhancing? Could those methods be improved? On this approach, then, the goals of the philosophy of science require that the philosopher provide a rational reconstruction of the practice of scientists so as to raise questions about the truth and warrant of scientific claims. This represents the normative face of the philosophy of science.

Another ambiguity contained in the characterization above concerns the scope of claims in the philosophy of science. Some philosophers have posed the problem of the logic of science in a global, foundationalist form.[2] They undertook to provide a reconstruction of scientific knowledge on a solid basis, with self-evident observations at the foundation, girders of symbolic logic supporting higher-level theoretical claims, and an abstract and universal scientific method of research and justification guiding the construction as a whole. This vision of the philosophy of science is untenable, however. A generation of philosophers of science have demonstrated that no such foundation exists. All observations are theory laden; any body of empirical claims may be contested or overturned; and there is no reason to believe that a single "scientific method" underlies and determines all scientific research.

In place of these global aims, I assume a localistic philosophy of science. My focal question is not, "How does empirical evidence justify scientific knowledge?" but rather, "How credible are the procedures and arguments advanced in resolving a given empirical dispute?" The aim of a localistic philosophy of science is to shift the focus from science as a whole to particular disciplines and to examine the rational force of empirical and theoretical reasoning in these areas. On this approach, the enterprise of science neither requires nor admits of foundation; instead, the aim of the philosophy of science is to assess the credibility of the techniques of research and forms of empirical reasoning that are current in specific areas of science.

Finally, we need to ask whether such a thing as a "scientific method" lies at the center of all scientific research. This question is misguided because it leads us to gloss over important methodological differences between areas of science. A more plausible view is a core-periphery analysis of scientific method; some features are common to all scientific enterprises, and a great many more are common to some but not all such enterprises. The former constitute the core criteria of scientific reasoning, whereas the latter represent something like family resemblance characteristics that weave throughout various scientific enterprises. And the most important methodological controversies arise in connection with peripheral features—not the largely uncontroversial elements of the core.

The core features of science include at least these criteria: empirical testability, logical coherence, and institutional commitment to intersubjective processes for belief evaluation and criticism. All sciences esteem empirical research and observation as a central means to evaluate scientific assertion and hypothesis.[3] All require that systems of belief be logically coherent and developed. And all proceed through a community of inquirers in which the individual's scientific results are subjected to community-wide standards.[4]

These criteria plainly represent not a full description of scientific inquiry but a set of minimal standards that any enterprise must satisfy if it is to be judged scientific.[5] Beyond these shared features may be found peripheral features that vary across scientific disciplines, such as the use of quantitative methods and models; a commitment to explain observed phenomena on the basis of underlying laws, processes, or mechanisms; a conception of theory as a unified system of hypotheses; use of controlled experimentation to evaluate hypotheses; extensive use of predictions based on theoretical reasoning; and a commitment to background metaphysical beliefs (for example, no action at a distance, no explanation of individual behavior presupposing pure altruism). These features are peripheral in that they are general and shared by many sciences; but obvious and important exceptions occur throughout the sciences. Thus throughout much of its history thermodynamics deliberately avoided hypotheses about underlying processes; cultural anthropologists rarely use complex quantitative models; and some areas of social science are concerned not with explanation at all but with descriptive accuracy.

I have identified some goals of the philosophy of social science; but how to pursue these goals? What are the methods of the philosophy of social science itself? The preceding suggests that the philosophy of social science should be based on close acquaintance with current social science. But progress in the philosophy of social science has often been limited by a tendency to consider highly abstract questions, inadequately examining existing social science research. This approach reflects a top-to-bottom strategy: formulate a general thesis (for example, about naturalism, methodological individualism, or the meaning of actions) and then illustrate it with examples from social science. The philosopher provides an abstract description of a "problem" for social science and then to resolve this problem refers to a philosophical topic that has been discussed in the main philosophical literature.[6] All too often this approach fails to reflect the practice of social research. Exceptions exist, of course, as, for example, Jon Elster's valuable work on the foundations of rational choice theory, Marxism, and other areas of social research (1978, 1979, 1985b). But the literature tends toward generality and abstraction rather than toward detailed treatment of features of social science.

The case-study method that I employ here is designed to avoid the pitfalls of excessive generality and neglect of scientific practice. It requires that the philosopher select several controversies in current empirical research and attempt to extract from these cases the features relevant to the philosophy of social science. For example, what types of explanation do the cases display? How do the researchers use empirical data? What logical or conceptual problems may be identified? The goal of this inquiry is to answer general questions about social knowledge, explanation, and empirical reasoning. But these

answers should emerge from a sensitive probing of the actual theoretical debates rather than from a priori philosophical construction.

In this book I approach the general problems of the philosophy of
social science from below, by examining particular social science
research cases. Progress on general issues will come only through a
more detailed conception of the models, explanations, debates, methods, and so forth to be found in areas of contemporary social science.
Such a study will lead, among other things, to a deeper recognition of
the important diversity to be found in social science.

The fruitfulness of the case-study approach has been demonstrated
in such other areas of the philosophy of science as the philosophy of
physics, biology, and psychology. There philosophers have emphasized the need for detailed studies of episodes in the history or current
practice of science in order to increase the level of detail of our understanding of the nature of science.[7] These lessons have not yet been
adequately learned in the philosophy of social science; philosophers
still tend to have an overly undifferentiated view of the logic of social
science.

Each case discussed here provides a strong example of the richness
of empirical and theoretical reasoning in current social science. By
considering these examples we will gain a richer and more complex
view of the social sciences and a deeper understanding of some of the
models and processes of reasoning that social scientists have constructed. Study of this diverse material will indicate that social science is not a single, unified discipline but rather a plurality of research frameworks that employ different explanatory paradigms and
conceptual systems and are motivated by varied research goals. I
believe that general observations emerge from considering these
cases—common features of explanation and reasoning. But these
generalizations are firmly rooted in the practice of social science.

Rational Choice Explanation of Social Phenomena

Social phenomena are constituted by the activities of human beings,
and human beings are *agents* who act on the basis of beliefs, meanings, interpretations, assumptions, and so on, in relation to goals,
values, prohibitions, and scruples.[8] Human beings, that is, are
intentional persons who act on the basis of reasons. This circumstance has several suggestive implications. First, it implies that social regularities derive from a different causal relation than do natural

regularities. Natural regularities derive from the fixed, objective features of the entities involved (atoms, forces, planets) and the laws of nature that govern them, whereas social regularities derive from the states of consciousness of the agents. Second, the intentional character of social phenomena creates the possibility of a type of explanation for social science unavailable in natural science: one in which social phenomena are construed as the unintended consequence of rational individual choices.

These considerations raise the possibility of a program of research for social science: to attempt to explain social phenomena as the aggregate consequence of the purposive actions of many individuals. By understanding what those persons wanted, what they believed, and how they expected their actions to accomplish their goals, it will be possible to explain the aggregate consequence. This model may be referred to as the method of *aggregative* explanation; and a central question raised in this book is how far this model may be used to explain diverse social phenomena in varied historical and cultural settings.

Controversy over the utility of rational choice explanations appears in the sociological literature as the debate between substantivism and formalism and in anthropology in the debate over the foundations of economic anthropology.[9] The bone of contention here is the explanatory relevance of individual rationality in premodern societies. Can economic rationality reasonably be attributed to participants within premodern societies? And can the tools of economic analysis and rational choice theory be applied fruitfully to these premodern institutions?

Two broad families of views of the role of rationality in social explanation have emerged in social science: formalism and substantivism. Formalists—whether economic historians, anthropologists, development theorists, or rural sociologists—hold that the assumption of rational self-interest by individual decision makers is crucial to understanding any social group in any historical circumstances. Their goal is to use the tools of economic analysis (including centrally the idea of rational calculation of action on the basis of individual material interests) to explain features of non-Western social life.[10]

Substantivists have maintained, against the formalists, that the concept of private self-interest is culturally specific and inapplicable to much of human history. Traditional societies are *communities*: tight, cohesive groups of persons sharing distinctive values in stable, continuing relations with one another (M. Taylor 1982:25ff.). The central threats to security and welfare are well known to such groups—excessive or deficient rainfall, attacks by bandits, predatory tax policies by the central government. And village societies have evolved *schemes of shared values* and *cooperative practices and institutions* that are well adapted to handle these problems of risk and welfare to protect the subsistence needs of all villagers adequately in all but extreme circumstances. The substantivists thus maintain that traditions and norms are fundamental social factors and that powerful traditional motivational constraints almost always modulate individual behavior. One consequence is that many societies do not distinguish clearly between group and individual interest.

The dispute between formalism and substantivism generally proceeds at a highly abstract level: Is human conduct motivated fundamentally by individual self-interest, or is individual rationality a cultural construct of modern market society? Once we descend from this level and look more closely at rational choice within specific institutional contexts, however, we find that this model has definite and surprising consequences for social life. The field of public choice theory is concerned with deriving these specific consequences. Dennis Mueller (1976:395) describes public choice in theory in these terms: "Public choice can be defined as the economic study of non-market decision-making, or, simply the application of economics to political science. The basic behavioral postulate of public choice, as for economics, is that man is an egoistic, rational, utility maximizer." Central tools of public choice theory include the theory of public goods and collective action, the theory of social decision rules and voting schemes, formal social welfare theory, and applied game theory and decision theory. The public choice paradigm attempts to construct explanations of noneconomic behavior on the basis of models drawn from these disciplines. A number of paradoxes of group rationality that appear to be relevant to empirical social science have been developed in this field. These results include Mancur Olson's collective action theorem, the prisoner's dilemma of formal game theory, the suboptimalities created by asymmetric information costs in market transactions (the market for lemons [Akerlof]), the Arrow paradox, and many others. Many of these formal results show that action according to private rationality leads to paradoxes of collective rationality, or that private rationality does not always aggregate to a collectively rational outcome.

Formalists have employed these "theorems" of economic rationality as explanatory tools to explain otherwise puzzling collective phenomena. Consider one representative example: Why do different cropping regimes throughout the world tend to correlate with different land tenure arrangements (sharecropping, fixed rent, corvée labor, peasant ownership)? A formalist explanation might go along these lines: Supervision and inspection costs vary sharply among different crops. For crops that require high-quality, intensive labor inputs (such as rice) corvée labor is not feasible, since supervision costs would be prohibitive, and private ownership or fixed rents are indicated. Crops that require only low-quality, extensive labor (such as cotton or coffee) are consistent with corvée or slave labor and may be produced on plantations or haciendas. This explanation turns on assumptions about how powerholders in a given regime would be inclined to structure production so as to best serve their material interests; they have a self-interested incentive to select tenure arrangements that give the producer an optimal incentive to produce at the appropriate intensity.

A central issue in public choice analysis is the conflict between individual and collective rationality—what is referred to as the theory of collective action. A generation of economists writing on public goods problems have shown that private rationality and collective action conflict: a group of rationally self-interested individuals will not act effectively in pursuit of indivisible and nonexcludable public goods.[11] (Russell Hardin has called this the "back of the invisible hand" [1982:7].) In a classic work Mancur Olson (1965) put forward a theory of groups and organizations that drew certain counterintuitive conclusions concerning group behavior. A longstanding tradition of thought took it as self-evident that groups and organizations would act collectively to pursue the group interest. Olson showed, however, that this assumption commits something akin to a logical fallacy, since groups consist of individuals who make independent decisions. Consequently, it is not sufficient to show that an action would serve the group's interest if all or most members of the group were to perform it; it is necessary to show also that all (or most) individuals in the group have a rational interest to act in that way.

Olson argues in fact that usually a group will *not* act effectively to pursue common interests. Rather, if we assume that a group is composed of rational agents concerned to maximize private interests, Olson shows that each member will have a rational incentive to take a "free ride," that is, to refrain from contribution and hope that sufficient other members make the contrary choice. This introduces what I refer to as Olson's "theorem of collective action": "In a large group in which no single individual's contribution makes a perceptible difference to the group as a whole, or the burden or benefit of any single member of the group, it is certain that a collective good will not be provided unless there is coercion or some outside inducements that will lead the members of the group to act in their common interest" (44). Olson's reasoning is complex, but it reduces essentially to the following: "Though all of the members of the group . . . have a common interest in obtaining this collective benefit, they have no common interest in paying the cost of providing that collective good. Each would prefer that the others pay the entire cost, and ordinarily would get any benefit provided whether he had borne part of the cost or not" (21). The theorem follows from two points: the rational, maximizing decision making based on private interests of the participants, and the fact that the common good is nonexcludable. Given nonexcludability, each individual can reason that the good will either be achieved or not achieved independent from his or her own choice of action. On either outcome, personal interests are best served by not contributing. If the good is achieved, the individual will enjoy the benefits without the cost of contribution. If it is not achieved, then the individual is spared the cost of contribution. Each member will thus decide not to contribute; the good will not be achieved; thus the theorem of collective action.

The collective action theorem has apparently paradoxical consequences for group rationality. It appears to show that groups composed of rational individuals will be incapable of acting to secure collective benefits. One might say that the rational individual is prisoner to individual rationality. And the only apparently available solutions to these problems in their most abstract form are either irrational conduct (each party choosing a less than optimal strategy) or coordination under coercive conditions (in which individuals can commit themselves not to defect from the collective action). A substantial literature on the theory of collective action has developed, and several authors have argued that Olson's conclusions are overly pessimistic about the possibility of collective action. These authors have analyzed the organizational and structural features that may help or impede successful collective action. (Important parts of this literature are summarized in chapter 2.)

Many of the arguments and explanations considered here depend on a rational choice framework of analysis. We will be able to evaluate the utility and limitations of the rational choice framework by considering the cases.

Materialism

Another major framework of explanation employed by several theories discussed here is historical materialism, the framework of classical Marxism.[12] The underlying view in this framework is that all human societies confront common problems of subsistence and security. Certain needs and constraints are shared by all societies; in particular, every society must use natural resources and tools to satisfy material needs. Analysis of these needs and constraints sheds light on all human societies. Thus, all societies must embody institutions, practices, or organizations through which to satisfy basic needs—food, clothing, shelter, health and education, and perhaps others. Materialist social science rests on the assumption that it is possible to derive generalizations from these material imperatives. On this approach, analysis of the social arrangements of production—agriculture, manufacture, distribution of income—will help explain such features of social life as religion and culture.

Materialism emphasizes the importance of two factors within the social process: the forms of technology in use within a given culture, and the social relations of power and authority through which economic activity is organized (the social relations of production, in Marxist terms). The latter refers to the property relations governing the use and direction of the forces of production—land, capital, investment funds, raw materials, and so on.

Technology and the material circumstances of production might be thought to constrain or influence social phenomena in several ways. First, it is sometimes held that an individual's experience of the dominant technologies that appear in everyday life and at the workplace directly influences consciousness. The subsistence peasant acquires a risk-averse value scheme (Scott); the hunter-gatherer gains a moral vision that emphasizes cooperation; the factory worker or machine operator achieves a form of consciousness that prominently features social alienation and consumerism. Charles Tilly's treatment of the cropping patterns and political attitudes of the Vendée (1964:113–45) illustrates this form of materialism. Marx's own treatment of the French peasantry illustrates a similar point; he held that the material circumstances of peasant cultivation—isolation, primitive technology, and a precarious subsistence—led directly to social conservatism.

Closely related is a parallel point about the technical organization of the production process. Some forms of workplace organization have dramatically different effects on worker consciousness than others. Thus, it is sometimes held that some occupational groups, such as miners, have a greater group solidarity and militancy than others because of the shared features of their work—risk, dependency on fellow workers, and close working conditions. Harry Braverman (1974) has explored implications of this aspect of materialist explanation.[13]

Both explanatory schemes fall under what is often described as technological determinism—the idea that important features of social life are influenced or constrained by the dominant technology and forms of organization through which the technology is employed. More important, perhaps, is what is called economic determinism.[14] This holds that the social relations of production are decisive in social change. In the classic Marxist view, the social relations of production simultaneously organize production *and* establish a division of society defined by access to the surplus product. Property relations, that is, define classes. Another way of characterizing this aspect of materialism is to say that materialism pays special attention to the system of surplus extraction in use in a given society and the division into extractors and producers defined by that system. According to historical materialism, the economic and political changes that follow upon the class conflict created by the system of surplus extraction have a central role in the process of historical change within a given society.[15]

The class relations in a particular economy may be analyzed more or less finely. Various authors considered here suggest, for example, that significant differences exist between poor peasant proprietors, poor tenants, and poor landless workers. Their absolute levels of welfare and security may be similar, but they bear varying relations to institutions in society and often react differently to common circumstances.

According to classical materialism, the arrangements that define the institutions of production, including the class system, impose a dynamic of development on other aspects of social life. Marx maintains that the forces and relations of production impose a pattern of development on the rest of social life. Thus Marx holds that the forms

of ideology current in a given social order have a functional relationship to the stability of existing property relations. In particular,
materialism maintains that political institutions, some cultural phenomena, and various institutions of consciousness formation are
strongly influenced by the "needs" of the economic structure and the
property relations. Gerald Cohen (1978:160–71) states, for example,
that Marxism postulates a functional relationship between such "superstructural" institutions and the economic structure.

Crucial to the adequacy of classic historical materialism is the
answer given to the question, what mechanisms link the needs of the
economic structure and the evolution of various superstructural elements—for example, political forms? The most convincing answers
involve several plausible social processes. First, members of the elite
class defined by the property relations can perceive the connection
between their interests and economic stability, and they typically
have substantial political resources to expend on defending their interests. Second, a more anonymous process is also at work: political
institutions that are *not* consonant with the needs of the economic
system will tend to produce adverse effects undesired by many or all
segments of society—not merely the elite class.[16] Thus a tax reform
package that favors the poor over the rich may create strong disincentives to invest, leading to poor economic performance—leading in
turn to widespread support to modify the reform package.[17]

Materialism gives rise to several hypotheses about social processes
and causal relations among social phenomena: (1) various elements
of local social structure and ideology can be understood as functional
adaptations to the needs of the economic structure and property system; (2) members of classes will tend to perceive their common material interests, so class membership is a significant basis for explaining
political behavior; (3) there is some correspondence between a class's
political power and its rights within the property system, and the
relationship between that role and the expansion of the forces of
production;[18] (4) large-scale causal regularities are at work between
technological development, the social institutions of production, and
the development of political, cultural, or ideological institutions.
Hypotheses of these sorts constitute a program of research for social
scientists: they lead the investigator to formulate questions about
the material institutions of a given society, to pay attention to the
particulars of local class relations, and to explore the causal relations
between these material factors and other social developments.

As a research program, then, materialism suggests that the investigator should strive to identify the forms of production that are current in a particular environment—technology, crops, forms of manufacturing—and the social relations of power and authority through which these forces of production are employed. These factors are postulated to be of substantial explanatory relevance in a variety of contexts and social patterns.

What sorts of predictions about social process does materialism arrive at? A materialist analysis of local property relations and technology is designed to provide a framework from which to characterize the interests, opportunities, and limitations of various agents. Seen from this perspective, materialism incorporates the core elements of rational choice theory. It postulates that individuals will act to serve their material interests, and it devotes considerable effort to describing the salient features of the social environment. The ways in which a landless worker pursues material interests differ greatly from those chosen by a poor peasant—let alone a lesser landlord. So, by providing an extended description of the social environment, it is possible to predict the forms of political and economic behavior to be expected from participants within this environment. Using this analysis, materialism postulates that it will be possible to construct an explanation of the particulars of a given political occurrence using information about the class interests and positions of the participants.

Such analysis is highly localistic. It does not presume to offer a general recipe for social change; rather, it asserts only that we can better understand the perhaps unique sequence of developments in question if we analyze the confluence of class interests and actions that underlie it.

Classical Marxism also makes large-scale predictions: about the development of modes of production as a whole (the laws of motion of capitalism, the falling rate of feudal levy), and about the "necessary" sequence of modes of production. These predictions derive loosely from the framework of class analysis described above, conjoined with a highly abstract model of the economies in question. It is likely, however, that actual economies are too various, embodying too many conflicting tendencies and processes, to permit us to attach much weight to any of these macropredictions. In any complex system—social or natural—we may understand causal factors in isolation, but because of their complex interactions and the sensitivity of the outcome to moment-by-moment particulars of the causal interaction, we may be unable to predict anything about the final state of the system. But we may still be able to explain transitions within the evolution of the system by appealing to the various factors.

It is thus plausible that capitalism itself contained more resources for continuing stability than Marx's model accounted for—with the result that the pattern of capitalist development may differ greatly from that predicted by Marx. And even more skepticism may today greet the assumption that a necessary sequence of modes of production, or even a short list of possible and discrete modes of production, exist. These forms of skepticism are probably justified; but this does not invalidate materialism as an analysis of the causal importance of class, technology, and control of surpluses to explain social development.

If we take this perspective, the significance of materialism is *not* its claim to provide a basis for large-scale aggregative predictions about modes of production, revolutionary transitions, or sequences of modes of production; it is rather the basis of analysis it offers of a cluster of important causal factors whose influence can be discerned at the local level and which contributes in important, but perhaps unpredictable, ways to the evolution of the system.

Results

The results of my analysis of the cases discussed below fall in several areas: contributions to the philosophy of social science per se; contributions to the theory of social metaphysics; methodological recommendations for the areas of social science under consideration here; criticisms of central theoretical approaches to social explanation (rational choice theory, Marxism, neoclassical economics); and a series of criticisms and elaborations of the detailed theories considered here. It may be useful to anticipate my findings briefly in each area.

Philosophy of Social Science

My findings within the philosophy of social science concern the logical character of conceptual frameworks in social science, the role of theory in social science, and the character of explanation and empirical justification in the social sciences. I argue for an approach that might be called empiricist, in this sense: I emphasize the centrality of factual empirical research in social science, I hold that disputes in social science are typically resolvable in principle through further factual inquiry, and I argue that at least some social concepts should be interpreted realistically, not as arbitrary constructs in terms of which to sort the phenomena. In particular, I reject the position that holds that social explanations and assertions are radically under-determined by the empirical evidence—with the result that there are in principle always alternative and incompatible ways to construe and explain a given range of empirical data. I thus maintain the pos-sibility of an "objective" social science.

A second feature that brings my analysis into proximity to em-piricist philosophy of social science is the position I take concerning methodological individualism. I show that most of the explanations considered here conform to an enlightened version of this doctrine, in that it is straightforward to specify the micromechanisms through which postulated social processes work; and I offer an account of the logical structure of explanation, and the relation between local and global social processes, that supports the doctrine. On this issue I thus side with such authors as Elster (1985b) and Przeworski (1985b) and against such authors as Miller (1978) and Levine (1986).

A third topic concerns the logic of social explanation. I argue that the forms of explanation to be found in virtually every case are log-ically rather simple. They typically take the form of *causal* arguments in which the investigator attempts to identify portions of the causal field—standing conditions, instigating events, or causal mechanisms—to account for the occurrence of an event or the per-sistence of a social regularity. Typically, moreover, these causal mechanisms work through the constraints that channel participants' choices; in place of natural necessity, these authors postulate social processes that depend ultimately on the perceptions, wants, beliefs, opportunities, and powers of the individuals who constitute the so-cial phenomena in question.

These positions bring me close to a fairly traditional empiricist philosophy of science. However, I also offer fundamental criticisms of the specifics of empiricist theory of social science. Most impor-tant, I argue that the model of scientific knowledge as a unified de-ductive theory from which observational consequences are derived is not generally illuminating in social science. Theoretical frameworks do not function in this way in the investigations I survey. Instead, a theoretical framework provides a basis for analyzing some parts of the social phenomena under study and suggests causal hypotheses about those phenomena. Each author considered in this study em-ploys theoretical constructs and assumptions; but in no case has the theory permitted the derivation of the behavior of the system as a whole. Rather, theory and factual analysis proceed hand in hand.

This position leads me to reject the central epistemological assumption of empiricist philosophy of science: the idea that knowledge claims are confirmed or refuted solely on the basis of the observational consequences of the comprehensive theories that they incorporate. I maintain instead that social knowledge—in these cases at any rate—takes the form of an eclectic set of hypotheses, analyses, and factual investigations, which can be empirically evaluated piecemeal. Rather than test a theory against its predictive consequences, I argue that many of these cases may be evaluated by a series of relatively independent empirical investigations. I thus hold that the most difficult epistemic problems of social inquiry fall at a low level of empirical investigation: research design and validation, assessment and aggregation of data, and arriving at judgments about the underlying empirical phenomena.

Social Metaphysics

In this study I arrive at positions relevant to social metaphysics, or the question of the nature of social entities, states, processes, and regularities. I argue, first, that there are *social kinds*: classes of social phenomena that recur and possess similar causal structures and histories. One example is a sharecropping land-tenure system. Second, I argue for an interpretation of the concept of a social structure as a set of constraints and incentives imposed on individual conduct and embodied in patterns of individual behavior. A marketing system is a social structure in that it presents agents with a set of goals, powers, opportunities, and constraints in the context of which individuals make choices. Third, I offer an interpretation of social causation in terms of the social regularities that follow from the assumptions of individual agency: individuals pursue goals within the context of institutions and structures, and their actions transmit influence from antecedent to consequent. In a given causal field we may judge that subsistence crisis causes rebellion; the mechanism of influence is that hungry people seek strategies, including the appeal to organized violence against landlords and the state, that permit them to satisfy their needs. This social ontology coheres with the principle of methodological individualism in that it grounds social causation and social structures and institutions in individual agency.

Methodology

A series of methodological principles emerges from the examination of the empirical debates below. First, analysis of the nature of generalizations in social science leads us to emphasize the importance of local studies in social research; even if the aim of social research is to arrive at broad generalizations, such generalizations must be based on careful studies of social phenomena at the local level. Second, analysis of the valid requirements of methodological individualism leads us to the importance of the local processes of change—local politics, features of organization, and the particulars of agent motivation. The best of the studies examined here—Scott, Popkin, and Perry—have argued for fairly general conclusions about certain processes of social change, but they have done so on the basis of detailed attention to data drawn from local studies and to local mechanisms of political and economic change. Third, investigators need to employ theoretical models and frameworks to explain the phenomena, but they should recognize the importance of being willing to be pluralistic. Social phenomena are not generally monocausal or uniform; rarely can one theoretical framework provide a full explanation. As we will see in the discussion of agricultural stagnation below (chapter 4), neither demographic factors nor surplus-extraction factors alone explain the phenomena; both are relevant. So a plurality of theoretical frameworks is neither an inconsistency nor a sign of conceptual indecisiveness; instead, it is a recognition of the multiple causation at work in most complex social processes. Again, some of the best work we have surveyed here—such as Philip Huang's study (1985) of the North China peasant economy—explicitly recognizes this point and attempts to incorporate as many theoretical perspectives into the account as needed to capture the complexity and variation among the phenomena. Related to this, it will emerge at various points—for example, in the discussion of the moral economy debate and peasant rebellions—that investigators need to examine apparently competing hypotheses to see that they are not in fact complementary. In the case of peasant rebellions, for example, we find that the class conflict theory, the local politics theory, and the millenarian theory may all succeed in capturing aspects of the phenomenon of peasant rebellion; only a mistaken desire for theoretical purity would lead us to demand that just one of the theories may be true. The investigator must recognize that the phenomena are complex, embodying a variety of social processes; a plurality of theories may well be needed to identify the causal properties of these processes.

Finally, I argue for the importance of careful validation of formal, quantitative models. Such models can illuminate social phenomena and can allow the investigator to discern causal relations among them. But it is easy for a formal construct to go wrong on formal grounds—it fails to identify the right data, it employs an improper mathematical technique of analysis, or it overextends the inferences that can be drawn from the model.

Theoretical Frameworks

The cases considered below use a number of higher-level theoretical frameworks—families of research hypotheses about social change and the regularities that underlie social phenomena that investigators may bring to bear on particular empirical problems. Central among these are rational choice theory, Marxism, neoclassical economic theory, and interpretation theory. In this study I identify weaknesses and strengths of each framework. I argue at several points that the rational choice framework is a powerful analytical tool for understanding social phenomena, but that this framework needs amplification in several ways. First, the narrow conception of economic rationality on which rational choice explanations depend is too restrictive as a theory of practical rationality; practical rationality incorporates not only means-end reasoning but deliberation about commitments, moral values, and self-conceptions. Second, rational choice explanations and collective action theory tend to give too little attention to the structures and institutions in the context of which decision making occurs. Thus, in the moral economy case we find that Popkin's collective action arguments do not go through if we build in more specific assumptions about the temporal and institutional structure of collective action.

We will also identify some of Marxism's shortcomings. The central research hypotheses of Marxism—that material institutions and class relations are particularly salient to political and economic phenomena and action—have been borne out in this study. But more specific assumptions—for example, that members of classes will tend to come to an accurate conception of their interests, or that individuals will tend to act politically on the basis of their class interests rather than patron-client relations or lineage ties—are not confirmed by my findings. Class consciousness is sometimes an important component of political motivation, but it is rarely the only component and sometimes is not present at all. Likewise, the cautions against monocausal explanations and theories in preceding paragraphs are pertinent to Marxism; to the extent that the Marxist investigator is committed to interpreting and explaining social processes in terms of classical Marxian categories, he or she will unavoidably overlook other significant causal factors, such as endogenous demographic processes, organizational competence, or local political cultures. Finally, I find that Marxist political theory confronts a problem of aggregation in basing its analysis of political behavior on the basis of class interests. We need to know more about the ways in which a group defines its identity, and at what level. How significant are occupational or skill differences within the English working class? To what extent do these distinctions constitute class differences? And in the Chinese context, we see that regional conflict of interest within the peasantry—a classically defined class—may mask the objective interests that the class holds in common.

I criticize neoclassical economic analysis on several grounds. First, as we will see in the analysis of Chao's construction, the neoclassical approach tends to abstract from historically specific institutional structures that are decisive in historical change. Second, we may repeat the criticisms of rational choice assumptions about rationality in this context.

Each of the major theoretical frameworks deployed by authors considered here may be criticized and extended. The point is not to discredit the theoretical frameworks; it is rather to indicate that none is—or should be expected to be—a wholly satisfactory basis to understand social phenomena. Instead, the defense of theoretical pluralism may be reiterated: there is no reason to expect that any single theoretical framework can explain a complex social or historical process.

The Cases

Finally, in this study I offer many criticisms, elaborations, and addenda about the specifics of the theories considered here. I argue that the moral economy theory is not wholly inconsistent with the rational peasant model, and I attempt to clarify the premises and assumptions of both frameworks. I show that a prominent attempt to refute Skinner's macroregions theory empirically fails on logical grounds and that Skinner's own causal analysis of urbanization is logically flawed.

Likewise, in my treatment of demographic and surplus-extraction theories of agricultural stagnation, I point out several methodological shortcomings in each theory; and my analysis of three models of peasant rebellion will show that each theory has much to gain from incorporating factors emphasized by the others. I hope that these points will be useful to scholars immersed in these empirical and theoretical debates.

Chapter 2
The Moral Economy Debate

In recent years an important debate over the basis of peasant behavior and social institutions has developed: one view is that traditional peasant society is organized cooperatively through shared moral values and communal institutions; an alternate view is that peasant society shows the mark of the rational individual striving for private welfare—even at the cost of village or community welfare. Two books have formulated these issues particularly clearly: James Scott's *Moral Economy of the Peasant* and Samuel Popkin's *Rational Peasant*.[1] Scott's analysis of Southeast Asian peasant society emphasizes shared moral values, group solidarity, and collective practices aimed at leveling out subsistence crises for all villagers. Popkin challenges this view of peasant society, presenting the peasant farmer as an economically rational agent motivated primarily by private interest. Popkin argues that Scott and other moral economists greatly overestimate solidarity and communal institutions in Asian peasant societies; instead, he points to internal inequalities and the extensive difficulties encountered by cooperative schemes. In particular, Popkin argues that familiar problems of collective rationality—public goods problems, free rider problems, prisoners' dilemmas—afflict village society and greatly undermine the stability of community welfare practices and institutions.

Both Scott and Popkin have an empirical story to tell; each attempts to provide an empirically grounded description of aspects of rural social life in Southeast Asia. More important, each seeks to explain important aspects of peasant society: social and economic arrangements of the village, social behavior among participants in local society (landlords, tenants, officials, notables), and rebellion and protest. And each believes that the structures and behaviors that he identifies can be found in a range of cultures and historical contexts—with the result that his analysis also explains other rural phenomena.

The moral economy debate revolves around two focal issues. First, are typical peasants in Southeast Asia motivated chiefly by self-interested rationality or shared communal values? Second, what social arrangements, institutions, and patterns of collective behavior do these motives foster?

This dispute raises important issues for the philosophy of social science. First, it poses problems concerning the logic of theoretical disagreement in the social sciences; the moral economy and rational peasant frameworks have more in common than may initially be apparent. Second, the resolution of theoretical disagreements in social science requires empirical data that may not be available. Finally, more than one way to explain social phenomena may exist: Popkin's approach represents a form of aggregative explanation, viewing social phenomena as the outcome of the rational behavior of individual participants within an environment of choice. Scott's approach, by contrast, has elements of functionalist explanation, arguing that some social phenomena are caused by the workings of a system of norms that are well adjusted to the community's subsistence needs.

The Theoretical Dispute

The Moral Economy Framework

In *The Moral Economy of the Peasant* (1976) Scott studies peasant social arrangements and political behavior in Southeast Asia, chiefly Burma and Vietnam. Scott focuses on the depression rebellions of the 1930s in the region. He intends to provide an analysis of the circumstances of peasant life and norms that will provide a basis for understanding these rebellions: why they occurred when and where they did, and why so many ordinary rural people made the costly and dangerous decision to revolt. Rebellions are moments of high drama, however, and Scott is also interested in explaining features of ordinary rural life: patron and client relations, duties of charity, and the normal functioning of village social and political institutions.

Scott holds that there is a normative scheme characteristic of peasants that is generated by their "existential situation"—the ecological, technical, and social circumstances which entail that peasant agriculture will fluctuate around the subsistence level (1–2, 13–15)—and that this scheme substantially shapes individual behavior. It is a subsistence ethic: a set of standards through which peasants evaluate the institutions and persons around them through the lens of risk and subsistence security. This ethic includes a right to subsistence and a set of obligations and rights associated with reciprocity. "We can begin, I believe, with two moral principles that seem firmly embedded in both the social patterns and injunctions of peasant life: the *norm of reciprocity* and the *right to subsistence*" (167). The subsistence ethic is cross-cultural, Scott maintains, because it derives from structural features of peasant life rather than cultural tradition or religious values.

Scott describes the social role of the ethics of subsistence in these terms: "What the subsistence ethic provides is a perspective from which the typical peasant views the inevitable claims made upon his resources by fellow villagers, landowners, or officials. It implies, above all, that such claims are evaluated less in terms of their absolute level than in terms of how they complicate or ease his problem of staying above the subsistence crisis level" (29). The subsistence ethic, then, constitutes something like a "sense of justice," determining the judgments peasants make and the circumstances in which they feel most aggrieved—and therefore most ready for rebellion and resistance.[2] Roughly, landlords, tax policies, and village institutions are good if they stabilize subsistence crises and bad if they exacerbate subsistence crises. Significantly, Scott holds that the subsistence ethic influences *all* strata of village society—not merely the poor but the affluent and powerful. The subsistence ethic constrains the actions and choices of the rich and mighty, compelling them to take some account of the needs of the poor.

To Scott, the details of the subsistence ethic offer the key to understanding peasant political behavior. He holds that the degree of dissonance between existing material relations (particularly taxation and conditions of land tenure) and the terms of the subsistence ethic is critical in explaining resistance and rebellion. Peasants whose sense of justice has been offended are more likely to rebel than those who regard existing relations as fundamentally fair. In describing his argument, Scott writes, "The purpose of the argument which follows is to place the subsistence ethic at the center of the analysis of peasant politics" (5).[3]

These features of the moral economy view concentrate on the normative basis of peasant decision making and political action. A complementary aspect of the view, however, concerns the economic and political arrangements of peasant social life. The moral economy view postulates that traditional social institutions are shaped to protect poor villagers from the effects of subsistence crisis. Scott maintains that peasant communities and villages embody institutions that provide collective welfare, smooth out subsistence crises, and assure a minimal standard of welfare for every village member. "Patterns of reciprocity, forced generosity, communal land, and work-sharing helped to even out the inevitable troughs in a family's resources which might otherwise have thrown them below subsistence" (3). Such institutions include: (1) client-patron relations in which the patron has the obligation to provide rent abatement, short-term credit, and so on, in times of dearth; (2) communal land and resources that are periodically redistributed among village families; (3) patterns of reciprocity, work sharing, and forced generosity through which wealth is to some extent redistributed and an income floor established (26–32); and (4) intra-village tax arrangements that favor the poor (43). Scott maintains further that the welfare assurance aspects of these institutions are reasonably effective. "The crisis value of such leveling pressures is most dramatically evident for a famine-stricken village in Tonkin where Gourou reported that only the equal distribution of hunger throughout the commune prevented anyone from starving" (43).[4]

Having described the main elements of the subsistence ethic and its corresponding social institutions, Scott evaluates the disruption of these institutions by the advent of more extensive market relations and a more efficient colonial bureaucratic state to replace the traditional political system. He argues that modern economic and political institutions have placed peasant communities under severe—perhaps fatal—stress. Thus Scott postulates a historical progression from traditional village society, in which communal norms and redistributive institutions work to secure the subsistence needs of the poor, to modern rural life, in which the modern state and a commercialized economy have fragmented this moral economy— both the institutions that embodied it and the values that supported these institutions.[5] At the same time, Scott recognizes that the premodern rural world varies greatly in terms of communal values and subsistence assurance institutions (60).

The Rational Peasant Framework

In *The Rational Peasant* (1979), Popkin provides an interpretation of the political economy of rural Vietnam (map 2.1) since the midnineteenth century. He describes the precolonial village—political arrangements, patterns of land use and cultivation, and tax system.

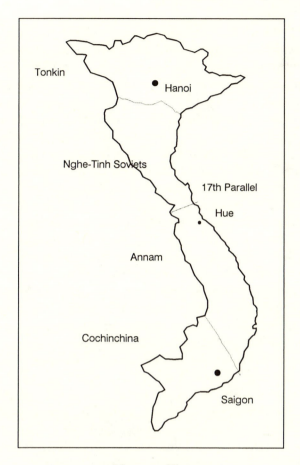

Map 2.1. Vietnam

He analyzes the effects of colonialism and commercialization on rural society, chiefly in the nineteenth century. And he chronicles the anticolonial movements of the twentieth century—the Cao Dai, the Hoa Hao, and the Communist movement. Like Scott, Popkin is concerned *both* to define the character of local economic and political arrangements and to explain peasant political behavior during periods of large-scale collective action (rebellion and resistance).

Popkin's account is framed as an extensive critique—both empirical and theoretical—of the moral economy approach. Empirically, he argues that the economic and political institutions of Vietnamese village life—precolonial, colonial, and postcolonial— did *not* have the redistributive and welfare-assurance effects that moral economists believe them to have had. He maintains that moral economy assumptions about the leveling effects of village institutions are thereby empirically refuted. Theoretically, he attempts to show that this empirical finding can easily be explained if we suppose that peasants are self-interested rational agents rather than communally motivated.

Popkin's central motivational hypothesis is that peasants are rational maximizers of personal or family welfare. They are motivated primarily by considerations of family welfare rather than group interests or moral values. "By rationality I mean that individuals evaluate the possible outcomes associated with their choices in accordance with their preferences and values. In doing this, they discount the evaluation of each outcome in accordance with their subjective estimate of the likelihood of the outcome. Finally, they make the choice which they believe will maximize their expected utility" (31). Since peasants are rational decision makers, Popkin holds that the tools of economic analysis ought to apply to peasant behavior and explain large-scale features of peasant society. "Economic theory . . . is a method of analysis: the postulation of a number of actors with certain ends and a deductive attempt to work out how persons will act in situations which present certain alternatives, 'on the assumption that they pursue their goals rationally'" (30–31).[6] This leads Popkin to a model of explanation of peasant society and behavior that is grounded in public choice theory: he attempts to explain observed outcomes as the aggregate of individuals' rational choices.[7]

In light of this theory of individual decision making, Popkin maintains that powerful results contained in public choice theory—game theory, collective action theory, decision theory, and microeconomic theory—ought to help explain village society as well. Most prominent among Popkin's applications from the literature is his use of Mancur Olson's collective action arguments, but he also applies the idea of a prisoners' dilemma (164), the problem of cyclical majorities (59), and the idea of a "market for lemons" [Popkin 1981]).

A particularly important application of public choice theory concerns the problem of collective behavior. Based on arguments deriving from the extensive public goods literature, Popkin holds that problems of collective action are central to peasant life. He asserts that the traditional village was conspicuously unable to secure collective action for shared interests, even when villagers recognized genuine shared interests (such as large-scale water management projects and defense against marauding tigers).[8] And the traditional village was incapable of creating effective subsistence assurance and welfare schemes because of problems of free riders, theft of collective resources, and mutual mistrust.[9]

These assumptions about individual motivation lead Popkin to dispute the moral economy view of the leveling effects of traditional village economic and political institutions. He distinguishes sharply between insurance and welfare institutions; insurance spreads risk among rough equals, whereas welfare redistributes income from rich to poor. Popkin holds that insurance schemes are relatively common in village life, whereas welfare practices are uncommon and limited in scope. Insurance plans can be supported by incentive schemes that make them attractive to those able to fund them, whereas welfare plans typically cannot.

Against the model of the communitarian village, Popkin views the traditional village in Vietnam as one in which rich and poor were sharply stratified; in which the rich and the notables took every advantage of their power to increase their wealth and position; in which institutions of collective welfare security were narrow, limited largely to providing relief for widows and orphans; and in which powers within the village would appeal to outside powers when it was in their interest.[10] Popkin argues that the characteristic features of social life within the traditional village contradict the central claims of the moral economy view: "Limited and specified reciprocities, low levels of welfare and insurance, outsiders, and the prevalence of market-determined credit rates (usury), all challenge the basis of moral economy claims about village welfare and insurance systems" (55). These factors are readily explained, moreover, on the assumption that participants are rational and self-interested.

Popkin denies that communal lands and village fiscal institutions typically level out material inequalities. Communal agricultural arrangements—even when potentially beneficial for all—tended to break down due to distrust and individual self-seeking.[11] Popkin quotes a Vietnamese proverb, "Why should I spread a banquet for someone else to eat," to account for problems of long-term investment in communal agriculture (104). This exemplifies the conflict between private and public interest and Popkin's skepticism about the capacity of peasant societies to solve such conflicts.

Popkin also casts doubt on moral economy assumptions about patron-client relations—that these were constrained by a subsistence ethic and generally worked to the advantage of both patron and client. Popkin argues instead that the terms of exchange between patron and client usually resulted from the balance of power between the two; in circumstances where patrons could effectively increase their share of the product, they did so. He maintains that patrons (in various times and places) made concerted efforts to reduce their clients' powers of resistance (by blocking a client's right to leave the relationship, by restricting access to literacy, and by preventing a client's access to the market [75]). In place of Scott's paternalistic model of the patron-client relation (1976:40–52), then, Popkin maintains that this relation was designed to further the private interests of the parties insofar as each had the power to insist on benefits for himself.[12]

A central issue between Scott and Popkin is the effectiveness of shared norms and values in regulating traditional village society. Of the moral economists Popkin writes, "In his relations with fellow villagers, the focus of the peasant is on adherence to norms and roles" (11). But Popkin expresses skepticism that norms and values effectively shape peasant social life, seeing them as largely subject to manipulation by self-interested actors. "I expect to find . . . that norms are malleable, renegotiated, and shifting in accord with considerations of power and strategic interaction among individuals. There are always tradeoffs between conflicting and inconsistent norms" (22). For Popkin, norms present ambiguous requirements, allowing contending parties to cite traditional grounds for conflicting self-serving policies. For example, the putative norm "every villager has a right to subsistence" might be taken by poor villagers to entail that tax burdens ought to be distributed progressively, whereas wealthy villagers might interpret it to mean only that widows and orphans should be provided with village support.[13] Norms and values thus play only a secondary role in explaining social patterns and forms of collective behavior in traditional society.

Another leg of Popkin's skepticism about the effectiveness of shared norms is his view that village institutions and practices are highly plastic, giving way easily to the arrival of a new set of social and economic forces—for example, market forces or colonialism. When local elites see opportunities to profit from wider commercial activities—even if these activities are forbidden by traditional institutions and practices—they will stretch institutions accordingly.[14] Likewise, if new economic opportunities become available to the village poor—as in the form of city labor—their individual choices will change custom and local institutions. This argument suggests that local customs, institutions, and practices have little constraining role in the face of large-scale changes in the economic or social environment; individuals pursuing private or family interests in the new context will alter customs and institutions along the way.

Popkin's analysis of peasant political behavior differs sharply from Scott's view. He maintains that peasants typically did not wage conservative or backward-looking struggles; rebellions and concerted movements of resistance were directed just as often against the most hated traditional village institutions, such as head tax assignment by the notables or redistribution of land (243–52). Vietnamese peasants in particular did not generally oppose modern market institutions and cash farming because the advent of market agriculture and the colonial state typically did not harm peasant welfare.

Popkin denies emphatically that communal interests or shared values motivated peasant rebels. Instead, he maintains that it is possible to explain peasant political behavior on the basis of an analysis of the incentives and deterrents present at the level of the individual decision maker—rank and file as well as leader. This account immediately confronts problems of collective action and free riding, since public goods problems ought to make such movements rare.[15] Accordingly, Popkin analyzes the organizational resources available to peasant political movements—the Catholic church, the Hoa Hao and Cao Dai sects, the Communist party—to determine what factors account for the success of these organizations at mobilizing peasant support and mounting major anticolonial collective struggles.[16] Here Popkin employs the concept of the political entrepreneur—the rational and self-interested leader who has a personal interest in founding and maintaining a collective activity and who can inspire trust in his followers that effective collective action will ensue (259–66).[17]

Prima Facie Disagreements between Scott and Popkin

The authors disagree first about the nature of motivation and decision making at the individual level. This dispute concerns the relative importance of prudence and norms to explain peasant behavior. This is in principle an empirical issue within comparative social psychology. But in practice, the disagreement functions as a theoretical rather than an empirical dispute; Scott and Popkin use their motivational assumptions to explain many social phenomena—the character of village institutions, the dynamics of peasant political action, and peasant response to modernization. Neither offers direct evidence at the individual level to uphold his analysis of peasant motivation; instead, each supports his position by referring to the predicted aggregate consequences that these analyses generate.

Scott and Popkin also disagree, on empirical grounds, about the character of peasant social, political, and economic institutions in Southeast Asia. The moral economy view asserts that such institutions have a prominent communitarian and redistributive character; the rational peasant view flatly denies this claim. This is a specific empirical and historical disagreement, to be resolved by historical research. Did precolonial village tax practices really benefit the poor? Did communal land arrangements have a periodic redistributive effect? Popkin argues at length that the data about Vietnam do not support the moral economy view.

Finally, the authors disagree about the motives, goals, and processes of peasant collective action (particularly revolutionary movements). Scott regards peasant collective action as largely reactive, responding to assaults on traditional subsistence rights; Popkin sees peasant movements as forward-looking, with peasant actors making decisions about their political behavior by estimating the effects of various movements on their future interests. On a different level, Popkin emphasizes careful analysis of the organizational resources and mobilization processes that underlie peasant politics. Whether a political movement will achieve a widespread following, according to Popkin, depends on the organizational resources available to its leadership. Scott, by contrast, presupposes a more direct relation between instigating event, peasant moral vision, and peasant political behavior.

The Social Basis of Cooperation

The problem of collective action is a central theme in *The Rational Peasant*. Popkin argues that peasant society will show the symptoms of public goods problems and that institutions and collective activities that might benefit the entire village will not emerge due to free-rider problems. When conflicts arise between common and private interest, decision makers will favor private interest. Irrigation and flood control projects, for example, have large potential benefits for the village (through increased crop yield), but these projects involve providing an indivisible public good (protection from flooding and waterlogging). And Popkin's analysis predicts that village society will find it difficult to overcome free-rider problems and that such projects will thus fail: "It is frequently the case that the actions of individually rational peasants in both market and nonmarket situations do not aggregate to a 'rational' village" (31). According to Popkin, if we concede that peasants are rational and concerned chiefly with familial welfare, then Mancur Olson's (1965) theory of collective action demonstrates that communitarian practices and institutions will collapse due to free-rider problems.

Recent work in collective action theory has identified important qualifications to Olson's analysis: circumstances that tend to make collective action in pursuit of public goods by rational decision makers more feasible than Olson believed. Popkin's analytic case is therefore unproven: it is possible to regard peasants as rational decision makers and still regard the traditional village as a social context in which cooperation, collective action, and communitarian practices occur relatively readily. This finding will suggest that public choice theory does not give rise to determinate predictions in the context of rural life—not because peasants are not rational, but rather because the social context of peasant social life is more complex than the public choice model can easily represent.

A Model Village

To consider the feasibility of collective action in traditional village societies, it will be useful to formulate an abstract description of a typical village. It is true of course that villages in different societies show tremendous diversity: Balinese, medieval French, and contemporary Mexican villages embody contrasting forms of agriculture, political organization, and religious and moral values.[18] Many of these differences, moreover, influence the solidarity and cohesion characteristic of the village. Bloch (1966:35–63) thus holds that the technical requirements of the heavy plow in northern France led to substantially more cohesive communities than peasant villages dependent on the light scratch plow in the south. And Hue-Tam Ho Tai (1983) shows that village society in Cochinchina was substantially less cohesive and communal than in Annam or Tonkin because peasants could emigrate cheaply to plentiful unclaimed land. Important dimensions of variation that influence village cohesiveness include residential patterns (dispersed or nucleated), commercialization, agricultural technologies, kinship organizations, religious practices, interaction between village and state, and wealth and income stratification.

Variations notwithstanding, village societies throughout the world share a cluster of features. Let us construct an admittedly idealized description of village society (a model village) and consider the degree to which these features facilitate or impede collective action. The features identified here reflect a variety of empirical village studies but are not intended to constitute a general theory of village society or to apply in all times and places. To the extent that particular village cultures diverge from this account, the arguments about collective action that follow will be less applicable. The purpose here is not to resolve the empirical issue between Scott and Popkin as to whether village societies typically embody communitarian features but to establish an analytical point: to the extent that traditional villages embody the features described in this model village, collective action will be substantially easier to achieve than Popkin expects.[19]

First, the model village is a relatively stable society; its institutions, social relations, and ecological and technical circumstances may be expected to change only gradually. Each member may confidently predict that today's decision whether to participate in collective projects will be paralleled in the future by other villagers' comparable decisions and that the circumstances of choice and problems of collective action to be found in the present will also be found in the future. Problems of water management, collective defense, and peak periods of demand for labor (harvesting, transplanting, and so forth) are examples of the opportunities for collective action that regularly confront the village.

Second, the model village is relatively isolated from outside intervention and resources, both economic and political. Villagers generally recognize their high level of economic interdependence. This is not to deny that peasant villages are located within wider market and political institutions; the reverse is generally true. Peasant communities are taxed and are usually involved in market agriculture.[20] Often, though, external economic and political forces constitute the environmental parameters within which village life proceeds but do not alter the everyday political and economic choices of villagers; they do not make available to villagers either new resources or fresh allies to pursue their ends. Describing prerevolutionary China, Philip Huang (1985:219) writes, "Even in the 1930's, all but the most highly commercialized villages of the North China plain were still relatively insular communities. Villagers had minimal social intercourse with outsiders, and village affairs were governed largely by endogenous leaders."[21] This relative isolation means that villagers are confident that they will continue to interact with one another. Each may rationally judge that his interests are tied to the success or failure of village practices.

Third, each villager has access to information about the history and present activities of others, reflecting the relatively small size of the village. The inhabitants know one another, and social relations are face-to-face. Villagers know one another's family histories; patterns of friendship and enmity have developed over generations; and villagers can keep track for years of records of contribution to collective village activities and have long memories for failures of reciprocity.

Fourth, the model village embodies many shared values (familial, moral, religious, and political), as well as organizations corresponding to these values (kinship organizations, temple groups, political parties). Clifford Geertz (1980:75–82) argues, for example, that the complex coordination required to maintain and use the system of terrace irrigation found in traditional Bali was secured largely through a stable system of religious beliefs and temple practices. "The hamlet shaped the everyday social interactions of a collection of neighbors into an harmonious pattern of civil attachments; the subak [water hamlet] organized the economic resources of a company of peasants—land, labor, water, technical know-how, and, to a rather limited extent, capital equipment—into an astonishingly effective productive apparatus" (50). And the main organizing device for both hamlet and subak, writes Geertz, was the intricate system of religious practices that Balinese farmers shared.[22] Shared values do not *assure* successful collective action, but they contribute to it in several ways: they increase the likelihood of diffuse social sanctions against those who offend the shared values, they motivate individuals toward collective welfare, and they provide points around which conventions may emerge to facilitate collective action.

Finally, social relations within our model village are multistranded, in that villagers share a multitude of relationships: kinship relations, religious practices, economic relations of reciprocity and dependency, shared political traditions, history of successful collective action, and simple neighborly acquaintance over time. The village leadership can use loyalties and commitments generated by this rich fabric.

Recent discussions of collective action have identified mechanisms within social groups that facilitate collective action by rational individuals and offset the workings of narrow individual rationality. Significantly, these mechanisms are supported by the main features of traditional village societies: stability, isolation, richness of information, shared values, and multistrandedness. Our model village thus embodies the social basis for at least some forms of collective action by rational peasants within the context of village society.

Reciprocity. Consider first patterns of cooperation based on strict reciprocity among individuals. A perspicuous formulation of the problem of cooperation between independent parties has emerged within game theory in connection with the prisoners' dilemma. The prisoners' dilemma is a two-person game in which each party has two strategies: defect and cooperate. If each cooperates, each receives a payoff of 1; if each defects, each receives a payoff of −1; and if one cooperates while the other defects, the cooperator receives −2 and the defector 2. Standard game theory analysis shows that the dominant strategy for each participant is to defect, since A reasons that, whatever B chooses, A is better off defecting than cooperating. Each thus receives −1, rather than the 1 that would have followed from joint cooperation. (See Shubik 1982:253−58 for further discussion.) This analysis appears to suggest that cooperation is irrational in many circumstances and will not emerge spontaneously among rational persons.

In an extensive analysis of the problem of cooperation Axelrod (1984:27−33) shows that the structure of the prisoners' dilemma changes in an open-ended series of plays of the game. He constructed a computer simulation of repeated prisoners' dilemmas involving many strategies. Each strategy played every other strategy in a two-hundred-game series of prisoners' dilemmas in a round-robin and received a score that was the sum of its scores in every contest. This tournament indicated that conditional cooperation (TIT FOR TAT) is the highest-ranking strategy and the most robust over a range of contexts. TIT FOR TAT opens with cooperation and then plays whatever its opponent played on the previous move—that is, it responds cooperatively to cooperation and immediately punishes defection with defection.

On this basis, Axelrod identifies a set of conditions under which cooperation (strict reciprocity) is the optimal strategy for each individual within the circumstances of repeated prisoners' dilemmas. Players must be able to recognize and reidentify their opponents from one play to the next, and they must be able to remember the opponent's previous history of play. These conditions are necessary to make the cooperator respond selectively to different strategies. Players must also judge that the probability of future interaction with the opponent is sufficient to justify weighing future gains from cooperation against present gains from defection. (That is, the "shadow of the future" must be long enough to permit cooperation on self-interested grounds.)

Under these circumstances, Axelrod shows that the optimal strategy for each individual confronted with opportunities for cooperation with others is conditional cooperation. The individual should cooperate with new potential partners, cooperate with partners who have cooperated in the past, and immediately "punish" players who defected on the previous occasion by defecting on this occasion. By pursuing this strategy the individual will achieve a higher gain over an open-ended series of plays than by any other strategy.

The assumptions of stability, isolation, and richness of information assure that these conditions will be satisfied in our model village; the village is small enough to make feasible the strategy of reciprocity. If each villager knows that his future lies within the village; if he knows that the problems and opportunities that confront individuals and the group in the present will continue to do so; and if he knows that villagers monitor one another's contributions to collective activities—then he may rationally conclude that conditional cooperation best serves his interests. Axelrod's analysis would thus predict that patterns of reciprocity and cooperation would emerge spontaneously in the model village and would persist stably until a change in social circumstances undermined the conditions of cooperation.[23]

Community. Michael Taylor (1976, 1982) has argued that some social groups ("communities") have features that facilitate cooperative behavior and collective action. For Taylor (1982:26), a community is a group that embodies a high level of shared beliefs and values among members, is characterized by direct and many-sided social relations (27), and relies on reciprocity as an engine of social coordination.[24] Taylor maintains that in such groups informal sanctions and rewards may effectively control free-rider problems.

Taylor identifies several mechanisms that secure individual contributions to collective projects in traditional societies. The "gift relation" expresses an extended form of conditional reciprocity; by making a gift the giver offers continued mutual aid. If the gift is not reciprocated appropriately, the offer is withdrawn.[25] In private retaliation, each individual (or family) tacitly promises to retaliate against injury or noncontribution to public goods. And a variety of informal social sanctions may be made against those who do not contribute to the collective good: shaming, gossip, and ridicule (1982:84, 89), accusations of sorcery and witchcraft (86), and ostracism and withdrawal of reciprocal aid (82). Members of a closed community who consistently pollute the water supply will be detected, and social disapprobation will result. Community sanctions and benefits thus offset the effects of free-rider impulses by members of the community. Olson himself mentions this avenue, for example, in the case of labor unions using coercion to secure contributions from their members. But Taylor argues that this mechanism has an extensive scope in mid-sized groups that have shared values (communities).

Taylor identifies several features of social life as central to successful collective action. First, successful collective action depends on the assumption that communities are relatively small social groups and that individuals have face-to-face, enduring relations. These conditions guarantee that each player will be relatively well informed about the contribution status of other players and will be able to practice selective reciprocity. Second, many mechanisms that Taylor cites work through diffuse social coercion: the community will identify and punish noncontributors. But for this mechanism to work, information about each player's history of play must be available. Finally, Taylor assumes that communities are coordinated partially through a system of shared values: individual conduct can be shaped through internalized constraints on action. This assumption implies that potential noncontributors are inhibited from noncontribution even where they could escape retaliation.

Our model of village life satisfies these conditions, postulating high levels of shared values and of interdependence—perceived and actual—among individuals. And the assumption of richness of information guarantees that villagers will be able to distinguish accurately between cooperators and noncooperators. These features make feasible the forms of diffuse social coercion that Taylor identifies as supporting communitarian institutions. The model village thus satisfies Taylor's terms, and we should expect the forms of reciprocity and collective action that he predicts to occur within the model village.[26]

Convention. Another important basis for collective action derives from analysis of games of coordination rather than games of competition. A coordination problem is one in which the best payoff to each individual depends on choosing an action that coordinates with the actions others have chosen—for example, finding a friend in a crowded train station.[27] Collective action may succeed if there are prominent features of a context of social choice that permit individuals to coordinate their actions to mutually beneficial outcomes. David Lewis has shown that *conventions* (known regularities of action in response to stereotyped problems of choice) can serve as such points of coordination.[28] In general, a convention may emerge around a family of coordination problems—for example, occasions when companions become separated in crowded places—which suggests a strategy to each individual around which collective action crystallizes ("meet at the ticket counter"). The convention does not need to identify the best collective outcome in each case; it needs only to coordinate individual action reasonably well over repeated occasions.

Imagine, for example, that there is a local practice among villagers of gathering at the river on holidays to fish in groups: some wade into the water and drive the fish toward shore while others wait with baskets at water's edge to catch the fish. This practice might be stable over a long time without any higher-level organization or agreement—just as a regular weekend softball game or café conversation may survive without explicit coordination. Each individual, knowing that the practice exists and that enough other potential players will orient their behavior to the practice to make it succeed, may rationally determine to participate. Without the convention, however, it might be difficult to initiate these activities.

Coordination by convention alone does not solve collective action problems directly, since coordination problems are defined as ones in which the individual payoffs depend on coordination with the future actions of others. This implies that the payoffs do not take the form of public goods (since in the case of a public good, the individual's payoff is the same whatever action he or she chooses). Convention does help with collective action, however, by facilitating action by individuals who are conditionally altruistic, that is, persons who are disposed to contribute to public goods if they are confident that sufficient others will also contribute to achieve the good.[29] If each potential contributor to a flood control project knows that (1) each household is required by custom to contribute one day's labor and that (2) villagers generally honor their customary obligations, then the conditional altruist will judge that success is sufficiently likely that he should contribute as well. Conventions can help maintain the assurance that collective action will succeed so that it is rational for conditional altruists to continue to cooperate.

These results are relevant to the moral economy debate because a shared system of values represents one possible convention for coordinating collective activity.[30] If a group shares an interest in a collective good (such as the purchase of a costly piece of fire-fighting equipment), successful action will depend on possible contributors dividing costs according to an agreeable formula. Equality of contribution is one such formula; but if religious or moral principles would clearly imply another distribution of costs (for example, in proportion to the amount of land owned), these principles may define a principle of cost allocation that is prominent enough to coordinate all parties' contributions. Action may thus coalesce around a set of shared values (for example, the subsistence ethic) simply because it is one clear point of coordination for group action. But having served this function, the ethic is more securely entrenched within social practices— and even more likely to serve as a focus for future action. Thus Hardin (1982:155–87) argues that in stable communities it is possible for "conventional contracts" to emerge around conspicuous solutions to public goods problems.

The requirements of coordination through convention are also reasonably well satisfied in the model village. The assumption of stability provides one important basis for conventional solutions to collective action problems: villagers are familiar with the collective action problems that confront them in their environment and the solutions that have been applied in the past, and they may be confident that these problems will recur. The experience of coping with collective action problems provides a basis for a convention to coordinate collective action in similar circumstances in the future. The assumption of shared values (moral or religious) provides another basis for possible conventions to coordinate collective action. If, for example, religious tradition designates the parish priest as the overseer of tithing in ordinary circumstances, this may suggest a point of coordination in less ordinary circumstances (for example, collection and distribution of grain for the most afflicted families in times of dearth). Finally, the richness of information postulated by the model village facilitates coordination through convention, since it assures that each agent will know a great deal about the beliefs of fellow villagers and will thus be able to identify salient points of coordination.

Group Size Considerations. Traditional village societies are relatively small social groups. Olson's original arguments (1965:22–23) for the collective action theorem stress group size; he argues that small groups may be *privileged*: they may contain individuals for whom the collective good is also a private good. That is, the individual's benefit from achieving the good may exceed the purchasing cost. Large groups, however, are unlikely to have such a structure and are likely to remain latent, (that is, unable to achieve collective goods).

Hardin (1982:40ff.) shows that this analysis of group size is too simple, however, and that a more complete examination demonstrates that size is also relevant in other respects. In particular, Hardin shows that more important than absolute size is the ratio of benefits to costs and the extent of stratification of benefits within the group. If the benefit-to-cost ratio is sufficiently high, the group may contain a subgroup that would benefit from the collective good even if it funded the entire project. "Let us use k to designate the size of any sub-group that just barely stands to benefit from providing the good, even without cooperation from other members of the whole group" (41). Hardin shows that the size of k rather than the absolute size of the group influences the feasibility of collective action.

These size considerations have direct application in small peasant communities: to the extent property holdings are stratified, it will be probable that there is a small group of large landowners who constitute a k-group for such collective projects as water management. Large landowners will derive disproportionate benefits from collective efforts to improve the conditions of agriculture and will thus have a rational incentive to arrange joint action. Whenever this condition is satisfied, the prospects of effective collective action are significantly enhanced.[31]

This does not cover every type of collective action that might occur within a peasant community; in particular, it would *not* facilitate collective action whose benefits are reverse-stratified—action designed primarily to secure the subsistence needs of the poorest villagers. Here the benefits of collective action accrue largely to the small rather than the great, and the primary beneficiaries are least able to pay for the good. This finding parallels Hardin's conclusion (43–45) that group size factors typically skew the advantages of collective action toward the interests of large contributors.

Organizations and Leadership. One final characteristic facilitates collective action within the assumptions of the model village: the coordinating role of informal, nonstate organizations. Village societies typically encompass local political institutions, often a village council dominated by prominent local figures. Such institutions perform certain recurring functions, for example, distributing tax burdens among villagers. But they also provide an institutionalized context within which to consider village interests and problems. As such, they provide the basis for a decision-making process that *may* possess the political skills and resources needed to secure cooperation on collective projects. Villages also typically embody a range of nonpolitical organizations to which villagers belong—kinship groups, religious associations, trade organizations, burial societies, and the like. These provide loyalties and commitments that influence individual motivation, as well as organizational and motivational resources to village leaders who attempt collective action. Such organizations can motivate individuals to participate (through loyalty, solidarity, or shame) and can enhance assurance by informing each villager of the likelihood that other villagers will contribute. Lineage organizations in traditional agrarian China provided a form of cohesion that cut across income and landholding strata and provided a basis for collective action even where conflicts of material interest were significant. Likewise, temple organizations may establish social relationships that cut across both lineage and class, providing yet another possible basis for securing collective action in pursuit of particular common interests.[32]

Varieties of Collective Action

These arguments establish that the traditional village possesses resources—institutional, structural, and normative—to solve problems of collective action. But many collective action problems may confront a traditional village, and the factors considered here do not facilitate all forms equally. The moral economy theory maintains that peasant societies will embrace several kinds of collective practices: labor and draft-animal sharing, crisis insurance among rough equals, agricultural development projects that benefit all villagers, *and* redistributive schemes to preserve the subsistence needs of poor villagers. The factors described above support some of these types; but one case crucial to the moral economy position remains problematic: redistributive and income-leveling practices to guarantee subsistence for the poor. Consider, then, the forms of collective action that these features of village society ought to facilitate: person-to-person mutual aid, disaster insurance, generalized cooperation, and intravillage redistribution from rich to poor villagers. Which would the mechanisms just described support?

Patterns of person-to-person mutual aid—labor exchanges, burial and ritual expense funds, banquets and feasts—should flourish in the model village. These practices embody the strict reciprocity that Axelrod describes, and noncooperators will be refused future aid. We should expect small groups of villagers to exchange labor, food, and small amounts of cash at need.

Risk-sharing arrangements—what we may call disaster insurance schemes—comprise two classes, depending on whether the participants' material circumstances are roughly comparable. Strict reciprocity would support disaster insurance schemes within groups of relatively equal farmers: each realizes that microdisaster may destroy a future crop (through flood, drought, or grazing animals) and that his long-term interests are better served by reciprocity than by noncooperation. But strict reciprocity would not support insurance schemes that include both landed and landless, because the relevant form of recurring reciprocal need is absent. The crises that may afflict the landless will *not* strike the landed, and the disasters that may afflict the landed could not be eased with resources available to the landless. The landed would lack any reciprocity-based incentive to support such schemes.

Consider also what might be called generalized cooperation: joint action by many or all villagers toward a common interest, such as relief from flooding or bandits. These projects may be classified further according to benefit distribution patterns. Benefits may accrue to all villagers equally (a road linking the village to a highway), may be stratified in the same direction as wealth holdings (erosion control), or may be stratified in the opposite direction of wealth (a free health clinic). Strict reciprocity would not support any form of generalized cooperation, since it involves contributions to pure public goods and is not person-to-person. Individuals cannot be denied the benefits of these types of collective action, either in the present or in the future. But several other processes discussed above can facilitate such projects: (1) Shared values can support generalized cooperation. If moral or religious values require every villager to contribute to projects that aim at perceived common interests, these direct and indirect incentives may be sufficient to produce the needed level of cooperation. (2) Positive stratification of benefits may encourage generalized cooperation by creating a k-group capable of funding or organizing the project. This form of collective action would not support reverse-stratified projects, however, since the groups best served by the project would be least able to fund them. (3) Local political features—leadership, integrative social organizations, and a process of consensus building—pertain specifically to village-level collective action directed toward public goods. Such projects possess structural limitations similar to the previous category; to the extent that political influence is stratified or that political leaders come from the richest segment of the village, we should expect politically selected projects to be biased toward notable interests.

Projects with positively stratified benefits will thus be easiest to achieve; equal-benefit projects supported by strong values and diffuse coercion will be possible; and reverse-stratified projects will be difficult to achieve without strong support from widely shared moral commitments. Collective action for public goods *is* feasible within the model village, even assuming individual rationality. But the types of collective action projects that extended individual rationality will support do have structural limits.

Redistributive collective practices, which favor the interests of the weak and poor over the rich, are essential to the moral economy view.[33] Examples include periodic redistribution of communal lands to benefit poor peasants, compulsory charity, preferential tax distribution that exempts the poorest peasants, and disaster funds to secure the poor against subsistence crises. Can the mechanisms identified here—reciprocity, community, coordination, stratification of benefits, and local politics and organizations—support genuinely redistributive practices?

They cannot. Redistributive schemes harm rather than enhance the interests of affluent villagers; in the strictest sense, a redistributive scheme does not provide a public good at all, since it does not benefit all contributors. Enlightened prudence will not lead affluent villagers to support such schemes. The conditions of reciprocity will not provide such an interest (unless rich villagers are in jeopardy of falling precipitously into a lower class). Coordination around conventions will lead to joint action only if all parties can improve their payoffs, which will not happen in redistributive schemes. Since redistributive schemes result in reverse stratified benefits, there will be no k-group to fund such a scheme. Political processes, both formal and informal, *could* organize and implement a redistributive scheme; but on our assumptions these processes are dominated by affluent villagers motivated by prudent self-interest. For redistributive practices to persist, rational self-interest on the part of all villagers will not suffice; the presence of moral values that work against individual rationality must be postulated.[34]

Before leaving the model village it is worth asking what circumstances might begin to undermine voluntary cooperation and collective action in village society. Incentives toward conditional reciprocity disappear as group size grows larger and social relations become more atomized. And familiar social forces at work on the traditional village appear to have just such effects. First, as traditional patterns of interaction destabilize, the shadow of the future shortens and cooperation becomes a less promising strategy. Extreme pressure on village survival created by famine, drought, or banditry can put continuing interactions under a cloud; likewise, market forces or extra-village politics (such as a more intrusive state) can disrupt traditional social relations and undermine cooperation by giving individuals a smaller stake in dealing with other villagers.[35]

Second, to the extent that villagers interact more heavily with outsiders they may have less to gain from cooperation with insiders. As individuals develop primary economic and political relations to outsiders (through day labor in the city, temporary migration, or affiliation with national political parties), both interdependence and information richness diminish. As the isolation of the village is lessened, then, so collective and communitarian practices are undermined.[36] Finally, exposure to a national economy and culture may be expected to reduce shared values within traditional village society, and these values will no longer be able to enhance cooperation through convention or community.[37]

Significantly, these are just the factors that Scott identifies as undermining the moral economy of the peasant: more extensive cash farming, larger market forces, privatization of land, proletarianization and semiproletarianization, and so on. As villages become more atomized under population pressure, market forces, and the colonial state, there is less face-to-face interaction, less room for coordination because of more extreme stresses on individual welfare, and less assurance that the community's practices will survive.

Rational self-interest appears to support a broader range of collective action in the circumstances of the traditional village than Popkin would allow. Yet this broader range falls short of the communitarian practices postulated by the full moral economy view. Some features of a social group enhance effective collective action, and these features are conspicuous in many traditional peasant societies. It is thus reasonable to expect that traditional peasant villages find it easier to achieve collective action and cooperative practices than Popkin would suggest. And rational decision makers in the traditional village have clear, compelling reasons to continue to contribute to reciprocal schemes of collective action. Patterns of ongoing reciprocity, shared values, and community sanctions and rewards may effectively offset free-rider tendencies within the traditional village and permit the village to secure collective goods that would be impossible in a more atomized, anomic society.

The moral economy approach, however, postulates a form of communal practice that does *not* derive from the assumption of extended individual rationality: practices that redistribute from the rich and mighty to the poor and powerless. This assumption postulates a moral scheme that is not grounded in rational self-interest. Its adequacy will depend on whether it is possible to provide some account of the emergence, effective operation, and regular reproduction of a set of moral values that orient behavior toward redistributive collective goods.

A gap still exists between the forms of collective action feasible through an extended rational choice model and the full moral economy hypothesis. Popkin's negative case is too sweeping; many types of collective action can be achieved within the traditional village on the basis of rational self-interest. But even if qualified along the lines suggested here, the rational choice model and the moral economy position still disagree. One type of potential collective action will not emerge from the assumptions of the extended rational choice model: redistributive action oriented toward the subsistence needs of the poorest villagers. And it is central to the moral economy position that such practices will emerge. To support that hypothesis a full-blooded and nonreducible theory of the influence of moral values on peasant behavior is necessary.

A methodological conclusion concerning the utility of public choice theory for constructing social explanations can be drawn. These arguments suggest that the public choice framework is currently too sparse to make predictions in real cases. It postulates narrow economic rationality in the individual and derives aggregate consequences at the social level: cooperation and collective action will be infrequent and difficult. But this discussion shows that the occurrence of collective action is indeterminate even assuming individual rationality. We must specify the circumstances of choice, the norms and values within which decision makers act, the temporal structure of social action, and the institutional context of action before we can make even a tentative conclusion about the likelihood of collective action and cooperation. The public choice paradigm must formulate more complex models of the institutional and cultural context of rational deliberation if it is to understand the forms that individual and collective behavior are likely to take within traditional village societies.

Normative Systems as Explanatory Factors

A complementary aspect of this debate is disagreement over the role of norms, values, and symbolic systems in determining the character of village institutions and practices. Do systems of values in traditional societies constrain and motivate individual behavior, thereby influencing social life? If so, through what social mechanisms? This question may be posed at either the individual or the social level. Is individual peasant behavior influenced by the norms and values of the society within which the individual exists? And are social practices, institutions, and patterns of development influenced by the matrix of norms and values that members of that society share at a given time?

A Social Action Model

Scott and Popkin differ sharply on the role of moral values in social life. Popkin assumes that moral values are negligible, asserting that village practices are determined primarily as the aggregate of the rational activity of many rational, welfare-maximizing villagers. He holds that village institutions will largely reflect the material interests of those most able to impose their will on the village and that practices that embody the welfare of the village as a whole, or its most needy members, will *not* emerge unless they correspond to material interests of powerful figures. This feature makes Popkin's a political economy approach; Popkin subsumes the explanation of patterns of village life under the framework of rational individual self-interest, just as the economist subsumes patterns of market phenomena under rational economic decision making. In this view, moral norms and values have negligible (or at any rate, secondary) effect on social life.

By contrast, Scott's position *depends* on the assumption that systems of moral values impose patterns on the societies in which they are found and that these normative systems are more fundamental than the patterns of decision making that constitute social action. To explain peasant behavior, it is necessary to understand the cultural values of the peasant. This view constitutes both a criticism of and an alternative to the rational choice paradigm as an account of action: peasants are not mere self-interested calculators but social actors. Their actions result from a complex process of deliberation that both takes account of and is structured by moral values, commitments to others, traditional practices, *and* self-interest. Certain behaviors are unthinkable—for example, serving pork at an Islamic feast. And others are highly inhibited though not impossible—such as flatly refusing to tithe. This part of Scott's position suggests that a richer model of peasant action than the rational choice model is needed and that once we have such a model we will see that the rational choice paradigm has limited application.[38] This could be called the social action model of choice: all action takes place within a universe of meaningful choices, background values and meanings determine the universe of the possible, and this universe imposes narrow constraints on the possibilities available to the individual. Culturally specific meanings and values structure individual action.

Scott holds that the values and meanings that constitute the context of social action play a causal role in determining aggregate patterns of village life and traditional society. (Call this the causal claim.) Voluntary charity, collective activity and work, religious activity, rebellion and resistance, individual violence and antagonism—these examples of aggregate patterns can, according to Scott, properly be explained by reference to a background set of meanings and values—a moral economy—shared by a community within the context of which the forms of individual activity that contribute to these patterns are predictable.

Scott's account of individual motivation is sketchy; accordingly, we must extrapolate to arrive at a more definite view. Nonetheless, the outlines are clear; Scott's position emerges from the following:

[A strictly materialist view] risks treating the peasant purely as a kind of marketplace individualist who amorally ransacks his environment so as to reach his personal goal. . . . The individual and society are set apart from this perspective and society is simply the milieu in which he must act. . . . To stop there is to miss the critical social context of peasant action. It is to miss the central fact that the peasant is born into a society and culture that provide him with a fund of moral values, a set of concrete social relationships, a pattern of expectations about the behavior of others, and a sense of how those in his culture have proceeded to similar goals in the past. . . . We are thus in the presence of cultural values and forms in all peasant social action. (1976:166)

The strictly materialist view to which Scott refers is the narrow political economy approach, which defines peasant goals as objective material interests (subsistence security, income, and political power and influence). All action may be understood as a calculated attempt to maximize attainment of these goals. Scott suggests that the materialist view is too narrow in two ways. Most important, Scott assumes that individuals are influenced by cultural values they have internalized through socialization. More radically, however, he suggests that actions, goals, and circumstances must be understood in terms of cultural meanings, not merely objective or material features. Action is not merely instrumental but may also have normative, symbolic, or expressive functions.

How might norms and values influence behavior? Scott suggests two distinct forms of influence. There is first direct normative constraint. The individual internalizes a sense of culturally specific prohibitions and obligations; these norms play a direct role in the deliberative process; and the individual is disposed (to some degree) to act in accordance with these norms. This form of influence is familiar from theories of moral psychology (call this the normative dimension of social action). It can be integrated into a rational choice model relatively straightforwardly by introducing a mechanism through which norms are weighed in the process of deliberation. Several recent efforts have been made to expand the concept of economic rationality in such a fashion, providing a means through which rational conduct may be influenced by moral principle and commitment (for example, Sen 1987, Harsanyi 1977, or Margolis 1982).

Less tangibly, Scott suggests in this passage that these cultural values influence action by shaping individual perceptions of the social world and of available options for action. Individual circumstances are not raw material "givens"; they are meaningful, interpreted social relations as understood by the individual. If we are to understand the behavior of landless tenants when confronted with changes in the land tenure system, for example, it is not enough to describe existing rent relations in material terms, such as fraction of the product going to tenant and landlord. The rent relation must be understood instead in terms of value-oriented assumptions about just and unjust rental relations, customary obligations of landlords and tenants, religious duties, and the like. The tenant perceives the relation as a meaningful element of his social world, in these terms, and they influence his dispositions to behavior. This model suggests that social action is structured by available categories of social perception. Certain kinds of landlord behavior provoke resistance not just because of their material implications for welfare but because of the meaning those actions have to the tenants (call this the meaning dimension of social action).

This account makes it more difficult to assimilate the workings of cultural meanings or norms into a rational choice model. For the rational choice model requires that we distinguish between form and content in rational deliberation: the decision-making process is the form, and the beliefs and values that constitute the inputs of that process are the content. The interpretation-theoretic view suggests instead that cultural facts operate at the level of form as well as content; they shape the *processes* of perception, belief formation, and judgment themselves. The actor whose social world is structured by the concept of just price (the medieval peasant, perhaps) does not *choose* to view a capitalist landlord or merchant as unjust; rather, the injustice of a (high) market-determined price is simply part of the medieval worldview.[39]

An adequate model of social action will need to be more complex than the rational choice model in at least two dimensions. First, the actor must be represented as responding to a meaningful environment of actions by others and cultural institutions and practices. The actor perceives the actions and practices of the community in a value-laden way and responds accordingly. Second, the moral norms (obligations and prohibitions) that constrain action at the deliberative level must be represented. Finally, the goals that the actor takes as fundamental, often such material factors as security, income, and family welfare, must be represented. An account of action that overlooks any of these factors will not be a satisfactory basis for explaining individual behavior in a given cultural context.

In practice Scott's account primarily emphasizes the normative and material dimensions. He provides a relatively full account of the norms that define the subsistence ethic and the implications these norms have for action when applied to changes in social practices and institutions generated by colonialism and market agriculture. And he details the material institutions, and material interests, of Southeast Asian rural society.[40]

At the level of individual action, then, Scott's position may be summarized as follows: (1) Peasants are intentional actors who (often) deliberate and choose in a rational way. (2) Peasants always live within a social world whose "facts" are determined by a matrix of norms and concepts that constitute the meaning of the primary social relations. Their actions and choices are constrained by their understanding of the meaning and value of events and practices in their world. (3) Peasants possess shared values and norms—in particular, norms defining just or civilized treatment of them by other actors in society—that are incorporated into the deliberative process. These values influence the deliberative process in that the eventual action depends (at least in part) on consideration of the relevant moral norms. (4) Peasants have material interests and are concerned to preserve them.

To explain individual peasant action, it is necessary: to understand the meaning of the social relations that constitute the context of the action, to know the norms that the actor would consider relevant to action in these circumstances, and to know the actor's perceived material interests. This is manifestly more complex than the theory associated with the political economy approach. But note that the social action theory reduces to the political economy model in a range of cases: cases in which no norms and values are outstanding, in which an act's sole cultural meaning is its material consequences, and in which the actor sees material consequences as the primary factor of deliberation. Under such circumstances the social actor would be expected to behave as the rational peasant is postulated to behave: to maximize personal or familial welfare.

Mechanisms of Social Causation

Scott maintains that the subsistence ethic affects social structure and collective behavior. It is plausible to require that causal explanations account for the mechanisms (natural or social) that connect cause and effect. Accordingly, the mechanisms Scott's causal arguments depend on must be considered. This analysis relies on two sorts of causal processes that correspond to two levels of analysis—individual and organizational. First is a prototheory of individual behavior (how norms and perceptions lead an individual to be disposed to resist). As we saw earlier, this theory is much more complex than the political economy model of rational decision making, but it serves the same explanatory function. The theory of social action is designed to explain individual behavior, given relevant background information (goals, beliefs, norms, and meanings). Second, a comprehensive account of collective political behavior (which Scott does not attempt to provide) would require a theory of how political organizations (the state, political parties, religious associations, councils of notables) manage collective behavior.

The mechanism that underlies the successful working of a value system is found at the level of individual behavior. Scott asserts that the subsistence ethic is a strong motivation: individuals are to some degree disposed to act out of regard for the requirements of the ethical system, and when a form of treatment clearly violates the ethic, the victim will be inclined to retaliate. Scott cites examples of peasant fury over a landlord's refusal to allow a rent abatement in a bad harvest year. The cause of the anger is not simply material deprivation, or even deprivation occasioned by a particular person; it is that the deprivation comes through a proscribed form of behavior. The values associated with the subsistence ethic constitute a normative framework for peasant behavior. "Woven into the tissue of peasant behavior, then, whether in normal local routines or in the violence of an uprising, is the structure of a shared moral universe, a common notion of what is just" (167).

Scott holds that virtually all parties—landlord, official, and peasant alike—in the traditional village accept the legitimacy of the main elements of the subsistence ethic. They modulate their behavior out of regard for these values: "It is critical to understand that the obligation of reciprocity is a moral principle par excellence and that it applies as strongly to relationships between unequals as between equals" (168). Each may see the requirements of the ethic in a different light, but few reject it out of hand. In particular, Scott argues that the subsistence ethic affects the empowered within peasant society—the landlord and the village notable. This may stem from the notable's sincere adherence to the values of the ethic or from a fear of the results of noncompliance. Scott cites gossip, boycott, ridicule, and the like as means by which the group can enforce the requirements of the ethic on the powerful.

These processes apply directly to the character of the client-patron relationship. Plainly, the patron wields the greater power. But the subsistence ethic requires the patron to extend credit to the client in times of need, to reduce rents in times of poor harvest, to offer bureaucratic assistance in the client's dealings with the state, and so forth. The patron as well as the client admits obligations, and through a mixture of internal and external factors (sincere adherence to the code and fear of consequences in light of nonconformance) the patron generally adheres to the code.

Scott cites two mechanisms that reinforce the subsistence ethic and its associated practices at the individual level; significantly, both are familiar from our earlier discussion of reciprocity and community. First, he holds that tacit reciprocity is a stable, continuing practice in traditional society: "It is also evident that as soon as a peasant leans on his kin or his patron rather than on his own resources, he gives them a reciprocal claim on his own labor and resources. The kin and friends who bail him out will expect the same consideration when they are in trouble and he has something to spare. In fact, they aid him, one might say, because there is a tacit consensus about reciprocity" (28). This observation is precisely what we would expect from Axelrod's account of reciprocity.

Second, Scott refers to a range of forms of social coercion that support shared values—treatments that punish those whose behavior does not conform to the subsistence ethic.

> Few village studies of Southeast Asia fail to remark on the informal social controls which act to provide for the minimal needs of the village poor. The position of the better-off appears to be legitimized only to the extent that their resources are employed in ways which meet the broadly defined welfare needs of villagers. . . . Most studies repeatedly emphasize the informal social controls which tend either to redistribute the wealth or to impose specific obligations on its owners. The prosaic, even banal, character of these social controls belies their importance.

> Well-to-do villagers avoid malicious gossip only at the price of an
> exaggerated generosity. (41)

Affluent villagers who refuse to contribute to ceremonial expenses or
landlords who refuse to provide small loans to their tenants in times
of dearth may be slandered, gossiped about, and ridiculed; and within
the traditional village these are relatively effective forms of sanction.
Note that these are just the mechanisms that Taylor identifies as the
means through which a community imposes its values on all its
members.

Here we may assume a mix of motives: a moral motivation deriving from the subsistence ethic (every villager has a right to subsistence, and may therefore claim aid from other villagers); and a rational interest deriving from the long-term benefits of reciprocity
(each villager knows that he may find himself in similar circumstances in the future and that noncontribution will be generally
known, so that he may not receive aid when needed in the future).[41]
Here again, then, Scott has grounds for holding that the normative
system affects the patterns of village society and, in particular, that
the subsistence ethic may stabilize village welfare practices by
providing an internal motive and a focus for sanction by other villagers against noncompliance; "An understanding of the informal
social guarantees of village life is crucial to our argument because, as
they are sustained by local opinion, they represent something of a
living normative model of equity and justice. They represent the
peasant view of decent social relations" (41). The normative system
has a primary influence on individual behavior and a secondary influence on noncompliance through threats of disapprobation by other
villagers.

A provisional conclusion may be drawn about the explanatory role
of values in social action. Popkin's approach disposes him to underestimate the causal role of a scheme of shared values within a traditional and relatively closed society. But the effects of such values on
aspects of village life can be observed. More important, it is possible
to give a theoretical account of the mechanisms of such causation
through individual decision makers. Two distinct mechanisms have
been identified. The individual decision maker, first, may adhere
sincerely to those values; he may structure his choices by considering the requirements of the subsistence ethic. And second, even
those who do not find moral reasoning a primary motivator may
nonetheless be constrained to comply with the community's value

system for fear of community sanctions—ridicule, gossip, accusations of witchcraft, social ostracism, or violent retribution. Shared values within a social group may establish diffuse coercive forces that reinforce the ethic even among nonadherents. Here the village ethic works indirectly, through the actions of villagers who accept the ethic and act against noncontributors.

Functional Assumptions in the Moral Economy Framework

The moral economy framework asserts that traditional social arrangements protect poor villagers from the inevitable subsistence crises of peasant farming. It assumes that social institutions and arrangements are functionally adapted to the needs of the population that lives within them. Scott writes, "If the need for a guaranteed minimum is a powerful motive in peasant life, one would expect to find institutionalized patterns in peasant communities which provide for this need. And, in fact, it is above all within the village—in the patterns of social control and reciprocity that structure daily conduct—where the subsistence ethic finds social expression" (1976:40). Scott makes two related assertions here: that the existence of needs at the individual level makes likely the existence of social structures that satisfy those needs, and that the existence of a system of norms makes likely the existence of a set of social practices that "express" those norms. Both assertions are problematic—not because such correspondences never exist but because Scott must describe the mechanisms through which needs and norms give rise to social arrangements that satisfy and express them. In other words, claims of a correspondence between individual needs and values and social structures must be underwritten by some more general account linking the two levels.

One way to underwrite these claims is to rest on the assumptions of a functionalist sociology. Crudely put, functionalism holds that a social system is a complex of functionally integrated institutions and practices. Each institution is postulated to have the properties necessary to satisfy some need of the entire system or an important subsystem. Examples of social needs that have been included in functionalist explanations are social cohesion (Malinowski 1922), the smooth workings of a market economy (North and Thomas 1973), and the reproduction of a set of property relations (G. Cohen 1978).

The functionalist framework purports to provide a basis for both explanation and prediction. To explain a social structure or practice, simply identify the benefits that structure confers on the system. And if one has identified a need of an important component of the system, then the functionalist framework predicts a corresponding social institution.

Functionalist explanation in social science has been subjected to devastating criticism, however, particularly through the writings of Jon Elster (1982, 1983). The general argument is this: Functional explanations are most plausible when applied to complex artifacts (such as nuclear power plants) and biological systems (such as species). Each of these examples is special, however, in that the functional claim is underwritten by a well-known causal story that explains why a given element has a functional role within the system. In artifacts, that story concerns the intentions of the designer of the system; the water tower has the function of dissipating excess heat within the power plant because the plant designer, recognizing that the plant will produce excess heat, designed the water tower to dissipate that heat. In biological systems, the story concerns the process of natural selection. Through natural selection the functional organization of the physiology of a given species is fine-tuned to a particular environment of selection.

In social systems, however, neither story applies. In general, social institutions have not been deliberately designed with the beneficial effects attributed to them in mind, and no process of social evolution analogous to natural evolution explains the adaptability of given institutions. Elster draws a convincing conclusion from such considerations: functional claims in social science must be accompanied by an indication of the mechanisms through which the functional relation in question began and is reproduced over time. "Microfoundations" must be provided for functional claims: an account of the specific pathways at the level of individual behavior through which institutions and practices are modulated to satisfy the needs of the system.[42]

Popkin's explanatory paradigm is a useful corrective in this context. He offers an aggregative model of explanation similar to Thomas Schelling's (1978). According to this model aggregate social phenomena are explained as the outcome—often unintended—of the rational choices of individuals within existing circumstances. Popkin aims to explain central features of Vietnamese village society as a result of problems of collective action. In effect, he puts forward deductive explanations that begin by assuming individual rationality, then describe the circumstances of choice surrounding the actors (peasant, lord, official, moneylender), and finally predict aggregate outcomes in village society. He describes such features as property stratification, exploitative credit and rent arrangements, tenurial arrangements that favor the landlord, absence of effective subsistence insurance systems, and difficulty of mounting collective projects (for example, water management projects) that would supply public goods. Popkin's explanatory paradigm, then, is deductive and microfoundational: he explains village-level social patterns through deductive arguments by assuming individual rationality and circumstances of choice and then describing the aggregate patterns that result.

The moral economy claim about the leveling effects of traditional social institutions must be supplemented by an account of the processes through which individual behavior leads to such institutions. This finding suggests an avenue of research for the moral economy theorist that would allow rational peasant criticisms to be addressed squarely; by laying out reasonable assumptions about peasant decision making and the social relations through which peasant action is organized, the moral economy theorist can refute the rational peasant theory. And by detailing the mechanisms through which rational individual welfare-maximizing behavior is offset or constrained to conform to collective welfare needs, the moral economy position can be made to withstand Popkin's theoretical criticisms.

Note that the moral economy argument is thus retained within a generally individualist framework. Social entities (systems of shared values) cause social changes (rebellions), but they do so through individual-level processes. Values influence individual choices, and the actions of individuals aggregate to large-scale social events. Whatever their differences, Scott and Popkin advance accounts that are in principle compatible with the requirement of microfoundations for macroexplanations.[43] Popkin offers such microfoundations explicitly, whereas Scott's account needs such foundations to obviate a charge of spurious functionalism.

The Empirical Dispute between Scott and Popkin

Popkin maintains that the moral economists—in particular, Scott—have got the story wrong in their account of village life in Southeast

Asia. The central empirical disagreement between Scott and Popkin is over the extent and nature of redistributive mechanisms within village life. Did land redistribution occur? If so, did the process tend to benefit the poor? Did charitable institutions within the village level out subsistence crises for the poor? Were tax burdens within corporate villages distributed to ease the subsistence crises of the poor? On each of these points Scott is affirmative, Popkin negative. More precisely, Scott holds (60–61) that the traditional village—precolonial and precapitalist—embodied redistributive institutions and that these institutions were undermined and eventually overthrown by colonialism and commercialization.

Is this a straightforward empirical disagreement? Could data resolve the issue in favor of one position? It should first be noted that the two accounts differ in scope. Scott offers a generalization about peasant life in Southeast Asia, illustrating his account with examples from Burma and Vietnam. But the hypothesis must be formulated more specifically in time and place before it can be evaluated empirically; historical evidence can only be provided with a more specific scope. And substantial regional and temporal variation in the data is likely. Suppose, then, that we confine the dispute to Vietnam (map 2.1). Scott claims that the villages of pre-twentieth-century Vietnam possessed substantial and effective redistributive mechanisms; Popkin denies it. Even here, however, two dimensions of variation impede empirical evaluation. First may be significant temporal variation; perhaps, for example, colonialism and commercialization had a devastating effect on redistributive mechanisms, so that data from precolonial Vietnam would support Scott, whereas data from colonial Vietnam would support Popkin. Second may be important regional variation; Cochinchina, for example, was a newly settled border area with little communal solidarity, whereas Annam and Tonkin were much older areas with strong communal traditions. Data drawn from the north might support Scott, whereas contemporaneous data from the south might support Popkin. In fact, Scott holds that the strength of the moral economy of rural Vietnam varied in just this way: "Where these norms were weak to begin with, notably in the relatively atomized frontier regions of Cochinchina and Lower Burma, they never had provided much social insurance for the peasantry" (60).

Let us take one factual disagreement and follow it through both Scott and Popkin. Scott asserts (43) that in Tonkin and Annam communal control over land was substantial (roughly 25 percent) and that this land was used (in part) for redistributive purposes: "Some of this land was allotted more or less on the basis of need to poor villagers. The rent from communal land was deployed in part to help the poor pay taxes and to support noncultivating widows and orphans" (43). Scott cites Yves Henry, *Economie agricole de l'Indochine* (Hanoi: Government Générale de l'Indochine, 1932), as his source for these data. These data are drawn from northern and central Vietnam, and Scott is not specific about the time. Later arguments make it plain, however, that this analysis applies to pre-twentieth-century Annam, for in discussing the Nghe-Tinh rebellions in northern Annam, Scott argues that by the 1920s "communal land that had once relieved the plight of the village poor had fallen increasingly into the hands of local notables and mandarins" (129). The redistributive effects of communal land institutions had thus lessened sharply by the 1920s, producing greater subsistence pressure on the poor and exacerbating the sense of injustice experienced by the landless.

Now consider Popkin's data. Popkin agrees (1979:91, 173) that there was substantial communal land (20–25 percent) in Annam and Tonkin and that this institution was never significant in the south (Cochinchina). But even in the north, Popkin disagrees over the effect of communal land institutions. According to Popkin, communal land was controlled by village political institutions; these institutions were dominated by village notables who sought advantages from their positions; and as a result, communal land redistribution was *not* typically oriented toward the subsistence needs of the poor. "Generally, village procedures gave important benefits to notables and protected—rather than leveled—wealth" (100). Popkin concedes that some communal land was reserved for the truly needy—"widows, orphans, and the aged without children" (101) but argues that the bulk of communal lands "were distributed not according to need, but ascriptively, on the basis of rank within the village" (101). Popkin's analysis throughout this chapter relies heavily on a work by Paul Ory, *La Commune annamite au Tonkin*.[44] Popkin describes Ory as "one of the most meticulous observers of the nineteenth-century Vietnamese village" (107). (Popkin also refers to Yves Henry's study [1931–32], which he faults for seriously underestimating the extent of large holdings in Annam [155].)

Here, then, is a fairly sharply defined empirical disagreement between Scott and Popkin. Scott maintains that in nineteenth-century Annam effective institutions of communal redistribution satisfied the subsistence needs of the poorest; Popkin offers evidence for the same time and place that contradicts this claim. But neither makes a compelling empirical case; on balance, Popkin offers more varied and detailed sources to support his position. In both studies the data are thin, subject to interpretation, and largely take the form of interpretations offered by other observers. The empirical cases offered by Scott and Popkin are indeterminate, and only further, fine-grained historical research at the local level can resolve even this single, rather limited question—whether there was a substantial redistributive effect of communal land within the precolonial Annam village. This suggests the unlikelihood that the moral economy debate can be resolved on narrowly empirical grounds.

The Relation between Scott and Popkin

Scott and Popkin appear to view their theories as incompatible. The most salient difference between them is at the level of their respective theories of individual motivation and action. Popkin assumes a narrow calculus of cost and benefit, whereas Scott postulates that individuals act within a set of cultural values that constrain and motivate action and thus offset pure self-interest. To explain peasant behavior, therefore, it is not sufficient to identify the circumstances of choice and derive the optimal action for the individual. Both the current circumstances of choice *and* the values and norms that define the action must be identified; then it may be possible to work out what the individual will choose.

Scott and Popkin offer aggregative explanations based on a theory of individual action. What Scott adds to the model is the assumption that individuals are motivated not only by rational self-interest but also by a set of culturally established constraints. This permits Scott to make a causal argument: the prevalence of certain norms and values is causally involved in the emergence of an aggregate pattern for a given social group. A subsistence-based sense of justice is thus a causal condition for peasant rebellion in twentieth-century Vietnam, according to Scott.

This treatment identifies an important disagreement between the two positions concerning the springs of individual behavior. But both have a place in a more comprehensive perspective, and they are thus complementary rather than contradictory. Of the two accounts, Scott's is the more general, and Popkin's analysis may be seen as an effort to specify one component of the full theory that Scott's account would need to become a comprehensive theory of peasant behavior.

Recall that Scott's account takes the form of a complex causal analysis. This treatment depends on several mechanisms, but central is a theory of individual motivation to provide an avenue through which social perceptions and values are transformed into individual and collective behavior. The second mechanism Scott's account requires is a theory of organizations and organizational behavior to explain the process of politics through which individual behavior is aggregated or dissipated into collective action. Scott pays little attention to this part of the comprehensive account, but he recognizes the need for such a theory.

Popkin's analysis contributes to both problems. He presents a simple model of individual motivation and decision making. Popkin's account is rational-intentional, and it depends on a narrow conception of rationality. Although this conception faces several serious problems, it applies directly to many aspects of social and individual life. Popkin attempts to discover the collective consequences of this theory of individual decision making within the circumstances of the traditional village; on the whole, his analysis is rigorous and insightful. Popkin's second contribution lies with organizational behavior. He provides a parsimonious and elegant way to analyze the behavior of organizations in terms of the interests of its leaders and members, and he details the unexpected consequences of aggregating private interests into collective organizational action. Here again, however, Popkin's account is flawed by thin motivational assumptions; as we will see in chapter 5, organizational behavior in Asian society displays much of the diversity and complexity of individual behavior.

Chapter 3
Regional Systems in Traditional China

The writings of G. William Skinner have profoundly influenced contemporary China studies. An economic anthropologist, Skinner has constructed a wide variety of formal models to analyze and explain important features of agrarian China: the hierarchical relations among villages, market towns, and cities, the temporal structure of market schedules; the physiographic macroregions into which traditional China may best be analyzed, the logic of administrative postings within the late imperial bureaucracy, the causes of differential rates of urbanization in different regions of nineteenth-century China, and so on. Skinner leads a generation of scholars who have forged a China-centered approach to this field by attempting to avoid traditional presuppositions about China and by adopting the theoretical tools best suited to the voluminous empirical and historical information about traditional China now available.[1]

Skinner's work is pertinent here for several reasons. He is unusually willing to use theoretical constructs and mathematical models to analyze and explain empirical social phenomena, and he is prepared to borrow these constructs and models from many disciplines. Examination of several of his models will shed light on the role and efficacy of formal models in explaining social phenomena. In addition, Skinner's research takes a sophisticated stance toward problems of generalization and specificity in social science. To what extent can generalizations be offered about such social entities as cities, peasant societies, or marketing arrangements? Can generalizations be established about all cities—modern and premodern, European and Asian, commercial and administrative? Or must attention be restricted to particular cases—the nineteenth-century Chinese commercial city, the Vietnamese peasant society of Cochinchina, or medieval French marketing arrangements? Finally, is even this level of description too general, since variations also exist within these categories? Must we restrict our attention to the particular: Hankou in the nineteenth century, or a specific Vietnamese village or medieval French market town? This issue also raises the question of the role of schemes of classification within social science.

Skinner's work raises anew the question of whether the concept of means-end rationality is relevant in explaining noncapitalist or non-Western societies. Skinner's analysis of regional systems in traditional China unavoidably assumes that consumers, farmers, administrators, and other participants are economically rational in their decision-making processes. But other writers hold that the concept of economic rationality is a specific psychological disposition found within the period of bourgeois market society, that it is a modern Western creation, and that it is ethnocentric to use the concept to explain the behavior of persons living in other social relations and times.[2] Instead, it is necessary to construct a radically different model of behavior, oriented by different conceptions of the individual and society, and a set of norms, traditions, and practices that elicit "nonrational" behavior. Is the concept of individual rationality an ethnocentric notion the Westerner imposes on the Chinese peasant? Or is it a justifiable theory of individual behavior everywhere—East or West?

Skinner analyzes three related features of Chinese society and economy: the functional differentiation imposed on places—villages, towns, and cities—by the economic and political behavior of individuals; the spatial relations among places that express this functional specialization in the landscape; and the effective regionalization of the Chinese economy as a result of these factors conjoined with physiography and existing transport technology.

The Hierarchy of Central Places

Skinner analyzes the functional organization of the economic geography of China in terms of several important forms of social specialization: economic, and political or bureaucratic.[3] Economic specialization finds expression in a hierarchical system of markets, whereas political or bureaucratic specialization takes the form of the bureaucratic hierarchy of the traditional state. Skinner first analyzed the structure of local marketing hierarchies: the orderly relations that obtained between villages, market towns, and large market towns in rural China. Central to the notion of a marketing hierarchy is the local marketing system. Consider a region of an agrarian society in which peasants both produce and consume a variety of goods: agricultural produce (grain, cooking oil, cotton) and handicraft products (pots, metal tools, cloth, yarn, ceremonial objects, clothing). We can ask a series of questions about this region:

- How dependent are households on commercial activity (that is, what fraction of household consumption depends on purchase of goods through a market)?
- Through what channels are products acquired from producers, processed and packaged, and distributed to consumers?
- What fraction of products consumed in the region are produced within the region, and what proportion are imported from other regions or other countries?

A pure subsistence economy in which each household is self-sufficient requires no marketing arrangements. Any more complex economy, however, requires a dual system of markets: one through which goods are purchased (or otherwise acquired) from producers for processing and packaging, and one through which finished goods are sold or distributed to consumers. The former system (the production-oriented market system) represents an upward flow of goods from producers to local markets and traveling purchasing agents to higher-level commercial firms that process and package consumer goods; whereas the latter (the consumption-oriented market system) represents a downward flow of goods from centralized firms through a distribution system to consumers.[4] Some goods, such as vegetables, may travel no farther than the local market; peasants bring surplus products to the market and sell or trade them with other local families for consumption. Other goods, such as cotton or tea, may be collected at a local market where peasant producers sell their products to agents for commercial firms; the cotton may then move through a series of hands—including wholesale cotton firms, putting-out firms for spinning, weaving, and finishing, and finished goods firms—and finally return to the local market for sale as cloth or clothing. This circuit may thus move from village to market town to city and back.

In an often-cited series of articles ("Marketing and Social Structure in Rural China," 1964–65), Skinner attempted to provide a basis to analyze the functional and spatial structure of habitation in rural China. He maintained that all central places in traditional China may be arranged in discrete hierarchies defined by economic function. The general ideal of a marketing hierarchy is that higher-level places serve a network of lower-level places by providing goods and services for all lower-level places within the larger system that cannot be supplied locally. Villages have no market facilities; no commodities can be obtained for sale or exchange. Villages are served by a nearby standard market town, which supplies subsistence goods to peasants: tools, grain (if needed), fruits and vegetables, and agricultural services. Skinner defines the standard market as "that type of rural market which met all the normal trade needs of the peasant household: what the household produced but did not consume was normally sold there, and what it consumed but did not produce was normally bought there" (6). The standard market is the lowest rung in the marketing hierarchy above the peasant household and village.

Above the standard market town are a series of higher-level economic units: intermediate market town, central market town, local city, and regional city (9). Intermediate market towns serve standard market towns and are distinguished from them in that they supply luxury goods to village notables, landlords, and officials. Teahouses and social meeting places serve these groups. And higher-level places provide a stratified series of goods and services for the places that they serve. There is thus a hierarchy of places defined in terms of (1) the commodities and services available, (2) the regularities of marketing behavior of the population within the region, and (3) the patterns of itinerant traders and peddlers. Skinner asserts that the trading systems found in a region impose a distinct form of organization on the economic geography of the region: the relations among cities, towns, and villages in the region, and the roads and transportation links that join them. Skinner's postulated hierarchical structure among central places may be represented as a tree diagram (fig. 3.1).

In "Cities and the Hierarchy of Local Systems," Skinner refined this classification of places by distinguishing among eight levels of economic function: standard market town, intermediate market town, central market town, local city, greater city, regional city, regional metropolis, and central metropolis (1977a:286). Each level is defined by characteristic economic functions. These include the range of goods available in its markets that are unavailable in lower-level markets,[5] position in transportation networks, level of postal service available, timing of market schedules, and level of financial service available (347–51).[6]

So far this account is abstracted from space. But cities and towns exist in a two-dimensional space, linked by a transport grid that

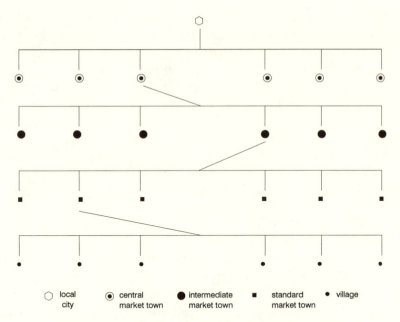

Figure 3.1. Tree diagram of central-place hierarchy

determines a central economic factor: transport cost. This fact implies that the functional differentiation will be manifested in specific spatial arrangements—ideally, ones that minimize transport cost for buyers and sellers. The most obvious implication is that higher-level places in the functional hierarchy will be surrounded by lower-level places, which are themselves surrounded by even lower-level places.

Skinner treats spatial relations among villages, towns, and cities through *central place theory*, as developed by Christaller and Lösch.[7] Central place theory may be characterized as the effort to construct an abstract representation of an economic landscape containing a hierarchy of places on the basis of a set of simple assumptions about economic relations. Central place theory chiefly considers transport cost and the demand threshold and range of a good. Skinner defines demand threshold as "the area containing sufficient consumer demand to enable the supplier to earn normal profits." And he defines the range of a good as "the circumscribed area beyond which buyers would not be willing to travel to purchase the good" (1977a:277). Demand threshold plainly depends on purchasing power per unit of area: a sparsely populated, poor region will provide much less demand for a good per unit area than will a densely populated, affluent area.

These assumptions lead to predictions about the spatial organization of central places. Imagine that villages and market towns are
distributed on a flat, featureless plain containing uniformly scattered
resources.[8] Transport cost is constant in all directions, and demand
density is uniform across the plain. Central place theory shows that a
unique pattern of placement of villages and market towns results,
consistent with plausible requirements of optimality: "(1) the most
disadvantaged villager in any given marketing area is no more and no
less disadvantaged than the most disadvantaged villager in any other
area, and (2) the distance from the market of the most disadvantaged
villager in each marketing area is minimal" (1964–65:17). The optimal arrangement is a set of hexagonal marketing areas with a standard market town at the center and villages distributed in a hexagonal pattern around it. Instead of a tree, we now have a concentric
hierarchy (which still conforms to the tree structure when unraveled;
see fig. 3.2).

Theoretical considerations do not determine how many villages
ought to be served by a single market town; this model is consistent
with one, two, or more rings of villages surrounding the market town
in a hexagonal array. Skinner argues, however, that the Chinese landscape typically provides evidence of a two-ring structure: an inner
ring of six villages and an outer ring of twelve villages (1964–65:18),
or a ratio of eighteen villages to one market town. On this model, we
would expect six paths to radiate from the central market town to
each village in the area.[9]

This same argument may be repeated for each pair of adjacent
levels within the hierarchy of places: standard market towns should
be arranged around intermediate market towns in a hexagonal pattern, and intermediate market towns around higher market towns in
the same pattern. The resulting landscape should consist of superimposed hexagonal arrays of places. And the terrain will be organized
into a hierarchical network in which higher-level places (cities, higher market towns) serve extensive marketing needs of lower-level
places within their marketing areas.

The assumptions that underlie this analysis—flat terrain, uniform
demand density, constant transport cost, and unboundedness—are
patently unrealistic. To apply this model to the Chinese countryside,
the effect of modifying the assumptions in the direction of realism
must be considered. Skinner regionalizes agrarian China into
macroregions of core and periphery regions. This modification introduces additional variables: boundedness, variation of demand and

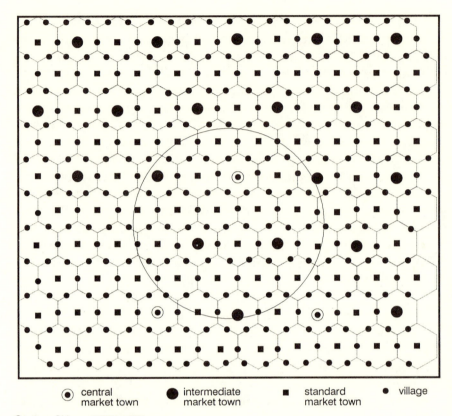

central ⊙ | intermediate ● | standard ■ | village •
market town | market town | market town |

Source: Skinner 1977a:279

Figure 3.2. A model of central places

population density, and variation of transport efficiency. First, the assumption of uniform transport cost should be modified. Agrarian China has a rich network of water transport facilities through rivers, canals, and coastal routes. This means that the cost of transporting a cargo between two cities several hundred miles apart on the Yangzi River may be substantially less that the cost of transporting the same cargo overland from the city to an off-river destination only twenty miles away. Such contrasts in transport efficiency unavoidably distort the idealized countryside. The model also assumes a featureless plain, but real terrain contains varied physiographic features: plains, forests, mountains, marshes, deserts. These also affect transport cost (and demand density). In an extreme case, a marketing system within a narrow valley surrounded by steep mountains and open only at the bottom will bear little resemblance to one situated amid a large plain. These considerations entail that the hexagonal market systems be "stretched" according to variation in transport cost in different directions and that market systems near extremes of physiography may be forced into a different topology altogether.

Skinner's research indicates that Chinese rural marketing systems conform closely to these spatial and functional expectations: "In six areas of China where I have been able to test the proposition, a majority of market towns have precisely six immediately neighboring market towns and hence a marketing area of hexagonal shape, albeit distorted by topographical features" (1964–65:17). Using a map of some twenty market towns and higher-level places of Sichuan, Skinner shows how these places are tied into a regular transportation network embodying the predicted hexagonal structure (22–23). And he later provides (1977a) a more detailed geographical analysis of the same region, showing through a progressive series of maps how the marketing structures are mapped out on the ground (294–95).

Mechanisms

This account postulates strong functional and spatial organization within the system of central places. But given that the location and functions of a central place only rarely result from deliberate design,[10] we need to ask what sorts of mechanisms might underlie the patterns that Skinner identifies. In other words, what *establishes* these relations, and what stabilizes and reproduces them?

These questions are important in part because of the shortcomings of functional explanation in social science generally.[11] Because a given spatial arrangement of central places is optimal for the efficient distribution of products does not guarantee, or even explain, that places will be distributed according to that arrangement. Consequently, if we are to assert that a given social system possesses functional organization, we must sketch the processes that establish and reproduce those functional relations. It is necessary to provide an account of the microprocesses that produce and sustain the macrolevel functional properties.

Skinner offers rudiments of a hypothesis on this issue: "It may be suggested that regularity in central-place hierarchies and consistency in the alignment of function with systemic position are enhanced by, if they do not actually result from, a condition of perduring 'entropy'—many forces acting on the system of central places in many ways over a period of many centuries" (1964–65:5). He suggests that a central-place system is a *stochastic* system in relatively stable equilibrium: a system subject to varied forces whose combined action over time tends to preserve the organization of the system. But what forces are at work here?

Settlement patterns depend ultimately on where individuals choose to live, and their choices are influenced by such economic factors as availability of land and work and convenient access to necessary markets. Other things being equal, deliberative persons will favor a settlement that has more of these requirements over one that has fewer. Critical to both employment and marketing is transport cost,[12] because—particularly in a preindustrial society without mechanized transport—transportation is a major component of a commodity's cost. The cost of transporting a volume of grain two hundred miles might exceed the initial cost of producing it (1977b:217). The more inaccessible a settlement is to the nearest markets, the higher the cost of living.

Differences in transport cost affect the consumer, who may desire to relocate to the more advantaged settlement; the merchant or entrepreneur, who may take advantage of poor settlement location by establishing the rudiments of a new market town; and the government official, who may encourage or discourage the establishment of a new settlement in a given place through a variety of means and interests.

Skinner (1964–65:196) holds that in normal periods new settlements are established gradually through economic considerations (land and transport costs): "My theory [of the pattern of settlement] assumes, then, that during periods unmarred by the wholesale devastation of rural areas, spatial development may be analyzed as a simple process of addition—the continual establishment of new households, new villages and new markets—and that the amount of settlement extinction may be dismissed as negligible." And as individuals contribute to this gradual process through residential and marketing behavior, their preference for convenience and low cost will lead, in the aggregate, to approximately optimal marketing relationships.

The analysis so far unavoidably assumes economic rationality on the part of peasants, merchants, and officials. To assume that spatial relations among places will approach optimal distribution over the long run, given technology, resources, and ecology, is to assume that economic rationality dominates all other features of individual decision making, including religion, necromancy, and kinship relations.[13]

We might ask briefly what forces would upset this functional and spatial organization. Particularly relevant in the course of Chinese rural history are ecology and rebellion. When major ecological disasters occur—regional flooding, drought, earthquake—the basis of the marketing system may be permanently altered: cropping patterns may be forced to change, people may be forced to relocate, and transport networks may be disrupted for a long time. Second, rebellion and war may devastate regions, destroying towns and cities and disrupting the economy an extended time. When a region is rebuilt after such a period of devastation, new functional and spatial patterns may emerge (taking advantage of modest advances in transport technology, for example). Chinese history readily demonstrates both processes: the meandering of the Yellow River in North China periodically forced major shifts in patterns of residence, whereas the destruction caused by the Nian and Taiping rebellions depopulated major cities and towns. Finally, radical improvements in transport efficiency or routes may be expected to alter the system of central places. The introduction of rail or steamboat links between cities may revolutionize the marketing systems found between them. And improving water transport—through canal construction, dredging, or desilting—may have similar effects.

Implications

How does this analysis lead to a better understanding of rural life in China? Skinner suggests several important implications. First, he states that marketing hierarchies have important consequences for the scope of rural social life. Whereas many historians and anthropologists have viewed rural life in China as centered around the village, Skinner asserts that the social horizon of the peasant was substantially broader, encompassing the standard market town, and that the horizon of the local elite extended to the intermediate and higher market town. "The standard marketing system in particular is a unit whose social significance for the peasantry and for peasant relations with other groups deserves major attention. . . . There is good reason, I believe, for attempting to analyze this type of community not only as an intermediate social structure but also as a culture-bearing unit" (1964–65:32). "Thus, marketing had a significance for societal integration in traditional China which at once paralleled and surpassed—which both reinforced and complemented—that of administration" (31). Since the standard marketing community encompasses roughly eighteen villages and a mean population of seven thousand (33), this hypothesis represents a significant broadening of the social horizon of the peasant. Skinner asserts that an adult would typically have a nodding acquaintance with virtually every other adult in all parts of the marketing system and would know a great deal about most families throughout the system. Further, Skinner holds that these forms of social relation and knowledge are limited to the marketing system: the peasant will know little about villages outside the scope of the standard market town—even if a village is nearby but oriented to a different market.

The marketing system is socially integrated by regular attendance by all adults within its scope at the standard market and through the teahouses, marriage brokers, and patron-client relations that are established in the standard market town (35–36). These towns are also the locus of temple organizations, occupational organizations, secret society lodges, and voluntary associations (38–39). Such extra-economic organizations reinforce the social significance of the market town as the basis of rural community.[14] "These examples indicate that a variety of voluntary associations and other formal organizations—the composite lineage, the secret-society lodge, the committee on arrangements for the annual fair, the religious service society—take the standard marketing community as the unit of organization" (39).

Ideas, political movements, and knowledge are diffused through marketing system channels. Itinerant merchants, artisans, and providers of service (letter writers, necromancers, fortune-tellers; 10) who travel on regular schedules through towns within the intermediate and higher marketing areas (28) create much marketing activity. These itinerant businesspeople provide news of the outside world, and the circuits they establish become natural conduits for noncommercial travelers—religious teachers, secret society organizers, and the like. This means that a regular channel of communication penetrated agrarian China and assured the diffusion of ideas, values, technical innovations, and social movements. So local society was less isolated and provincial than it might appear, and political and religious movements had relatively easy access to local society.[15] Winston Hsieh explores implications of these processes in the diffusion of rebellion, holding that rebellious activity in the Canton region in 1911–12 divided sharply along lines of local marketing systems. "Tracing the movements of insurrectionary armies on the map of local marketing systems helps to reveal the channels through which these bands were drawn to the centers of conflict and the patterns of mobilization at various levels of the marketing hierarchy" (1974:120).

Let us recap. Through his analysis of the market structures of rural China, Skinner shows that China was not an undifferentiated, randomly connected mass of places but was a hierarchical system arranged in regular spatial configurations. He suggests that the marketing system structure has important implications for cultural, political, and religious organization at the local level; consequently, to delineate the marketing arrangements for a given region is to lay the basis for explaining a variety of social phenomena and historical processes.[16]

Macroregions

Much of this discussion has proceeded from the local level of rural society: the village and standard market town. In more recent work, Skinner (1977b) takes these tools and argues for a comparable functional and spatial thesis for the Qing Empire as a whole. He suggests that China was not one unified society and economy but a collection of regionalized rural-urban systems that were functionally distinct and experienced different cycles of change. He thus argues that the economic geography of traditional China is best understood as a set of nine macroregions defined by physiography and marketing hierarchies.[17] (See map 3.1.) Each macroregion is a functionally integrated system consisting of an urban core and peripheral hinterlands. The functional organization of each macroregion is constituted by the marketing hierarchies that exist among villages, market towns, and cities. Macroregions are distinct in the sense that it is possible to discern relatively sharp boundaries between them defined by the orientation of local marketing systems. And economics—largely the constraints of transport cost—influences the formation and identity of each macroregion. Skinner thus provides a framework to analyze the distribution of cities, transportation networks, trade networks, and so forth. And he argues that through this framework the spatial patterns of such social phenomena as the allocation of administrative resources, the spread of heterodox religion, or the recruitment of rebel forces can be analyzed.

The macroregions are defined as a "partition of activity-space showing the interrelatedness of things . . . producing a set of functional or nodal regions" (216). Skinner prefers this functional ap-

Source: Skinner 1977b:214

Map 3.1. Macroregions of Qing China

proach to one defining regions in terms of "homogeneity of things considered, producing a set of formal or uniform regions," which would regionalize China in terms of soils, climate, agriculture, or ethnicity. By contrast, "functional regions are internally differentiated and constitute systems in which activities of many kinds are functionally interrelated. In the regions of China under discussion here, cities are the nodes of the systems, the 'command posts' that serve to articulate and integrate human activity in space and time" (216). By offering a core-periphery analysis of the interior of a macroregion, however, Skinner can identify regions that are homogeneous for some purposes—degree of commercialization, degree of urbanization, population density, intensity of cultivation, and so on.[18]

We may summarize the macroregions theory in these terms:

A *macroregion* is a physiographically defined region that contains an integrated urban system, possesses a core-periphery structure, and is largely isolated from other such regions in a national system.

An *integrated urban system* is a system of places arranged in a marketing hierarchy through which commodities flow from producer to processor to consumer.

This definition requires that we define *core-periphery structure:*

Regional *cores* are extensive pockets of high resource density: per capita income; demand density; value of production per unit of land; proportion of land that is arable (1977b:281–82); level of capital investment; level of commercialization (284–85). These variables are indexed by population density.[19]

Regional *hinterlands* are the complement of regional cores.

The macroregions thesis is this:

Traditional China consists of eight macroregions.[20]

Using the above definitions, this thesis may be expanded:

Traditional China contains eight physiographically distinct regions; these regions contain functionally integrated, largely independent urban systems; and these regions possess pockets of high resource concentration that correspond to urban concentrations.

This framework constitutes a theory of the economic geography of China; call it the central thesis. But Skinner offers this thesis in the context of a larger research hypothesis: that noneconomic phenomena in Chinese history may be better understood if they are placed within this spatial framework. He maintains that the pathways of commerce and trade in these macroregions condition a variety of cultural and political phenomena—such things as the spread of heterodox movements, the occurrence and diffusion of rebellion, the structure of the imperial bureaucracy, and the cultural horizon of the peasant.[21] This research hypothesis is necessarily more diffuse and less specific than the core ideas of the economic geography; Skinner is aware that diverse factors influence these noneconomic phenomena. Nonetheless, the extended research hypothesis has stimulated much fruitful work and insight into a range of phenomena.

The plausibility of the macroregions framework depends heavily on Skinner's criteria for distinguishing among regions. His regionalization proceeds through four related schemes of analysis (1977a:281–82). First, through analysis of urbanization in China he discovers twenty-two city systems. By tracing the maximal hinterlands of these city systems (some of which join into larger urban networks), a smaller number of regional city systems can be discerned. Skinner then considers the functional integration of these city systems by estimating the volume of trade between various points in the urban system. This feature establishes a high degree of independence of regional city-systems. Third, Skinner maps the distribution of economic resources (per capita income, population density, irrigation density) across the landscape. When these variables are plotted by county, a distinct separation results between core and periphery of various regions, defined in terms of resource concentration. Finally, Skinner analyzes the terrain of China in terms of its large-scale physiographic features, chiefly river systems and barriers to transportation (mountains, marshes, deserts). The indications of regionalization produced by the preceding criteria conform closely to the physiographic regions defined by river systems and boundaries. Skinner describes his results: "When these four approaches are followed in regionalizing nineteenth-century China, the results are in large part mutually reinforcing and/or complementary. Nine major 'islands' of relatively dense population were identified, each surrounded by concentric gradients of declining densities. Each high-density 'core' was wholly contained within one of the nine physiographic macroregions" (1977a:281–82). Map 3.1 represents the macroregions that emerge from this analysis.

Note that each technique for identifying functional regions is best applied using detailed maps of the Chinese landscape. The first criterion would require that we plot high-level urban systems on the basis of the sort of information about the circulation of commodities described in the previous section. The second requires that we plot the flow of trade between all pairs of places, using line-width to indicate volume of flow. The third requires that we represent the concentration of economically significant parameters in their distribution over the landscape: population density, demand density, per capita income, agricultural yield (this is typically done county by county). Skinner suggests that this inquiry will lead to a relatively smooth set of gradients over the landscape, falling off to low-densities at the periphery of each region. Finally, the fourth criterion requires that we add such important physiographic features as mountains, rivers, and transportation routes to our map and define regions in terms of drainage basins.

A priori, these four criteria could have led to significantly different patterns of regionalization, and they might not have produced patterns of regionalization at all. The fact that they do not lead to inconsistent results has several implications. It suggests that the empirical case for this regionalization of China is substantial and convincing. And it implies that we need to explain the convergence among the criteria. Skinner views the last criterion as fundamental, because it defines the constraints of transport cost. The regularities identified by the first and second criterion ultimately depend on this factor (as we saw in the previous section). The third criterion displays regularities that depend on the system identified by the first and second criteria: soil fertility, for example, is enhanced at the urban core through the use of night soil and as a result of a "transfer of fertility" from periphery to core.[22]

Skinner holds that this regionalization provides the basis for a better analysis of aggregate economic and demographic data than province or other political units provide. In relation to urbanization rates, he asserts that "in premodern times urbanization rates for China as a whole are very nearly meaningless and that the question should be reformulated in terms of regions. . . . Accordingly, I have ordered my data on cities regionally, approached urban history in the context of regional development, and analyzed urbanization separately for each physiographic region" (1977b:211–12). The eight resulting macroregions cut across provinces (compare provinces and macroregions on maps 3.2 and 3.3). "Thus, it is methodologically indefensible and generally misleading to compare provincial urbanization rates, for the explanation of differences found is a function not of what the characteristics of the provinces as systems were but simply of how the boundaries happened to be drawn" (218).

Once China is regionalized according to these criteria, Skinner asserts, "In each of the major physiographic regions there developed a reasonably discrete urban system, i.e., a cluster of cities within which interurban transactions were concentrated and whose rural-urban transactions were largely confined within the region" (216). Moreover, each macroregion has a core-periphery structure: "The concentration in a central area of resources— . . . arable land, . . . population and capital investments—and by the thinning out of resources toward the periphery" (216). The core regions have greater

Map 3.2. Provinces of Qing China

population and agricultural productivity and lower transport costs. Distance and mountainous terrain isolate these macroregions, limiting interregional commerce. "Transport costs of this order of magnitude effectively eliminated low-priced bulky goods from interregional trade" (217).

Skinner's regional analysis of traditional China illustrates the importance of choosing an appropriate framework of analysis to explain social patterns. Skinner's data involve population statistics and commercial patterns associated with places—villages, towns, cities, provinces, and China as a whole. He asks what patterns of urbanization may be discerned in these data and what explains the emerging patterns. But the data may be sorted in a variety of ways: by province, by cities according to population size (large, medium, small), by cities according to function (commercial city, administrative city), or by macroregions. And Skinner holds some schemes of analysis superior in revealing patterns of population growth and movement that correspond to genuine underlying social structures and causes. Thus Skinner argues that macroregions defined in terms of physiography and functional connectedness are appropriate units of geographical analysis and that when demographic data are arranged in these terms,

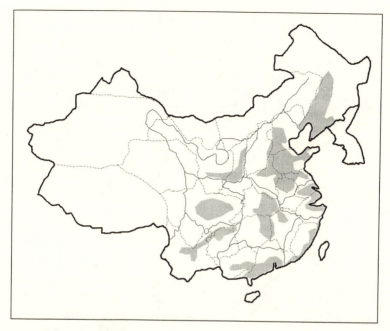

Source: Skinner 1977b:215
Map 3.3. Provinces and macroregions of Qing China

significant patterns of urbanization emerge. This may be Skinner's most important contribution: his insistence on the spatial and temporal differentiation discernable in Chinese history and the importance of analyzing economic and social data within the context of an appropriate spatial and temporal framework.

An Empirical Test

How can the truth or falsity of this construction be evaluated empirically? Note first that Skinner's construction poses narrow and wider issues of confirmation corresponding to the core thesis (the analysis of the regional systems of China) and the broader research hypothesis (the view that important noneconomic processes are better understood when analyzed within the macroregions framework). Many researchers have accepted the main elements of the core thesis and have done one of two things: either contest certain details (for example, certain boundaries between macroregions are not accurate [Rozman 1977–78:671–72, Esherick 1987:3–7]) or argue that the extended research hypothesis cannot be applied to some specific noneconomic issue (for example, the diffusion of rebellion in a particular area [Naquin 1981:35–36]). Barbara Sands and Ramon Myers (1986), however, challenge the core theory, stating that available empirical data refute Skinner's construction.[23] If their arguments are successful, then the larger research hypothesis is also seriously undermined. Moreover, given Myers's stature as an economic historian of China, these criticisms are likely to have some influence. Sands and Myers are unsuccessful, however, because their empirical "refutations" of Skinner's construction do not bear the right logical relation to Skinner's theory. This indicates some of the difficulties involved in constructing an empirical test of a complex hypothesis in social science.[24]

Interregional Trade

Sands and Myers begin with the question of the hypothesized independence of macroregions: "Did each macroregion really have this degree of independence, so that the production, trade, and consumption characteristics of other macroregions did not affect its evolution?" (724). They attempt to support a negative answer by showing that there was more interregional trade than Skinner believes. But this finding (supported by other researchers as well) does not seriously harm the macroregions model, because the assumption of interregional trade isolation is not crucial to the theory and can be readily modified or abandoned in light of contrary evidence.

Sands and Myers offer several types of data to support their contention that interregional commerce in late Imperial China was significant. They identify grain, salt, copper, and cotton as important interregional commodities and show that trade between regions was significant in these commodities (724). They also calculate that between two and four macroregions were not self-sufficient in grain production—implying that food grain was imported into these regions from other regions.[25] They assert that grain commodity prices in different macroregions are closely correlated over time—once again implying a national market in grain. They conclude, "When we examine the historical trading patterns, foodgrain production, and market price correlations we must conclude that this combined evidence does not support the economic criterion Skinner used to define his macroregions" (726).[26]

Does a finding of extensive interregional trade significantly disconfirm the macroregions theory? It does not because Skinner's thesis is not logically committed to negligible interregional trade. It maintains only that (1) macroregions are defined by physiographic features that significantly increase transport costs between macroregions; (2) each macroregion contains an urban-rural hierarchy within which commodities flow along paths connecting cities, market towns, and villages in volumes determined by demand level, commodity price, and transport costs; and (3) to the extent that interregional trade exists, it will occur between high-level central places within different macroregions. This set of factors defines the functional integration of the separate macroregions. It is an open question how much interregional trade will occur. The theory predicts merely that the commodity system will be organized at the macroregional rather than national level. Any exports from a macroregion, for example, will not flow directly into a national market system but will first be concentrated in the central cities of the macroregion core, and from there pass to central cities of other macroregions for distribution within those regions' own market systems. (Rowe 1984:52–68 provides an analysis of such interregional linkages.)

Substantial interregional trade can be easily accommodated within the macroregions framework, and Skinner himself has done so. Given that high transport costs are the chief factor limiting interregional trade, Skinner notes a key exception: "navigable water routes linking macroregions" (1977b:217n). He describes the interregional networks: "Because of the overwhelming importance of water transport in interregional trade, its spatial structure was dominated by the great sideways **T** that tied together five of China's eight regions. The Lower Yangtze was the cross of the **T** whose leg to the west was the Yangtze, whose arm to the north was the Grand Canal, and whose arm to the south was the sea route to the major ports of the Southeast Coast and Lingnan" (234).

Most of Sands and Myers's evidence for interregional trade is precisely along this "sideways **T**." They cite (724) Han-sheng Chuan and Richard Kraus on grain trade, the same source that Skinner (1977b:713n) cites approvingly in his argument. They cite (726) Loren Brandt's work demonstrating high correlations of grain prices in major cities along the **T**, and they cite interregional trade in salt and cotton, most of which also moved along these routes.

Some macroregional cores, then, were clearly linked by cheap, efficient water transport, which facilitated interregional trade. These considerations show that the mere existence of interregional trade is not an empirical problem for the macroregions thesis. The macroregions framework makes a prediction and generates a research question in connection with such trade. The prediction is that trade between macroregions will occur between appropriate points of the corresponding marketing hierarchies and will proceed along water transport paths, for example, regional cities located on interregional transport links (primarily waterways). And the research question is this: Can the particulars of interregional marketing systems and paths be reconstructed?

The data that Sands and Myers offer thus miss the mark. The central commitment to which these data pertain is the thesis of functional distinctness of macroregions. Sands and Myers have taken this to imply that absolute levels of interregional commerce should be low. But the theory does not imply this, so the data establishing relatively high levels of interregional commerce fail to disconfirm the theory.

The Urban-Rural Argument

Sands and Myers's second line of argument is an ambitious piece of statistical reasoning; they attempt to show that Skinner's construction has certain implications for rural society that are not borne out. They use *discriminant analysis,* a technique of regression analysis designed to explain a given classification of items in terms of a set of features that some of those items possess. (One might, for example, classify books into two categories—those favorably reviewed in the *New York Review of Books* and those unfavorably reviewed—and then try to find a set of properties that allows us to predict which books belong to which category.) Sands and Myers argue that if macroregions are functionally organized systems, then urban and rural characteristics within regions should display a perceptible relation. But they hold that no set of rural characteristics properly sorts counties into macroregions. This failure, they conclude, casts serious doubt on the empirical standing of the macroregions theory.

My response here is twofold. First, discriminant analysis cannot be used to support the conclusions Sands and Myers want to draw. Second, even if the technique could be justified in this context, the range of variation among the urban properties of macroregions is narrow, so we would expect only a narrow range of variation of rural properties, even supposing that urban and rural properties are causally related. It is dubious whether discriminant analysis is suitable here; it is too blunt an instrument to do the required work. Even if there were interesting urban-rural correlations, they might well disappear when aggregate county data are produced.

The logical basis of the urban-rural argument occurs in the following:

> Although his macroregional scheme was developed mainly on the basis of urban demographic evidence, Skinner argued that the macroregions represented integrated "socioeconomic systems" of rural and urban sectors. If true, the macroregional framework ought to be empirically justified by rural as well as urban data. Given Skinner's emphasis on systemic integration, the relations between the rural characteristics and the rate of urbanization within the macroregions should not be completely random. Further, there should be some correspondence between Skinner's ranking of macroregions according to their urban characteristics and the ranking of those same macroregions by some pattern of rural characteristics. (727)

This argument depends on a dubious connection between Skinner's framework and the sort of data the authors will put forward. If the logic of the argument is not sustained, however, then the painstaking statistical argument, and the extensive survey of rural data that it represents, fails to make contact with Skinner's theory.

The authors' procedure is this. They assign to each of China's 1,897 counties a set of rural economic and demographic measures, based on the above-mentioned survey by the Nationalist government's Statistical Bureau. These measures are the "rural characteristics" that Sands and Myers judge to be relevant features of rural society: irrigation intensity (Irg), population density (Pop), percentage of farming households (Farm), percentage of food grain cultivation (Food), total food grain surplus (Surp), and cropping intensity (Crop) (729). Sands and Myers then separate all counties into sets that correspond to Skinner's eight macroregions. They now have eight sets of counties, each with its own data for the six rural features. They next construct a "discriminant function" based on these independent variables. This is a "weighted linear combination of the independent variables that best reproduces the hypothesized grouping" of counties by macroregion (727–29). Sands and Myers produce this function:

F1 $$D_i = 0.83107(\text{Irg}) + 0.46145(\text{Pop}) + 0.24311(\text{Farm}) + 0.02748(\text{Food}) - 0.01135(\text{Surp}) + 0.00075(\text{Crop})$$

Sands and Myers make several observations about this function. First, the size of the coefficients is a measure of the significance of the given factor as a determinant of its classification; thus only Irg and Pop (and perhaps Farm) are significant in accounting for membership in a given macroregion. Second, this function does better than the pure chance criterion, but not dramatically so: it provides only a 46 percent success rate in classifying counties into macroregions (where pure chance would predict a 26 percent success rate). The authors therefore take this to show that membership of a given county in a given macroregion is not successfully predicted by its rural characteristics, which they take to empirically discredit the macroregions framework.

When we examine this analysis, however, it emerges that this procedure should not be expected to lead to success. Sands and Myers have classified all counties by macroregion; they have identified six salient "rural characteristics" for each county; they have constructed an index value that is the linear function of these values best able to reproduce the macroregional classification of counties; and they have shown that the new classification creates groupings of counties in which slightly over half of the counties are not placed in the correct macroregion. What, however, is the logical connection between this statistical argument and the validity of the macroregions framework? This technique presupposes that some weighted linear function of rural characteristics should allow us to sort counties by macroregions. But just because county X belongs to macroregion M does not mean that X must have a set of features that distinguish it statistically from all other counties not belonging to M. The features that determine whether counties belong to the same macroregion are geographic position and containment within a particular urban marketing system—not any set of features that make those counties more similar to one another than they are to counties in other macroregions. Sands and Myers have utterly ignored Skinner's explicit distinction between his "*functional* or *nodal* regions" and "*normal* or *uniform* regions" (1977b:216). Only *uniform* regions, each defined by certain shared characteristics, should be distinguishable by discriminant analysis.

Sands and Myers's six rural factors are more likely to be associated with the conjunction of core-periphery status and macroregion membership than with membership alone. The irrigation intensity, population density, percentage of farm households, food grain production and surplus, and cropping intensity of a poor core county in the dry-farming area of the North China macroregion should not be expected to differ markedly from those of a peripheral county of the richer and more commercialized Lower Yangzi macroregion; and there is no reason to expect that these measures will be similar for a core county and a peripheral county within a given region. This finding suggests that counties cannot be sorted into macroregions on the basis of these rural properties; the range of values assigned to counties within macroregions is likely to be as great as the range across macroregions. So Sands and Myers's negative conclusion based on discriminant analysis is entirely unsurprising. Discriminant analysis is thus the wrong tool for the job. There is no reason to believe that interregional differences should disaggregate into differences among counties in distinct regions.

Sands and Myers also make an aggregate claim about correlations between urban features and rural features at the macroregional level that can be formulated without using discriminant analysis. They assert that a macroregion's urbanization rate and its index of these rural factors ought to show high correlation (727) and in consequence that the ranking of macroregions by rates of urbanization and by this set of rural factors ought to correspond. To justify this assumption we must accept an unsubstantiated causal assumption about the relations between urban and rural properties: that *any* difference in urban properties in a macroregion ought to produce discernible differences in the values of *these* particular rural factors in that region.

This causal claim is objectionably vague: what variations of urban characteristics are significant here? What effects should urban variations have on rural characteristics, or vice versa? Through what mechanism? Even if we accept the point that the macroregions theory is committed to the existence of some systemic relations between urban structure and rural characteristics, which urban features ought to be expected to influence which rural features is an open question. This raises problems for Sands and Myers on both sides. They have not established that the rate of urbanization is the appropriate urban variable to consider, they have not shown that their rural features are the appropriate rural variables, and they have not indicated any hypothesized mechanism through which the rate of urbanization should be expected to influence these rural variables. Once again, their test lacks logical force.

Further, even if this claim about rankings by rural and urban factors were plausible, rates of urbanization differ little except between the top and bottom groups (table 3.1). The bottom five macroregions

Table 3.1. Urbanization rates and a rurality ranking

Rural Characteristics Ranking by Macroregion

Macroregion	Skinner urbanization rate	Sands-Myers ranking by rural characteristics
Lower Yangzi	7.9	1
Lingnan	7.0	3
Southeast coast	5.9	2
Northwest China	4.9	7
Middle Yangzi	4.6	4
North China	4.2	8
Upper Yangzi	4.2	6
Yungui	4.1	5

Sources: Skinner 1977b:235; Sands and Myers 1986:730

in particular are closely bunched; variation among macroregions even by urban features is minimal. This implies that applying the discriminant analysis technique even to urban features might fail to sort counties into macroregions accurately. If the urban features of macroregions vary systematically with rural features, and if the urban features differ only slightly from macroregion to macroregion, then we would expect that rural features will also differ slightly. And when we compare Sands and Myers's ranking based on rural data with Skinner's based on urban data, we find that the groups are classified correctly: the bottom five and top three each fall together.

These considerations show that Sands and Myers's application of discriminant analysis sheds no light on the empirical adequacy of the macroregions framework. It represents the application of intricate statistical machinery without the correct logical relation between theory and data. This example shows that it can be as easy for an empirical test to misfire for reasons of logical adequacy as for the theory itself to do so. The critic must pay attention to the logic of the argument and the presuppositions on which it depends as well as the volume of data. We may draw another lesson from Sands and Myers: a simple attempt to refute a complex theory empirically is likely to miss the mark unless the critic pays attention to the logic of the theory being addressed. Sands and Myers failed in part because they did not recognize the complexity of Skinner's construction and looked precipitously for a quick empirical refutation.

Empirical Standing of the Macroregions Framework

Sands and Myers have not provided an appropriate empirical evaluation of Skinner's account. They are certainly correct, though, in holding that Skinner's theory of macroregions is an empirical hypothesis
and therefore stands in need of empirical justification. So how should
Skinner's account be empirically evaluated?

The central hypothesis of the macroregions theory is the functional integration of regions as economic systems. This functional
integration may be tested by examining price correlations within a
given macroregion. Current research by Peter Perdue, James Z. Lee,
and R. Bin Wong examines price data (derived from memorials report-
ing prefectural-level grain prices) to determine the degree to which
prices correlate across the marketing hierarchy in various regions.[27]
Their preliminary findings suggest that price movements correlate
closely among higher-level places in regional cores and poorly in
peripheral areas—a finding that appears to support the macroregional
framework. This would appear to be a theoretically appropriate form
of empirical test for the macroregions theory: it identifies a core
implication of the theory (that prices will be correlated among high-
ranking places within the regional system) that was not part of Skinner's original construction and attempts to discover data that permit
the researcher to evaluate this aspect of the theory.

Another critical element of the macroregions framework is the
distinction between core and periphery. Skinner adopts a criterion
based entirely on population density to draw this distinction, and he
asserts that the resulting differentiation of the countryside is economically, socially, and politically significant. Is this prediction
borne out? In his extensive review of Skinner's *City in Late Imperial
China* Rozman (1977–78) expresses some reservations about the
core-periphery distinction: "The core-periphery distinction should
be of value when used cautiously, but at this juncture it lacks empirical support and has been overstated in a form that does not encourage careful comparisons of prefectural level units in order induc-
tively to establish a continuum of local variations, i.e. a true local
studies approach" (671). In later work, Rozman (1982) provides a
sustained effort to determine whether available demographic data
supports or disconfirms the core-periphery analysis in North China.
Rozman employs a variety of county- and prefectural-level data to
arrive at estimates of several important demographic parameters—
population density, population per market, mean household size, and

sex ratio—and plots his data. He then summarizes his conclusions: "The spatial examination of data reveals in most instances a series of inner and outer belts—at times even a concentric-circle effect—and in many instances also a north-south differentiation" (94). But he also finds that the patterns of core and periphery do not coincide entirely with those provided by Skinner: "I use the labels core and periphery to describe the findings for North China, but the areas so differentiated are neither coterminous with G. William Skinner's core and periphery in his North China macroregion nor used as fixed categories that obviate the need for alternative spatial divisions" (96). Rozman's conclusion, then, is that the macroregions framework, and the associated core-periphery distinction, is an illuminating approach to the analysis of Chinese society but one that must be developed and extended through more local studies and county-level data.

Another empirical investigation pertinent to assessing the core-periphery distinction is an important study of elite behavior by R. Keith Schoppa (1982). Schoppa argues that Skinner's core-periphery distinction is a good beginning but that it is insufficiently differentiated to serve as an adequate basis for understanding elite political behavior in Zhejiang: "A study of Zhejiang's seventy-five counties in the two macroregions supports the general accuracy of [Skinner's] continuum concept. However, for a systematic analysis of elites and their political and social structures, this conception is inadequate: it is too vaguely and insufficiently differentiated to represent a range of elite structural types, allowing only polar types to be presented clearly and offering description only in terms of broad social and political parameters" (16). This research offers qualified empirical support for Skinner's construction; Schoppa suggests that the macroregions framework draws the correct distinctions within the economic space of traditional China and recommends that the analysis be given finer structure for some purposes.[28]

These examples show that the macroregions framework might be empirically tested and extended in many ways. Sands and Myers have not refuted the macroregions theory, but much empirical work remains before Skinner's account can be thoroughly evaluated.

Urbanization

A theory must face other criteria of adequacy besides empirical confirmability. It must be logically adequate: its formal constructs must be coherent, they must depend on plausible background assumptions, and so on. To illustrate this dimension of theory assessment, I now treat in detail one of Skinner's formal models, his analysis of the causes of regional differences in rates of urbanization. (The rate of urbanization is defined as the percentage of the population living in urban places [1977a:223–27].) Skinner's quantitative causal analysis of urbanization contains several flaws. Although I have chosen a point of defect in theoretical reasoning for close attention, I regard this as an exception and do not mean to discredit Skinner's formal work more generally. On the contrary, Skinner's fertile application and rigorous development of abstract models to studies of China shed original light on Chinese society and economy. I select this example because it illustrates nicely the importance of logical analysis of the assumptions that underlie a mathematical model.[29]

When population data and urbanization rates are analyzed by macroregion, it emerges that different macroregions have markedly different patterns. What explains these differences? Skinner argues (1977b:230–36) that it is possible to identify a small set of institutional and commercial factors that jointly constitute the cause of variation in rates of urbanization across macroregions.

Skinner's data set consists of 2,500 cards covering every city and town in traditional China that (1) served as a county- or higher-level capital or was designated a municipality (1893–1953); (2) attained economic central functions symptomatic of "local" and higher-level cities; (3) reached a population of four thousand by the Qing period; and/or (4) had a population of fifty thousand by 1953; and (5) had a post office of any grade by 1915 (221ff.). Each card provides population estimates and other data indicative of central functions: level and rank of every capital, official categorization of top bureaucratic posts, circumference of city wall, postal status, trade statistics, date of steamship and rail service initiation, and the like. Using these data, "each central place was classified on a number of dimensions, only three of which need to be mentioned here, all estimated or standardized for the year 1893: population class, administrative status, and level in the economic hierarchy" (221–22).

Skinner next estimates the rate of urbanization—what proportion of the population lived in urban places—in China in 1893. To estimate this, two sorts of work are needed: fairly complete population data for different places and a definition of *urban place*. Skinner shows that a range of possibilities exist, given the variables of population class, administrative status, and economic position. More inclusive definitions will incorporate more places and a larger total urban population. The range extends from 20,807,000 (5.3 percent) to 25,673,000 (6.5 percent). Skinner argues for an intermediate criterion, which gives rise to 23.5 million urban dwellers and a 6.0 percent urbanization rate.[30]

When these population data and urbanization rates are disaggregated by macroregion for 1893, it emerges that different macroregions had markedly different urbanization rates, ranging from 7.9 percent in Lower Yangzi to 4.1 percent in Yungui. (These data are provided in table 3.2 and summarized in figures 3.3 and 3.4.) Skinner advances a model of urbanization intended to explain these differences on the basis of a quantitative causal analysis. He argues that it is possible to identify a small set of institutional and economic factors which jointly cause the observed variation in rates of urbanization across macroregions: population density (PD), extent of division of labor (DL), level of technological development (TE), volume of intraregional and extraregional commerce (IC and EC), and degree of ad-

Table 3.2. Determinants of regional urbanization

	Macroregions							
	LY	L	SC	NWC	MY	NC	UY	YG
Population density	7.00	1.50	2.60	0.80	2.50	3.30	2.50	0.50
Division of labor	3.50	5.00	4.00	2.00	2.50	1.50	3.00	2.50
Application of technology	6.00	5.00	3.50	3.00	3.00	2.50	2.50	1.50
Intraregional commerce	6.00	4.50	5.00	3.00	2.50	2.50	2.50	1.00
Extraregional commerce	8.00	8.00	6.00	5.00	5.50	4.00	3.50	1.50
Administrative component	1.80	4.30	3.00	5.00	2.60	3.10	2.40	9.00
Sum of six weightings:	32.30	28.30	24.10	18.80	18.60	16.90	16.40	16.00
Index (sum * 0.248):	8.01	7.02	5.98	4.66	4.61	4.19	4.07	3.97
Urbanization (actual):	7.90	7.00	5.90	4.90	4.60	4.20	4.20	4.10

Note: LY: Lower Yangzi; L: Lingnan; SC: Southeast Coast; NWC: Northwest China; MY: Middle Yangzi; NC: North China; UY: Upper Yangzi; YG: Yungui
Source: Skinner 1977b:235

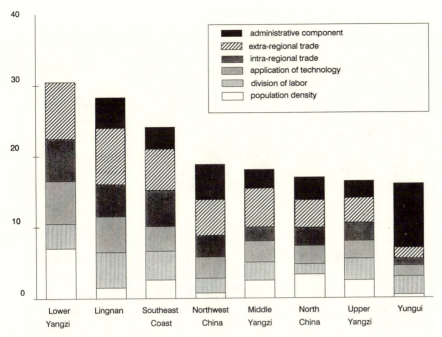

Source: Skinner 1977b:235

Figure 3.3. Determinants of urbanization

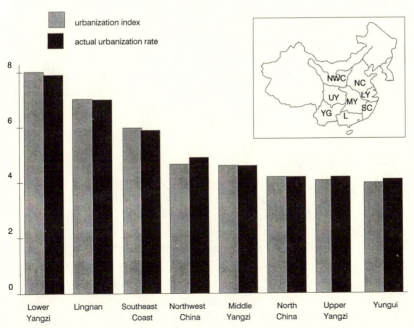

Figure 3.4. Correlation of urbanization index with observed rate

ministrative involvement (AC) (230–36). He provides quantitative estimates for each factor for every macroregion, aggregates these values, and shows that the resulting "urbanization index" correlates closely with variation in rates of urbanization across macroregions (see fig. 3.4). Skinner argues that together these factors explain varying urbanization rates across macroregions.[31]

This argument proceeds in two stages. Skinner first shows informally how each factor should be expected to be a positive causal influence in urbanization. Population density facilitates commercial development, revenue extraction, and administrative efficiency. Intraregional division of labor leads to higher levels of commerce and efficiency and more extensive marketing arrangements. Application of technology both boosts and is boosted by transport and agricultural efficiency. Commercialization and intraregional trade depend on transportation efficiency as well as such things as absolute distances and comparative advantages of climate, which "together create a potential for territorial specialization" (234). Extraregional trade has the same consequences for urbanization and likewise depends on transport.

The next stage of the argument is quantitative. Skinner constructs a quantitative measure for these factors, assigning values to each for each macroregion, he aggregates the factors through simple addition (fig. 3.3) and compares the normalized sum with observed urbanization rates.[32] The results conform closely to known rates of urbanization (fig. 3.4). This model appears to represent an effective example of rigorous quantitative causal reasoning. But the model's quantitative side is unsatisfactory.

The Logic of Measurement

To assess the adequacy of this model, the logic of measurement and aggregation must be examined. Skinner's background assumptions are these: First, he hypothesizes that these six factors causally influence the rate of urbanization. This means, at a minimum, that if two macroregions are similar in every other respect and one possesses more of one of the factors, then it should have a higher rate of urbanization. Further, he assumes that meaningful quantitative measures of each factor can be provided. Next, Skinner assumes that the contribution of each factor to the rate of urbanization is a linear function and (implicitly anyway) that the factors do not interact.[33] Finally, he assumes he can provide a mathematical function that both permits him to aggregate the measures of these factors into one composite value and is consistent with the assumptions just identified. He must (1) construct a technique of measurement for each factor and (2) formulate a reasonable aggregation function to arrive at an index based on the six factors. Skinner's handling of both tasks has serious problems, however.

Consider first problems of measurement: scaling and error assessment. How are quantitative values assigned to each factor? What types of scales do these factors represent—ratio, interval, or rank order? And, given the technique of measurement, what level of precision may be assigned to the numerical values provided for each factor?

Three factors permit fairly direct measurement: population density and intra- and extra-regional commerce (though the latter two require somewhat arbitrary assumptions to assign values). More imagination is needed, however, to construct measures for technological development, division of labor, and administrative component (AC). Skinner achieves a value for AC by assigning a value to administrative places of different ranks, summing these values for all administrative places in each macroregion (230), and normalizing the sum to a ten-point scale. Both division of labor and technological development are given only impressionistic measurements, representing Skinner's qualitative judgment of relative positions of the eight macroregions on these dimensions (233). These scales are thus similar in form to judging such sports as diving, in which the judge has a list of features and assigns a numerical value on the basis of a qualitative judgment of performance on those features.

What are the logical features of these different measurements? The different measure scales—cardinal (ratio and interval scales), and ordinal (rank order scales)—are well known to represent descending amounts of information.[34] On a ratio scale (for example, mass) the ratio of two values of different quantities is significant. On an interval scale (for example, temperature), only ratios of differences between quantities are significant. On a rank order scale (for example, baseball standings), only the order of the quantities is significant; we cannot estimate how close two measured quantities are, only which is greater. Each measure is invariant under a different mathematical transformation: ratio measure is invariant under multiplication by a constant, interval scales are invariant under linear transformations, and rank order scales are invariant under all monotonic increasing transformations.

To know what sort of scale a given measurement technique represents, we must ask two questions. First, given the definition of the variable being measured, is it meaningful to compare ratios of values, ratios of differences, or only rank order of individuals? This question involves the logic of the defined variable within its theoretical context. Second, we must ask about the "information richness" of the measurement technique: what level of comparison will the information generated by the technique justify?

Some of Skinner's six factors—population density, intraregional commerce, and extraregional commerce—may plausibly be interpreted on a ratio scale. That is, it is meaningful to judge that South China has twice as much intraregional commerce as Middle Yangzi or that North China is half as densely populated as the Lower Yangzi. Administrative component (AC) would appear to be measurable at best on an interval scale. We might conclude on the basis of comparative study that Peking has greater administrative component than Shanghai, that Shanghai has greater than Hankou, and that Shanghai is substantially closer to Peking than it is to Hankou. This judgment entails that ratios of differences are significant. Division of labor (DL) and technological development (TE) are the least tangible factors and the most difficult to measure—only rank order scales are available for TE and DL. It is possible to judge that Southwest China is more technologically developed than North China and North China more than Yungui, but we cannot assign quantitative values to either relative values or values of differences.

These considerations show that the six factors represent varying kinds of information and correspond to measurements based on differing scales. This implies that the data are not directly commensurable. By analogy, suppose we have data about members of a graduating high school class: age, average number of hours of study time per week, grade point average, SAT test scores, class rank, and gender, and suppose that we want to produce an index to predict lifetime earnings. Given the logical diversity of these different data, any such index will obviously require careful construction and formal decisions about scoring. Skinner's construction possesses a similar range of data; but because each data element has been assigned a numerical value in roughly the same range (0–10), the reader can overlook the logical problems associated with combining the data into one index.

Turn now to the problem of error assessment in measuring these factors. As Oskar Morgenstern (1963) demonstrated several decades ago, social scientists must follow the lead of natural scientists and pay attention to the level of precision their techniques of measurement allow. There is a regrettable tendency to draw inferences from quantitative reasoning that are wholly unsupportable if measurement error is appropriately accounted for. In the present example, the correlation between rates of urbanization and the sum of these six factors is highly impressive in figure 3.4, but if the data represented there are recalculated to reflect even fairly conservative error estimates, the correlation disappears (fig. 3.5). Figure 3.5 represents the range into which each value may fall on the assumption of a hypothetical error estimate. (This graph is based on the assumption that the precision of the actual value of the urbanization rate is greater than that of the aggregate index, reflecting the fact that the aggregate depends on six pieces of data, some of which unavoidably have wide error ranges.) Only the most general conclusions may be drawn from Skinner's data when error estimates are provided. In particular, the first three and last five macroregions fall within two bands of values, within which each region could have virtually any value. By the data represented here, Northwest China could have a lower actual urbanization rate and a higher index than Yungui; the reverse combination is also possible. The apparent correlation between index value and actual value virtually disappears when we account for error ranges. The close fit in figure 3.4 appears to be an artifact of the values assigned to each factor.[35] Apart from problems about the meaning of the different measure scales, then, estimates of error for each factor's measure indicate broad bands of possible aggregate sums and correspond only loosely to observed patterns of urbanization.

Aggregation

How should these six causal factors be aggregated? Is it meaningful to add the quantities? Given Skinner's qualitative assumptions (that these factors are positive linear causal factors), we may infer the mathematical form the aggregation function must take. This function must (1) show positive slope in each of the six dimensions and (2) be linear in each of the six dimensions. The aggregation function must therefore be a linear function. Skinner adopts one such function when he postulates that the factors may be added to arrive at an urbanization index:

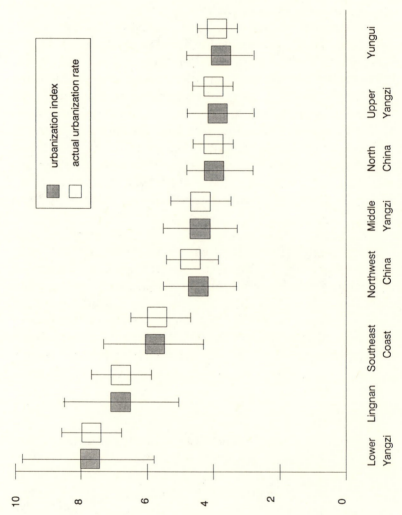

Figure 3.5. Urbanization estimates with error rates

F2 $$V_i = PD_i + DL_i + TE_i + IC_i + EC_i + AC_i,$$

where V_i is the computed urbanization index. Each macroregion i with its own vector of causal factors may now be assigned its urbanization index V_i. But a significant error has already crept in; the assumptions identified here require that the function be linear but do not fix the coefficients. The aggregation function should be this:

F3 $$V_i = a*PD_i + b*DL_i + c*TE_i + d*IC_i + e*EC_i + f*AC_i + K,$$

where $a, b, c, d, e,$ and f are constant coefficients and K is a constant.[36] By assuming that these coefficients are unity, Skinner makes an unmotivated assumption about the causal weight of each factor and the objectivity of the scales that have been constructed for them.

But our problems get worse. We saw above that it is implausible to assume that all the measure scales of the six factors are of the same logical type; some are ratio scales, some interval scales, and others simple rank order scales. This implies that no theoretical rationale exists to aggregate the numerical values through addition—any more than adding the temperature and mass of an object is likely to be a meaningful aggregate of its physical properties. The problem is this: unless the quantities can be interpreted on a ratio scale, they cannot be regarded as contributing linearly to a given effect.

Finally, even supposing each scale can be given a ratio value, a problem of scaling remains.[37] Skinner has constructed each scale so that measurements fall roughly in the range of 0–10. But given that a ratio scale is invariant under ratio transformation (multiplication by a constant), the absolute values assigned to each factor are not significant; it is thus arbitrary to treat a numerical value of 5 on the AC scale as equal to a value of 5 on the TE scale. This problem arises from Skinner's setting the coefficients in the general linear function (F3) to unity. This is not a problem within a given scale, since this transformation preserves proportions among all values on the scale, but it is a problem if we wish to aggregate measures drawn from different scales (for example, aggregate the PD value 7.0 and DL value 3.5 for LY). So it is necessary first to arrive at a reasonable basis for normalizing the six measure scales so that values for different quantities are comparable. (This problem is roughly equivalent to assigning weights to the factors.) But Skinner has provided no argument to motivate his choice of measure scales and aggregation function.

We thus arrive at a blank wall on the aggregation problem. The measurements provided for the six factors are shaky; the scales of measurement provide logically different kinds of information; Skinner does not provide us with any justification for aggregating these disparate values; and if such were provided, we would still lack justification for aggregating these specific scales (or setting the linear coefficients to unity).[38]

What conclusions can be drawn about the urbanization model? Not much quantitative reasoning survives; in particular, Skinner's quantitative case does *not* show that these six factors are the causal factors that explain differences in rates of urbanization. That Skinner succeeded in assigning measures to these factors and aggregating them in a way that reproduces the pattern of urbanization does not support his conclusion that these factors are the relevant causal factors; we must first be satisfied that the model is logically adequate. To draw such a conclusion we would have to confirm that reasonable and accurate measurement procedures are in place, that the decisions made along the way in constructing these measurement operations were not arbitrary, and that the aggregation function can be justified. These requirements are not satisfied, given what Skinner has written about his techniques. The argument as a whole thus lacks any inferential weight. All that survives is the qualitative reasoning (which presumably could be extended) showing how these factors ought to work to increase urbanization, given other assumptions about economic organization and development. The formal work in this case appears to be misleadingly precise.

Do these criticisms justify a more general skepticism about the utility of Skinner's formal mathematical models in application to historical phenomena? They emphatically do not. This model of Skinner's is flawed, but it simply illustrates the point that the social scientist must work through the presuppositions of a model carefully and ensure that these presuppositions are coherent and plausible.

Chapter 4
The Breakthrough Debate

An important puzzle in Chinese economic history is the failure of the medieval Chinese agricultural system to break through to self-sustaining growth, rapid technological innovation, and ever-higher levels of productivity. This failure is perplexing because the Chinese economy possessed many advantages that would seem to have favored such a breakthrough. The economy was much more developed than its European counterpart. Agriculture was substantially more productive per hectare; commercial development and wealth were more concentrated; the labor pool was large; and technical knowledge was capable of supporting industrial development. Yet the Chinese agrarian economy witnessed half a millennium of technical stagnation and modest growth, whereas the European economy witnessed a breakthrough to high-yield agriculture, rapid technological innovation, and self-sustaining growth. Given its material advantages in the sixteenth century over Europe, why did the Chinese agricultural system not move into a process of technical innovation and economic growth?

The problem of economic stagnation in traditional China is a huge issue with a correspondingly enormous literature. In this chapter I therefore concentrate on a smaller, but strategically central, problem: what prevented the emergence of the profit-oriented capitalist farm in traditional Chinese agriculture? I have posed the question this way in consideration of a plausible theory of the starting point of the economic revolution in England, according to which the impetus to economic breakthrough was the replacement of peasant agriculture by the capitalist farm. Capitalist farmers could introduce technical innovations into agriculture on a more suitable scale, farm output increased while food prices declined, and this made possible a more extensive urban manufacturing sector.[1]

The question of technical stagnation in China has provoked many answers, from supposed obstacles to innovation raised by the imperial bureaucracy to cultural hindrances internal to Confucianism. I focus on two theories that attempt to explain Chinese economic stagnation in terms of the Chinese economy itself and that are premised on the assumption that cultivators make rational decisions within the institutions in which they find themselves. I begin with a neo-Malthusian theory advanced by Kang Chao, according to which a low land–man ratio led to such low labor rates as to make technical innovation unprofitable. Then, with sidelong looks at the contrasting experience of early modern Europe, I consider a neo-Marxist model that places primary emphasis on surplus-extraction and the material institutions of production. These theories represent two poles of a common distinction drawn by economic historians of China between *technological* and *distributional* theories of economic change in China. Technological theorists hold that China's economic stagnation is best explained as the result of resource scarcity and population growth that led to widespread poverty, low economic surpluses, and a consequent inability to introduce modernized production technologies. Distributional theories hold, by contrast, that the traditional Chinese economy generated substantial surpluses that could in principle have funded economic development but that the elite classes used those surpluses in unproductive ways.[2]

The Chinese Agrarian System

Agriculture in traditional China, most observers agree, was organized primarily around peasant farms, not manors or capitalist farms.[3] Myers (1970:211) and Huang (1985:85–89) offer evidence that small family farms provided the overwhelming preponderance of the rural product in late Ming and Qing China, with various kinds of rent relations constituting the main regional variation.[4] These farms had characteristics that distinguished them from such other types of farms as the capitalist farm or feudal manor: small scale, traditional cultivation techniques, labor-intensive cultivation, and production oriented toward the subsistence needs of the family rather than profits. One noteworthy distinction between the Chinese peasant economy and other peasant regimes, however, was the extensive level of commercialization. Peasant farms in China operated within the context of active markets and generally attempted to produce a marketable surplus.

A second important feature of Chinese agriculture was technical: the farming system showed a finely tuned adjustment of agricultural practices to ecological variation and a large supply of labor. In a survey of traditional Chinese agriculture Mark Elvin writes, "Chinese farming was more like gardening. It produced high yields per hectare from a multitude of adjustments to local conditions arrived at through a constant empirical experimentation. . . . Late-traditional Chinese farmers were neither 'primitive' nor caught in an unthinking technological conservation, but their methods were not scientific in the modern sense of the term" (1982:13–14).

On Dwight Perkins's accounting, this system of agriculture made considerable achievements. He holds that traditional Chinese agriculture was highly efficient and well adapted to local environments and available resources and techniques.[5] He maintains (1969:8) that Chinese agriculture from the fourteenth century to the present was forced to expand gross output eight to ten times, in order to support increasing population; and that it did so largely through expanding inputs rather than changing the techniques of production. "The central proposition of this book is that Chinese farmers were able to raise grain output and that they did so in more or less equal measure by expanding the cultivated acreage and by raising the yield per acre" (13).

Perkins also holds, however, that technical stagnation generally accompanied agricultural development in China: increases in output were achieved through applying existing techniques more intensively rather than through technical innovation. "Most of the increase . . . seems to have resulted from greater capital and labor inputs in conditions of a stagnant technology" (38). "It is quite clear, however, that the increase in the number of tools was not accompanied by any great change in their quality or variety. Farm implement technology was generally stagnant" (56). Perkins accounts for this technical stagnation in terms that parallel Theodore Schultz's analysis of traditional agriculture:[6] the exhaustion of technical innovations that were feasible in the absence of modern scientific and technical knowledge. "A more plausible explanation [than simple traditional inertia] is that there weren't many further advances that could be made without a major technological breakthrough, a breakthrough that could be achieved only by means of the techniques of modern science" (58).

A Demographic Theory of Stagnation

Several efforts have been made to explain this pattern of agricultural stagnation. One model assigns primary responsibility to a long-term increase in population.[7] In *Man and Land in Chinese History* (1986), Kang Chao argues that the main elements of China's economic history, including the dominance of small producers, labor-intensive techniques of production, and technological stagnation since the twelfth century, are the effects of a steady population increase over a period of two thousand years and a consequent decline in the land–man ratio. As labor became abundant and resources—particularly land—grew relatively scarce, Chinese farmers and handicrafters were under increasing incentives to adopt labor-intensive production techniques and were presented with corresponding disincentives to introduce efficient, labor-saving innovations. Chao puts his central conclusions in these terms:

> Why did an industrial revolution take place in eighteenth century England but not in Sung China? . . . Sung China had already [by the twelfth century] approached the threshold of technological invention and was far more advanced than Europe in craftsmanship and engineering skill. By this time, however, the Chinese population had grown to the point where there was no longer any need to save labor. There was no longer a demand for labor-saving devices because people were concerned with the problem of how to dispose of unused labor gainfully. . . . China, meanwhile, had fallen into a trap of overpopulation, and institutional flexibility only worsened the situation. Overpopulation induced the populace to adopt more labor-intensive technology and labor-absorbing institutions, which in turn raised the limit of tolerance for overpopulation. (227–28)

Chao bases his case on two extended pieces of analysis: a theory of the nature and causes of demographic change in traditional China, in tandem with a reassessment of existing estimates of the growth of the Chinese population over the past two thousand years, and a formal marginalist economic analysis of the unit of production (farm, workshop) under conditions of a falling land–man ratio. This analysis is designed to show that the peasant farmer is under overwhelming incentive to select labor-intensive production techniques and under no incentive at all to introduce labor-saving innovations.

The Effects of Population Increase

Like Malthus, Chao postulates a close causal relation between population growth and economic arrangements. Malthus maintained that
population and economy were in a dynamic causal relationship. Rising population would stimulate more intensive productive efforts,
with falling marginal returns, to the point where rising mortality
rates checked further population increase. Yet increases in the food-
producing capacity of the economy (increases in arable land, more
efficient farming techniques) would stimulate population growth.
Thus population change and economic growth are interactive causal
variables, each influencing the other over time.[8] Malthus posited
that this causal connection between economy and population works
through positive and negative checks. Positive checks include
sources of increased mortality resulting from overpopulation (civil
strife, famine), whereas negative checks include culturally specific
checks on fertility (delayed nuptiality, birth control, and the like).
And in fact demographers have discerned a variety of mechanisms
within the cultures of Western Europe that modulate fertility rates in
response to economic circumstances (Schofield 1986).

Chao holds, however, that the demographic experience of China
differs sharply from that of premodern Europe. He maintains that
European cultural values regulated nuptiality and family creation,
effectively establishing the negative checks postulated by Malthus:
European men were culturally discouraged from entering into marriage and family until they had attained an economic position capable of supporting a family (8). In China, however, according to Chao,
the cultural values defining nuptiality and family-formation differed
fundamentally and were essentially disengaged from economic factors.[9] A very powerful cultural value was attached to having heirs,
which led young people into marriage without regard to economic
prospects. Chinese traditional society, Chao maintains, thus embodied a culturally specific mechanism of family formation that led to
population increase without regard to the economic opportunities
available to new families. And powerful cultural values dictating that
members of a family help support poor kin provided the redistributive mechanism that permitted the surplus population to
survive. Early marriage and extensive family interdependence and
loyalty led to more rapid population growth than was characteristic
of premodern Europe. Thus, Chao writes, Malthus's negative checks

were effective in premodern Europe (along the lines described by Schofield [1986:14]) but were looser in traditional China. This led in China to chronic overpopulation in relation to land and available production techniques.[10]

Chao also reappraises available population data on China for the past two thousand years. He argues that by the twelfth century China had reached such a population that it was largely immune from the positive checks that could substantially affect population size over fifty years—war, famine, emigration. "The crucial turning point finally occurred when, after steady growth for 150 years during the Northern Sung, the population surpassed previous peaks by a sizable margin so that major wars and natural disasters became relatively less destructive" (42).[11]

This tendency toward population increase led eventually to a secular decline in the land–man ratio. Though land reclamation was a natural response to rising population, particularly in the Sung dynasty, there were narrow limits to this response, given China's boundaries and ecology.[12] As population rose rapidly and cultivated land rose slowly, the per capita acreage unavoidably fell.

For culturally specific reasons having to do with the values defining family structure, then, the Chinese population tended to rise more rapidly than available cultivated land. This led to a persistent tendency toward a falling land–man ratio, and this fundamentally shaped economic institutions and production techniques in Chinese agrarian society.

Marginalist Analysis of the Peasant Economy

Chao describes the traditional Chinese economy as essentially homogeneous for two millennia: a highly commercialized market economy in which the vast majority of production was undertaken by small units of production run by family labor—the peasant farm and the handicraft shop.[13] Moreover, Chao maintains that all participants were economically rational: they made production decisions on the basis of calculations of price and profits. Family units farmed small plots of land and engaged in sideline handicraft enterprises, such as textile goods, within the context of a highly commercialized market.[14]

Chao maintains that the tools of marginalist economic theory permit important implications to be derived about the patterns of development that may be expected from these economic institutions given falling land—man ratios. In these circumstances the optimal choice for peasant cultivators is to adopt production techniques that absorb the maximum amount of family labor, even in circumstances when the marginal product of labor is well below subsistence. This is because the family is obliged to support all family members; labor costs are thus fixed, and any additional expenditure of labor that increases output even slightly is rational because it increases total family income. This outcome the Russian peasant economist, A. V. Chayanov (1925:70–89) described as the "self-exploitation" of peasant family production.

One important consequence of the self-exploitation of family labor is that family production units will use scarce resources—particularly land—more efficiently than labor-hiring enterprises. This, Chao maintains, is because the labor-hiring enterprise must pay a wage no lower than subsistence, whereas the peasant family can rationally continue to expend family members' labor until the marginal product of labor approaches zero. Consider two farms side by side, one a peasant family farm, the other a capitalist farm. The capitalist form uses hired labor, whereas the peasant farm uses family labor. Assume also that laborers are hired full-time and have no other sources of income (such as family earnings). The capitalist farm will expand its use of labor until the marginal product of labor equals the subsistence budget of the worker (on the assumption that the wage cannot drop below subsistence and still be attractive to the worker). Assuming that the same techniques of cultivation are in use, the yield per acre of the peasant farm will be higher, whereas the yield per man-day of the capitalist farm will be higher.[15] Thus family peasant production when the land—man ratio is low leads to a production system that is land efficient (producing a high yield for a given quantity of land) but labor inefficient (absorbing great labor for a given unit of output).[16]

This producer preference for labor-intensive methods has implications for the development of the Chinese economy. Chao holds that tenurial landlordism drives out managerial landlordism under these circumstances; a landowner can earn a higher rate of return by leasing his land to a peasant family than by managing the land himself using hired labor. This is true because the tenurial landlord can appropriate part of the surplus created by the highly intensive labor of the peasant family, an amount greater than that created by a hired work force.[17]

The marginalist analysis has a second implication that is most relevant for our purposes—the explanation of technological stagnation. Chao argues that peasant production is led toward intensified application of labor rather than toward labor-saving innovation.[18] This implies that there is no niche in which an innovative managerial farmer may profitably introduce capital-intensive, labor-saving techniques; the extremely low cost of labor swamps the possibility of technical innovation. The twelfth century represents the demographic turning point in Chao's account: the land–labor ratio then dropped low enough to trigger labor intensification rather than technical innovation as the peasant cultivator's primary response to the need for increased income.[19] As Chao describes it, "The other profound impact of overpopulation was on the technological preference of producers. . . . The primary direction of Chinese agricultural development after the twelfth century was towards intensified farming" (224–25)." He writes that "generally speaking, agricultural production in China followed a pattern of extensive development before the Southern Sung but gradually changed thereafter. Taking cultivating implements as an example, we may observe that virtually all important innovations and inventions took place before the fourteenth century, at the latest, and all were labor saving in nature" (194).

Here, then, is Chao's analysis of technical and economic stagnation in the traditional Chinese economy: population increased, relatively immune from check by economic factors; the ratio of land and resources to population fell; and peasant cultivators were increasingly compelled to adopt labor-intensive techniques of production rather than technical innovations that would increase labor productivity.

Assessment of Chao's Analysis

Chao's work is an ambitious effort to synthesize a great sweep of demographic data and to explain some of the most important features of Chinese economic history. But his account has serious shortcomings, both demographically and economically. Chao's demographic argument has two parts: a causal hypothesis about Chinese demographic change, according to which population tended to increase without regard to economic variables, and a reconstruction of China's population history to support this causal hypothesis and to establish Chao's central contention: the land–man ratio witnessed an economically devastating drop between the twelfth and twentieth centuries.

Consider first the causal analysis of demographic change—the thesis that Chinese population growth was not controlled by Malthusian economic checks. (Call this Chao's population dynamics hypothesis.) Put more explicitly than Chao does, the claim is this: changing economic circumstances did not affect traditional Chinese fertility rates. This claim is simply not demonstrated in Chao's work. To support this claim, time series of population statistics and relevant economic variables—per capita income, grain prices, or economic opportunities—must be provided. But for several reasons Chao's land and population data do not succeed in testing or exploring the population dynamics hypothesis. First, Chao's population estimates themselves presuppose the assumption that nuptiality rates were not affected by economic changes, since Chao uses the construct of a "stable population," one of the assumptions of which is that reproduction rates are constant (1986:28). But this assumption may seriously bias the data; if nuptiality and fertility were sensitive to fluctuating economic circumstances, then one would predict lower rates of population growth at various stages.

Second, Chao implicitly takes nuptiality as a proxy for fertility in his argument, but there is substantial current controversy over the level of marital fertility in traditional China. In their reassessment of the population data contained in the Lossing Buck farm surveys, Barclay et al. (1976) argue the fertility rate was substantially lower than other estimates have found and that universal early marriage was accompanied by customs that lowered the rate of marital fertility. (But see also criticisms of these findings in A. Wolf 1985.) If demographic data ultimately show that gross fertility and marital fertility rates were lower than traditionally thought, then Chao's reliance on the practice of universal early marriage to predict rapid population increase is unpersuasive.

Third, Chao's emphasis on land data provides insufficient information about family income to evaluate his claim about the lack of connection between nuptiality and economic change. To evaluate the demographic hypothesis we must have information comparable to a real wage index of family income over an extended time. But farm income is *not* a function solely of farm size (as Chao himself recognizes). It is a function of farm size, techniques of cultivation, cropping index, and market circumstances. If crop prices and the cropping index were rising gradually, this might compensate for falling farm size, and family income would remain constant. Likewise, gradual innovations in farming technologies could prop up family income in circumstances in which average farm size is falling. So Chao does not establish that a falling land–man ratio implies falling family income; and if family income is not falling, then evidence of population increase is not evidence for the population dynamics thesis.[20]

Finally, Chao's data set is too thin to test the population dynamics hypothesis. He has only a few data points for population and land figures separated by hundreds of years (eleven points covering almost nineteen hundred years on his table 5.1), whereas the relevant economic trends ought to be of shorter duration. Given that the correlation between nuptiality and the changing economic environment is established by individuals deciding on marriage in light of their perceptions of available economic possibilities in the near future, correlated movements, if any, should be on a time frame of twenty-five to fifty years. But even if such movements existed in China's population history, Chao's analysis would miss them because his data have centuries-long gaps. What is needed is a detailed study of the historical demography of various regions of China based on detailed family-level data, for example, extensive genealogies, which permit the demographer to reconstruct the central demographic variables—age of marriage, sex ratios, marital fertility, and the like. Significantly, Chao does not make substantial use of these data.[21]

In short, Chao's analysis lacks the quality and quantity of data to make this type of causal argument. Chao's central demographic hypothesis—that Chinese nuptiality and fertility were unresponsive to economic opportunities and limitations—is empirically unsupported.[22]

We may also ask how credible is Chao's analysis of the cultural determinants of nuptiality in traditional China. Chao maintains that the cultural values defining family relationships were sufficiently powerful as to offset the inhibitions to nuptiality created by economic constraints. Other research seems to indicate the contrary; Burton Pasternak's study (1978) of rural Taiwan in the 1930s, for example, reveals that family arrangements were quite flexible in the face of changing economic circumstances.[23] This account suggests that family relations, and the values constraining and guiding traditional family practices, were adaptive to changing material circumstances. If this example is at all representative, then Chao's claim for the priority of traditional family values over economic rationality within Chinese society is overstated. Again, Chao does not address the substantial current literature on these points.

Turn now to the data. A summary of Chao's reconstruction of the

population and land data for China over a two-thousand-year period
(table 4.1) shows a high land–man ratio before the tenth century. The
ratio then fluctuates sharply between the tenth and seventeenth centuries from a high of 8.7 shi mu per person to a low of 3.96. Finally,
though, the land–man ratio falls to roughly 3 shi mu per person in the
eighteenth century, where it remains with further erosion over the
next century. By the nineteenth century the land–man ratio is about
one-third what it was in the first century.

Chao puts these data forward to demonstrate a decisive downward
trend in the land–man ratio; his interpretation is that the agricultural system went from relative abundance in the second century
(10 shi mu per person) to surplus population in the nineteenth century (2.7 shi mu per person). These data are less convincing than they
first appear, however. First, the high ratios found between the first
and tenth centuries indicate—as Chao points out—that land was
abundant during this period and that cultivation could expand fairly
readily. So it is misleading to use this period as a baseline in terms of
estimating the effect of modern land–man ratios on population welfare. Second, the wide fluctuations of per capita acreage (such as
during the period of 1072, 1393, 1581) reflect extreme changes in
population: the population drops from 121 million in 1072 to 60
million in 1391 and then increases more than threefold by 1592. So
the peaks in 1391 and 1657 represent the effects of population catastrophes—not gradual processes of either population growth or land
reclamation. The most representative comparison appears to be of-

Table 4.1. Per capita acreages of cultivated land, A.D. 2–1887

Cultivated land		Population		
Year	Amount (million shi mu)	Year	Number	Per capita acreage (million shi mu)
2	571	2	59	9.68
105	535	105	53	10.09
146	507	146	47	10.79
976	255	961	32	7.97
1072	666	1109	121	5.50
1393	522	1391	60	8.70
1581	793	1592	200	3.97
1662	570	1657	72	7.92
1812	943	1800	295	3.20
1887	1,154	1848	426	2.71

Source: Chao 1986:89 (table 5.1)

fered by the years 1109, 1581, and 1800. All three fall within periods
of steady population growth. When we compare these years we find
that Chao's generalizations obtain: population increases and the
land–man ratio falls. Population increases by roughly 50 percent in
each interval, and the land–man ratio drops from 5.5 to 3.96 to 3.19.
But this drop is much more modest than the extremes of Chao's data
would suggest (from 10.78 to 2.70). For population welfare to remain
constant through such changes, only relatively modest gains in agricultural productivity are required, and in fact Perkins shows that the
agricultural system responded with such innovations, so as to keep
per capita income roughly fixed. The Chinese population clearly increased more rapidly than land reclamation proceeded; but what economic consequences this trend had is unclear. When Chao's argument is examined more closely, therefore, his data do not appear to
establish his central conclusion: that population growth imposed a
crushing obstacle to the capacity of the economy to introduce innovation and increase productivity.[24]

Finally, Chao's land–man computations themselves are questionable when we consider other authoritative estimates of the land–
man ratio. Dwight Perkins, for example, provides data that permit
the computation of land–man ratios for the last five centuries (1400–
1933) of the time period (table 4.2). However, Perkins's data do not
show the same steep trends that Chao describes. He finds a land–man
ratio that varies from 5.10 shi mu per person (1400) to 3.46 shi mu per
person (1873)—in contrast to Chao's findings of a decline from 8.70
to 2.7. He thus arrives at a moderate decline of roughly 32 percent
from the fifteenth to the nineteenth century rather than Chao's catastrophic decline of 69 percent. Even more striking, Perkins finds an
increase in per capita acreage from the seventeenth to the nineteenth
century. Perkins's data thus suggest a much slower and more moder-

Table 4.2. Perkins's land–man ratios

Year	Cultivated land (million shi mu)	Population (million)	Per capita acreage (shi mu)
1400	370	75	5.10
1600	500	160	3.13
1770	950	270	3.52
1873	1,210	350	3.46
1933	1,470	500	2.94

Source: Perkins 1969:16 (table 2.1)

ate process of population growth in relation to arable land. If these estimates are correct, it becomes even more plausible that innovations in agriculture could have kept pace with a gradual decrease in the land–man ratio.

At best, Chao has provided data for the general trend of movement in population and cultivated acreage over two thousand years. But he has not given data to support or refute a causal hypothesis about the relations between demographics and economic change. And he has not established his central economic claim: that falling land–man ratios led to involution and a marked preference for labor-intensive techniques of cultivation.

Turn now more briefly to Chao's economic analysis. A central shortcoming of this part of the theory is its failure to provide an institutional context for the agricultural system. Chao postulates a sea of small peasant proprietors involved in labor-intensive cultivation. He does not give an important causal role to the institutional arrangements through which farming takes place, however. He downplays the significance for the explanation of economic stagnation of the varieties of land tenure arrangements, the extent of smallholding and distribution of land, the availability of credit and the level of indebtedness, and the role of the state in affecting agrarian change, for example, through changes in taxation policies. Instead, he regards these as dependent variables that should be expected to adjust to demographic trends.[25] It seems reasonable, however, that these institutional factors are themselves important causal variables in determining the economic effects of demographic change. A farm economy is an organized system of social relations and independent decision making; it is highly implausible to suppose that the long-term trends of such a system can be explained by demographic factors alone.

A second problem has to do with Chao's implicit assumption that barriers prevent family members from selling their labor to managerial farmers below the subsistence rate. Chao assumes that the wage on managerial farms will fall to the subsistence cost but not lower, but this assumption is implausible. Consider the problem from the point of view of the peasant farmer: is it preferable to expend a young boy's labor time in weeding, leading to an increment of ten catties of grain over the course of the season, or in wage labor at a very low wage, but one sufficient to purchase fifteen catties of grain? The choice would appear clear; but this would imply that labor power will be available at a wage substantially below subsistence cost.[26] And this is in fact the finding that propels the proto-industrialization model: rural subsidiary production was much cheaper than urban manufacture because the depressed peasant economy drove rural wages below subsistence level.

A Class-Structure Explanation of Stagnation

Chao attempts to account for economic stagnation in terms of population increase, high levels of commercialization, and the like. The surplus-extraction model, however, attempts to explain economic growth and technical innovation in terms of local class relations and the particulars of an existing system of surplus extraction.[27] According to this model, the key to understanding the process of economic development in a given economy is to examine the social relations of production—the social institutions that surround the production and distribution of wealth—through which productive economic activity proceeds, on the ground that these relations are a crucial part of the institutional context of economic activity. Any economy produces goods to satisfy human wants and needs, and for any economy we can ask how the production process is organized and how the surpluses created by productive activity are distributed across society. The surplus-extraction model postulates that an economy typically embodies a class system dividing the immediate producers (farmers, workers, artisans) from the elite, who confiscate part of the surplus for their own uses. The direction that economic development takes depends heavily on the incentives, opportunities, and powers conferred on the class parties by the class system; class relations thus impose a logic of development on the system. This model directs us to consider the system through which various elements of the elite class are enabled to seize part of the surplus created through productive economic activity. How is the surplus appropriated and by whom?[28]

Robert Brenner (1976, 1982) has taken a leading role in applying this mode of analysis to premodern European economic development. Brenner's thesis is that the central causal factor in the pattern of agrarian development in Europe—the factor that varies most closely with patterns of development, regression, and stagnation in agriculture—is the character of class relations in a region and the incentives, opportunities, and powers imposed by local property relations. Brenner thus bases his explanation on a *microclass analysis* of the

agrarian relations of regions of Europe.[29] The processes of agricultural modernization in England unavoidably favored some class
interests and harmed others. Different property arrangements give
rise to different interests and incentives for the various actors, and
they determine the relative power of the classes defined by those
relations in particular regions.[30] Thus capitalist agriculture required
larger units of production (farms), the application of larger quantities
of capital goods to agriculture, higher levels of education and scientific knowledge, and so on. This required the expropriation of smallholders and the destruction of traditional forms of agrarian relations.
Whose interests would be served by these changes? Higher agricultural productivity would result, but the new agrarian relations
would pump the increased surpluses out of the producer and into
elite classes and larger urban concentrations. These changes thus did
not favor peasant interests, at least in the medium run. It is Brenner's
view that in those regions of Europe where peasant communities
were able to defend traditional arrangements—favorable rent levels,
communal control of land, and patterns of smallholding—those arrangements persisted for centuries. In areas where peasants had been
substantially deprived of tradition, organization, and power of resistance, an enlightened gentry and budding bourgeoisie were able
through capitalist agriculture to restructure agrarian relations in the
direction of profit and scientific innovation.

For agricultural modernization to occur in a given area, therefore,
Brenner argues that there needed to be a group (a microclass) that had
both an economic interest to further these changes and the political
power to do so. On Brenner's account, the decisive factors were the
property arrangements and the distribution of the means of power in
a given region. Where landlords could force peasants to accept changing property relations, the transition to capitalist agriculture could
proceed. But where peasant communities could resist changes in
property relations—in particular, abolition of communal lands, expropriation of small peasant property—they could block the
emergence of the property relations within which capitalist agriculture, wage relations in the countryside, and more efficient production could emerge.

Victor Lippit (1987) employs a surplus-extraction framework to
analyze the traditional Chinese rural economy. The main elements
of Lippit's theory of underdevelopment may be put in these terms:
First Lippit maintains—contrary to Chao, Elvin, and Myers—that
the traditional agrarian economy had a sizable surplus and that an

elite class effectively extracted this surplus from peasants and artisans. The mechanisms of extraction differed—rent, interest, taxation and corrupt tax practices—but the effect was the same: to transfer from the immediate producer to a small elite class some 25 to 30 percent of total rural product. This concentration of income within a relatively small class could have provided the investment funds needed for agricultural modernization, but the elite did not use its wealth in this way.[31] When we examine the class system of traditional China, Lippit argues, the elite constituted a rentier class, deriving income from office and ownership of property, and this class was largely separated from the production process. Absentee landlords lived in towns and cities and did not concern themselves with technical change; they already controlled a large surplus and because of Confucian disdain for farming and manufacture lacked an incentive to modernize production. "Thus in China there were no distinct elements within the elite to champion development. Rather, there was a strong consensus in favor of preserving the status quo" (97). "In this sense, the development of underdevelopment in China is more properly attributable to the domestic class structure and relations of production than to external influence. As a consequence of both its objective interest and its self-image, the gentry class was committed to preserving the existing order" (99). Lippit thus rejects the population-driven explanation of stagnation:

> I do not wish to argue that population growth created no difficulties, but merely that the population growth rate was modest and that the central issue is why the moderate levels of capital formation and technological progress necessary to raise output more rapidly than this modest rate were not forthcoming. . . . Yet even this modest rate of progress [needed to keep up with population growth]—or the industrial capital formation that could in part have substituted for it—proved unattainable, not because the best innovations were "used up," but because the social and class structure discouraged the development of new ones. (85)

The surplus-extraction model has three chief premises: The traditional economy created a sizable surplus over and above the subsistence needs of the cultivators and producers; rural society was heavily stratified, containing a small elite class and a large peasant class, and the elite managed to appropriate the surplus for its own purposes; and the cultural and economic values that governed the consumption behavior of the elite discouraged it from investing the surplus in productive economic ways—infrastructure, capital improvements, irrigation, and so forth. If these assumptions are substantiated, then a pattern of economic stagnation follows fairly directly. Producers (peasant farmers) lack funds to invest in more efficient technologies, whereas the elite lacks incentive to do so. The spectrum of innovations that would lead to economic development are blocked.

Each of these premises has been questioned, and some authors have held that the categories of class, exploitation, and surplus-extraction cannot be reasonably applied to traditional China. Ramon Myers (1970) describes the traditional farm economy as a sea of small peasant proprietors involved in an inherently poor economy, resulting in insignificant levels of surplus. Elvin, Buck, and others have described rural society as substantially flat, with only a narrow (and frequently reversed) range of inequalities of wealth and land ownership. Finally, some have held that landlords and lenders *were* prepared to invest in the production process but were inhibited by some other institutional factor (for example, the superior profits available in merchant activity [Elvin 1973]). To assess the cogency of the surplus-extraction framework, then, we need to see whether available empirical data support these three premises.

Size of the Surplus

The clearest case to be made for any of these premises concerns the extent of the surplus. Compelling studies make it plain that a substantial surplus was available within the farm economy and that this surplus was extracted from farmers through various mechanisms. In a work of 1974, *Land Reform and Economic Development in China*, Lippit offers a careful and extensive study of the sources of income in the Chinese rural economy in order to calculate available surplus. Working through economic statistics for 1933, Lippit arrives at these income estimates as a proportion of national income: land rent (10.7 percent), farm business profits (3.4 percent), and rural interest payments (2.8 percent). These data suggest that 16.9 percent of the national income was available as rural economy surplus in 1933.

Carl Riskin's (1975) careful assessment of the potential surplus in the Chinese economy in the early twentieth century supports Lippit's analysis. Riskin defines the "potential economic surplus" of the Chinese economy as the "difference between total potential current output and the *actual* level of labor and peasant income, assuming that those whose entire incomes take the form of returns to property (i.e., pure rentiers) are limited to the same consumption as wage and salary recipients (or peasants) in their sectors of the economy" (51). Potential current output is the sum of current output and an estimate of the output of currently underutilized resources, particularly unemployed labor. Riskin estimates a 36.8 percent surplus for 1933, of which 24.5 percent was generated in agriculture; if that portion of the surplus reflecting unused resources is excluded, he estimates a surplus of 27.2 percent (74).

Riskin and Lippit show convincingly that the rural Chinese economy created a substantial potential surplus in the early twentieth century. Given the turmoils of this time, dramatic growth is unlikely to have occurred, so these data imply that comparable surpluses were available in the previous century. A number of other studies support these findings. Philip Huang (1985:182) finds this estimate consistent with his study of the rural economy of North China, and Perkins's (1969) data on land tenancy rates also appear consistent with this perspective. Finally, the People's Republic of China's sizable investments in agricultural development in the decade after the revolution suggest that substantial surpluses were available for the state to capture and channel into productive investment (Lippit 1974).

A compelling case can thus be made that the rural economy supported a substantial surplus, which took the form of income to landlords, moneylenders, and labor-hiring managerial farmers. "Income from agricultural land remained the principal source of unearned income in the countryside. In the agricultural sector of the 1930s, land rent constituted 10.7 percent of national income, farm business profits or the surplus produced by annually hired labor above its own consumption 3.4 percent, and rural interest payments 2.8 percent" (Lippit 1987:40).

Degree of Stratification

Turn now to the second premise: the assumption that rural society in China was significantly stratified and that a small elite class controlled the bulk of the economic surplus. This assumption is independent of the first, since farmers and artisans could retain the surplus in the form of a standard of living significantly higher than subsistence. Lippit argues, however, that this is not the case, and that the surplus was largely appropriated by an elite class. The elite extracted the surplus through various means—rent, interest, forced labor, and corrupt exactions. Is Lippit's estimate of the degree of stratification of wealth within the traditional Chinese economy reasonable?

Lippit (1987:41) breaks down the pyramidal class structure of eighteenth-century China with a population base of 300–400 million as follows: gentry and landowning class (3.5 percent), rich peasants (7 percent), middle peasants (20–30 percent), and poor and landless peasants (60–70 percent). At the top of this pyramid was a compact elite class of landholding and wealth-holding gentry.[32] Lippit estimates the amount of income flowing to the gentry in the late nineteenth century (some 1.9 percent of the population) at 719 million taels, or 22.3 percent of the net national product (90–91). This income breaks down into three chief sources: service income (312 million taels), land rents (293 million taels), and merchant profits (114 million taels).[33] Lippit thus maintains that traditional Chinese society was highly stratified, with a class of large landlords who owned a substantial amount (perhaps 33 percent) of the cultivated acreage. By the eighteenth century, this group had become a rentier class, separated from the production process.[34]

How does this analysis square with other available information about the traditional Chinese economy? Several aspects of stratification are significant in this context: stratification of landholding, of income, and of other forms of wealth. The economy could, for example, have a narrow range of land inequalities but a wide range of wealth and income inequalities if there was a high level of indebtedness. Let us begin, though, with land inequalities and the associated problem of assessing tenancy rates in different regions of China.

Myers (1970), Elvin (1973), and Chao (1986) doubt that the range of land inequalities was wide in the traditional economy. As Joseph Esherick (1981) points out, these assessments rely heavily on the Buck land surveys of the 1930s. Esherick shows in convincing detail that the Buck surveys and other contemporary studies were tilted in such a way as to underestimate the holdings of landlords (396)—by excluding absentee landlords from the data, for example. Esherick painstakingly recomputes probable tenancy rates on the basis of Buck's and other data from the 1930s and arrives at the estimate of 42 percent of land rented, or 489 million mu (399). This figure is substantially higher than Buck's estimate of 28.7 percent. Esherick further estimates that 85 percent of this land was rented from landlords

Table 4.3. Class structure of Republican China

	Households (%)	Land (%)
Landlords	4	39
Rich peasants	6	17
Middle peasants	22	30
Poor peasants	60	14
Agricultural laborers and others	8	0
Total	100	100

Source: Esherick 1981:405

(excluding rich peasants, widows, and the infirm [400]) and judges that some 4 percent of rural households owned 39 percent of the land. (See table 4.3.)

Philip Huang's (1985) study of North China lends further support to the view that the Chinese rural economy was highly stratified. Huang provides data on land ownership for the eighteenth century in Huailu county, Hebei, in North China (table 4.4). According to these data, 25 percent of households owned no land; another 35 percent owned less than 10 mu; and 4.2 percent of households owned 35 percent of the land (104). Plotted crudely by percentile (fig. 4.1), these land distribution data can be converted into a standard Lorenz curve with a Gini coefficient of 0.68.[35] This is remarkably high and indi-

Table 4.4. Land distribution in Huailu county, Hebei, c. 1725–1750

Land (mu)	Households (N)	Households (%)	Total land owned	Land owned (%)	Mu per family
0	5,331	25.30	0	0.00	0.00
<1	555	4.20	439	0.20	0.79
1–5	3,507	16.70	10,207	3.20	2.91
6–10	3,172	15.10	22,948	7.30	7.23
11–15	2,137	10.10	26,157	8.30	12.24
16–30	3,332	15.80	70,006	22.20	21.01
31–40	967	4.60	33,205	10.50	34.34
41–50	498	2.40	22,313	7.10	44.81
51–60	334	1.60	18,195	5.80	54.48
61–70	540	2.60	40,534	12.80	75.06
>100	340	1.60	71,225	22.60	209.49

Source: Huang 1985:104 (table 5.5)

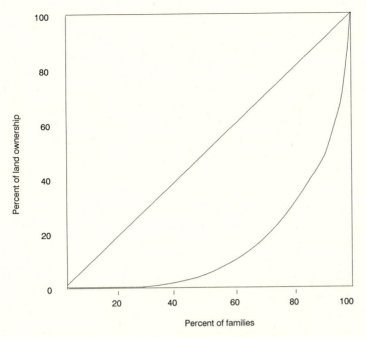

Figure 4.1. Lorenz Distribution—Huailu county

cates an extensive range of inequalities of land ownership. (By contrast, the Gini coefficients for Java and Bangladesh in the 1970s were 0.49 and 0.45 [Hart 1988:251].)

These data demonstrate high tenancy levels throughout China (with important regional variations, to be sure).[36] On all accounts, however, China had a sizable class of small owner-cultivators. Were owner-cultivators (that is, the nontenant sector) the source of substantial surpluses for others? The primary forms of surplus extraction from this group include usury, taxation, forced labor, and banditry, with indebtedness constituting the largest drain on family income. Huang (1985) holds that usury was an important source of income for the wealth holders of North China. Land pawning and money lending were lucrative practices in the impoverishment created by the ecological extremes of North China (176). "Interest rates in these villages generally varied from 1.2 percent a month to 3 percent a month, with most loans made at 2 percent. The lowest rates were generally obtained by the most well-to-do households, because they had the influence to procure them and were considered good credit risks; the highest rates were borne by the poorest households, considered the worst risks" (189). Perkins writes that "the rates of interest on such loans were commonly 30 or 40 percent per year and more. If the initial loan were large or if it were not quickly repaid, the peasant found himself increasingly in debt" (1969:92). Peter Perdue describes official efforts in eighteenth-century Hunan to "reduce landlord usury by enforcing a limitation of interest rates to 3 percent per month. They hoped thus to prevent the loss of land due to indebtedness" (1987:161). Likewise, Mark Selden finds that indebtedness eclipsed tenancy as one of the greatest drains on peasant resources in Yenan (1971:7–13). None of these authors provides any quantitative estimate of the level of indebtedness within the peasant economy, but each offers reasons for supposing that indebtedness significantly drained average peasant income.

In short, these data support Lippit's contention about the level of stratification in the Chinese rural economy. Huang, Perkins, Esherick, Perdue, and others emphasize extensive inequalities of landownership, substantial indebtedness, and high rents. These severely drained the rural surplus, confirming the notion that the rural economy was a class system, which empowered an elite class to extract much of the rural product for its own consumption.

Elite Consumption Behavior

The final premise of the surplus-extraction theory of stagnation concerns the consumption behavior of the elite class—the ways through which this class disposed of the surplus under its control. Lippit argues that the critical question in explaining economic stagnation in China is how the cultural and economic environment led surplus-extractors to dispose of the surplus. He maintains that this class expended the great bulk of the appropriated surplus in economically unproductive ways—not as investment in agriculture or manufacture but as luxury consumption, ceremonial expenditures, and the like.[37] Lippit describes the pattern of elite luxury consumption in these terms:

> The large house, its maintenance, landscaping, and furnishing were major outlets for luxury expenditure, as was a food-consumption standard far above prevailing norms. Expenditures on clothing that far surpassed in quantity and quality what the typical peasant could buy were also characteristic. The keeping of a rickshaw meant the need for a laborer to pull it. Personal

services were also supplied this family by its maidservants; the cost for this was only their room, board, and presumably some clothing, however, as they were given no salary. (1974:40)

Exclusive focus on consumption patterns makes the stagnation of the economy depend on a fairly superficial feature of Chinese society: the norms regulating elite behavior. However, a structural feature of the traditional economy further inhibited productive investment of the surplus. This was the separation that the economy embodied between the elite class and the process of production. The improving landlord and the small manufacturing capitalist were uncommon forms of wealth holding in traditional China; rather, the Chinese elite took the form of a rentier class, deriving income from ownership rights rather than managerial and entrepreneurial skills. "Mercantile profits were in distribution, and merchants tended to remain ignorant of the production processes for goods they traded. The major wholesale cotton cloth dealers of Suzhou, for example, had nothing to do with production; they paid labor contractors a fixed price per piece rather than hire labor directly. Under these circumstances, the merchants remained largely ignorant of the techniques of production and were hardly in a position to improve them" (83–84). Instead, small family units—peasant households, artisans, and the like—produced goods using traditional techniques. The resulting surplus was effectively extracted through the mechanisms already described, but the elites who ultimately received the income generated in this way had little practical or institutional connection to the production processes that created it.[38]

Chao's argument (1986) that population pressure makes tenurial landlordism preferable over managerial landlordism for the wealth holder (discussed above) is relevant in this context; this may be a point at which the two theories converge. Chao holds that, as the marginal product of labor drops below subsistence, the returns from managerial farming will be lower than land rents. This would constitute a further economic incentive, then, for absenteeism rather than direct management of cultivation.

Philip Huang's discussion of the agricultural economy of North China offers the basis for a similar argument. Huang holds that technical innovation was blocked in traditional Chinese agriculture by (1) disincentives created by social property system and (2) need for state intervention (flood control and irrigation) to alter ecological circumstances (1985:183). The more serious obstacle to capitalist agriculture derives from the two-tiered structure of wealth in traditional China: the commercial and bureaucratic elite might receive thirty thousand taels, in contrast to a small managerial farmer's several hundred. Consequently, rising managerial farmers had an overpowering incentive to become lease-holding landowners, giving them time to pursue commerce, education, or office (178). "Managerial agriculture, therefore, tended to return via landlordism to the same small farming from which it arose" (169).[39] Managerial farms reached a limit of roughly two hundred mu because plots were fragmented and hired laborers required close supervision. Doubling acreage would require increasing hired labor beyond the capacity of the owner to supervise; hiring a foreman would eat up the margin (172).

This analysis of landed property, the low income that even large managerial farmers could derive from land and the much larger incomes and status available through imperial office or commerce, illustrates Lippit's point: in the circumstances of traditional Chinese social relations, agricultural innovations were not the best way for the landlord to advance materially; landed income served rather as a base for launching the lord into higher status and income in commerce or office. Consequently, agricultural innovations did not occur.[40]

Lippit's account of stagnation may be summarized in these terms: The property arrangements through which rural economic activity took place defined a system in which vast numbers of small cultivators produced a surplus product. These property arrangements also enabled a small elite class to appropriate the bulk of this surplus through a variety of mechanisms: rent, interest, forced labor, corrupt tax practices, monopoly service charges, and so forth. Wealth flowed from the bulk of the rural population to a small class of wealth holders. Rather than invest this surplus in productive economic channels, this class tended to consume it in luxury consumption. These consumption preferences resulted from a confluence of cultural and economic factors: culturally, the elite was conditioned to prefer to keep its distance from farming and manufacturing, and economically, once a rentier economy was in place, members of the elite had little incentive to involve themselves in managing and modernizing production. As a result, the investment in production was minimal; predictably, the rate of innovation and modernization was extremely low. Property arrangements imposed a logic of stagnation on the traditional economy through the set of interlocking incentives, opportunities, and powers it imposed on participants.

Assessment of Lippit's Analysis

Recent scholarship on the Chinese rural economy appears to support Lippit's central claims. His analysis is subject to serious criticisms, however. First, by the standards established by recent work on the economic history of China—for example, Perkins, Huang, Rowe, Perdue, or Myers—Lippit's analysis is extremely sketchy. He offers a characterization of the Chinese economy over a thousand-year period in a single chapter, and he provides little detailed analysis of any region or time. His study functions more as a research hypothesis or framework than as a fully developed empirical analysis. Where Lippit's account does become more specific—for example, when estimating the size of the rural surplus—his analysis is premised largely on twentieth-century data. Given that the early twentieth century was a period of severe political and social tumult, economic data from this period are unlikely to be representative of earlier periods. (This criticism may also be addressed against Myers [1970].)

This shortcoming raises an important related lacuna: Lippit ignores regional and temporal variation. Much recent work on China has demonstrated that regional variations across the empire were significant (a point emphasized in the preceding chapter). But Lippit offers no regionally specific analysis; instead, his claims are couched at the level of China as a whole. Such generalizations are likely invalid, and it is possible to do better using the detailed area studies now available.

Different regional experiences demonstrate important exceptions to Lippit's generalizations about surpluses and elites. In his analysis of seventeenth- and eighteenth-century Hunan, for example, Peter Perdue (1987) shows that the elite invested extensively in land reclamation and waterworks, leading to rapid expansion in the rural economy. And Philip Huang (1985:72–84) argues that managerial farming was a persistent presence in North China—implying the presence of a group of village rich who had both opportunity and incentive to invest productively in their farms. Each point undercuts Lippit's generalization that elites were largely averse to involving themselves in productive activity or investment of the surpluses that they controlled.

It would appear, then, that Lippit's account raises a number of questions that can be addressed only through intensive regional studies. One important question has to do with the form and availability of rural credit. Lippit views indebtedness as a symptom of excessive surplus-extraction; seen from another perspective, however, the availability of rural credit is necessary for technical innovation and economic growth. So it is crucial to an adequate analysis of the rural economy to have fuller knowledge of the rural credit system.[41] Likewise, we need to know more about landlord-tenant relations to determine which party captured the gains of rising productivity. When double cropping or new seed varieties resulted in increased yields, did rents rise sufficiently to transfer the new surpluses to landlords? Or did rents remain fixed, leaving the surpluses for tenants or other locals? Absentee landlords would appear to be in a weak position to pursue increases in productivity vigorously through raising rents; if this should prove true, however, we should expect a shift in the proportions of the surplus controlled by landlords, creditors, and peasants. Given the nature of Lippit's model, these questions are crucial, but it is possible to answer them only on the basis of detailed local studies.

Lippit's social analysis of rural elites, finally, is critically underspecified. He refers to the elite without much differentiation, but it is clear from other studies that elites were strongly differentiated and that their differences were economically significant. (See Schoppa [1982] and Rankin [1986] for careful studies of elite political behavior in Zhejiang.) Degree-holding gentry, officials, landlords, merchants, and moneylenders all fall within the elite for some purposes, but they have substantially different economic roles and interests. Further, Lippit's generalizations about the "cultural values" of the elites are too encompassing, asserting that all elites throughout China disdain farming, are detached from the production process, and prefer luxury consumption. Not only do different economic strata within the elite group have different interests and patterns of behavior, but important regional variations may well exist even within a given stratum (for example, the landholding class). On his own assumptions, then, Lippit's analysis needs a fuller and more detailed treatment of the social composition and forms of variation of the elite class; different strata of this class may be expected to engage in distinct forms of political and economic behavior.

Relation between Chao and Lippit

What is the logical relation between the demographic and surplus-extraction theories? Do they offer contradictory theories of economic and social change? It would appear not; Chao and Lippit agree about most of the same factors and disagree about their relative causal importance. Chao emphasizes the importance of demographic factors in constraining economic growth and limiting innovation, whereas Lippit holds that the particular features of the surplus-extraction system determine growth. Lippit sometimes writes as though his account is a strict alternative to the demographic model; in fact, Lippit's chief contribution is to specify an important causal factor that the demographic model omits: the role that class and property play in determining the local effect of large-scale economic forces.

In particular, Lippit's account should not deny the importance of population increase and resource scarcity within the Chinese economy. However, according to the surplus-extraction model, these factors become background conditions in the environment of which property relations and economic institutions exercise their causal influence. The demographic model specifies economic forces that bathe the landscape of China on a large scale. Chao tacitly presupposes a simple, uniform, and transparent local mechanism through which this influence is translated into economic effects: rational individuals pursuing their material interests and responding rationally to changing economic circumstances. Lippit shows, however, that the institutions defining the local environment of choice vary significantly and that the outcome of large-scale economic forces is highly sensitive to those differences. Property relations and economic institutions thus constitute the local mechanisms through which demographic factors exercise their influence. This suggests not that the demographic explanation is false but that it is incomplete and must be supplemented with local and regional analysis of the political and institutional environment within which these objective economic factors exercise their influence.

It would seem natural to say that the demographic theory describes a widespread causal factor that exercises its influence across regions possessing different local properties; as a result, the effects of the objective economic factors differ across the landscape. Lippit's case (if empirically well founded) adds to our knowledge of local mechanisms, but does not invalidate the causal role of the objective economic factors.

Lippit's analysis and the demographic model actually have a great deal in common: each depends on the assumption of individual economic and material rationality, and each gives central place to the role of economic parameters (rents, prices, wages) in explaining social change. These two approaches share the assumption that the incentives and opportunities defining the circumstances of action of the individual decision maker (cultivator, inventor, manufacturer, merchant) determine large-scale patterns of development. And they share the belief that material interests (income, property rights, security) largely determine the motive structure of individuals.

Neither account is fully satisfactory. Each raises serious problems of empirical adequacy, since neither adequately analyzes the regional and temporal variation in traditional China. And each may be faulted for assuming that there should be a single-factor analysis of the causes of stagnation.

Problems of Empirical Reasoning

How should the issues raised between Chao and Lippit be resolved? At one level at least, this debate is the most sharply drawn of any considered here; the authors disagree over the correct causal explanation of an important feature of the Chinese economy, and they disagree about a number of important factual judgments (for example, the size of the rural surplus, the degree of stratification in rural society). What would be needed to determine which hypothesis is correct?

Several considerations are relevant. First, each theory may be criticized on internal grounds. Chao's demographic estimates appear to rest on a rather thin set of population data, Lippit's analysis is almost entirely based on secondary sources rather than primary research, and so forth. Such criticisms affect the credibility of the theories and may sometimes suffice to exclude a given theory from further consideration.

Second, these theories clearly share a number of points. Lippit largely embraces Chao's demographic data and disagrees only about what effects these population trends had, Lippit and Chao view the structure of the peasant household in much the same way, and so forth. So we do not have to evaluate incompatible competing theories; rather, we need to make a judgment concerning disagreements over the relative causal importance of a variety of factors whose presence is largely conceded by both theories.

Speaking abstractly, each case consists of several parts: (1) a range of empirical data that the author analyzes and presents to support his case; (2) a set of analytical tools to be used to draw inferences from the data and other assumptions; and (3) an organized argument showing how the assembled data strongly support the author's causal hypothesis. Chao's argument fits this scheme closely. He assembles a time series of population and land data for a two-thousand-year period; he presents a set of marginalist economic tools in terms of which to characterize the behavior of peasant farmers; and he offers an extensive argument showing how the falling land–man ratio leads, through rational peasant behavior, to technical stagnation. Lippit's case can also be analyzed along these lines. For him, the core empirical data concern the size of the economic surplus and the class relations governing agriculture. His analytical framework combines historical materialism with current economic theory. And his extended argument attempts to show how the institutions he discerns in the traditional economy lead to stagnation.

The most direct way to evaluate the competing hypotheses is through further empirical research. There may be a critical area of empirical disagreement between the theories—a crucial empirical question that, if firmly resolved, would favor one theory decisively over the other. In this case, the size of the agricultural surplus is such a critical test condition; if further research establishes that Lippit's estimates were correct, then Chao's case is weakened, and vice versa. Future investigators should attempt to identify the crucial empirical assumptions of the two theories and then attempt further to evaluate the adequacy of those assumptions or claims. This approach is similar to the use of experimentation in the natural sciences and has much in common with the aim of constructing a "crucial experiment" that will decide between two competing theories.

This debate, more than any of the others considered in this book, depends heavily on quantitative reasoning. Each theory is a study in the economic history of traditional China; as such, each is obligated to estimate various economic variables—population size, extent of arable land at a given time, average crop yields, average rent levels, aggregate debt levels, and so on for a long list of quantities. Estimates of these variables provide us with an econometric representation of the traditional economy and permit judgments about important economic trends, such as welfare levels, degree of stratification, land and labor productivity, and investment rates. Ideally, data would be extensive and representative at the county level over a long time series and would permit revealing aggregate statistics about the economy over time.

However, the data available to economic historians of China (or of any other country, for that matter) are vastly less complete than this idealization requires. The problem of data collection in a historical research discipline is quite different from that of a natural science because the circumstances to be investigated lie in the past; it may never be possible to improve the accuracy of knowledge of some periods of China's population history, for example. So some important empirical issues may never be settled because of gaps in the historical record; it is plausible to suppose that further research will not resolve the empirical disagreement over the size of the agricultural surplus.

Even if data are available, they may systematically misrepresent the underlying variable. One form of data generally available throughout Chinese history is the amount of cultivated land in a county; this information is available because it was needed to collect land taxes. But it is well known that land registers underreported cultivated land, as landowners undertook to minimize their tax burdens. The degree of underreporting depended on a host of local factors—the recency of land settlement, the vigor of local tax officials, the resources available for checking land registers, and so forth. So the modern investigator is forced to make a series of judgments about the sources of bias and misrepresentation contained in the data.

Another data problem concerns comparability of separate data sources. Even when the investigator possesses data on a variable—for example, levels of tenancy in different regions—the data may not be directly comparable. Usually the data have been collected by different institutions for various purposes, using diverse methods. One data set may define tenancy in different terms; another may exclude absentee landlords; a third may do its accounting by farm rather than by family; and so forth. So the investigator is forced to find ways of increasing the comparability of the data, which may involve making assumptions that cannot themselves be empirically evaluated.

Finally, many empirical issues raised by these theories are themselves highly theory dependent. To form an estimate of aggregate economic variables—population size, rate of urbanization, real wage, relative rent burden, level of indebtedness, and so on—it is almost always necessary to construct a model of the variable in question, based on a number of assumptions about the context, and to arrive at proxy variables for the primary variables under scrutiny.[42] Consider the difficulties of forming a real wage index for urban workers, given available information about wages and prices. Urban workers are occupationally stratified, so we must single out a sample of occupations to represent the group as a whole. Each of these occupations will have average money wages that we must try to determine (along with an estimate of average periods of unemployment in different occupations). If we make a series of assumptions about the size of various occupations within the work force we can finally estimate the average money wage for the urban worker. Now turn to the price side; since we are concerned with the real wage, we need to know how much the money wage can purchase. At a given time, though, some commodities may be increasing in price, some falling; workers may be substituting cheaper commodities for more costly; and so forth. So to construct an estimate of average price movements, once again we must make a selection of commodity prices to form a price index, as well as some assumption about consumption patterns. With all these assumptions in place, and estimates for the money wage and the price index, the real wage may be estimated and judged to be rising or falling. But this estimate is highly complex and sensitive to assumptions made along the way.[43]

Considerations of this sort suggest, once again, that resolving many disputes of the sort studied here is unlikely to be a simple matter of coming up with new incontrovertible data; instead, economic historians will offer new studies, based on new assumptions and (sometimes) new data sources, making a case for one position or the other.[44]

The Role of Theory

Clearly, Chao and Lippit both bring an explanatory framework and a set of theoretical categories to bear on empirical data. Lippit works within the general theoretical framework of historical materialism and class analysis, whereas Chao brings to his research the tools and assumptions of marginalist economic analysis. To what extent do these antecedent theories affect the author's analysis of the data?

Chao's relative neglect of institutional features appears to conform to his implicit assumption that any economy consists of a large number of independent decision makers within the context of a market economy. From this perspective, the features of the local economy are relatively unimportant; it is the logic of a market economy rather than the particulars of the property system, land tenure arrangements, and the like, that determines the development of the economy. Correspondingly, Lippit's surplus-extraction framework leads him directly to analysis of the institutions of production and the social relations of power and authority through which the economy proceeds; but he finds it difficult to take data about population change into account. And neither approach considers factors outside the theoretical framework: for example, the role of the state, the significance of Chinese cultural attitudes toward innovation, or the importance of such historical circumstances as the Qing conquest in explaining features of the rural economy. Each author offers a monocausal theory of economic stagnation.

A more satisfactory example of how theory should be employed in economic and social history is found in Philip Huang's study of North China (1985). Huang's analysis reflects his awareness of several competing theoretical frameworks of analysis; consequently, it is sensitive to local variations in economic and social organization. In his hands, social theory—the theory of the rational peasant, class interest, the self-exploiting peasant—constitutes a source of explanatory hypotheses, without the presupposition that one theoretical model will fit all the data. This suggests that the social investigator needs to be prepared for a high level of eclecticism when selecting a theoretical explanation of a social phenomenon. Rather than looking for a single explanatory factor, to be explained by one comprehensive theory, the investigator should be sensitive to multistranded phenomena and prepared to employ a variety of theoretical constructs.

These studies illustrate that explanation can proceed only on the basis of theoretical hypotheses and constructs. Each author makes a causal argument connecting a feature of traditional Chinese rural society with a pattern of economic stagnation. But such an argument can only be made out on the basis of a hypothesis about the underlying processes that link explanans and explanandum. Explanation requires providing some account of the lawlike processes of change that underlie the observable; and hypotheses and theories serve to attempt to satisfy that goal.

The Validity of Historical Constructs

The object of analysis in this debate is a large-scale feature of Chinese society—a deeply entrenched tendency for the farming system to become more labor-intensive and more land-productive without significant technological innovation. This pattern extends over a thousand years and encompasses the economic activities of hundreds of millions of rural people in dozens of regions of China. Two sorts of questions arise: What is needed to establish the meaning and truth of the claim that such a pattern exists? And what is needed to explain such a pattern adequately?

The circumstance to be explained by these theories can be formulated as follows: The farming system in traditional China became more labor-intensive and land-productive without significant technological innovation between the twelfth and nineteenth centuries. This statement identifies a social entity, the farming system of traditional China, and attributes a long-term pattern of change to it. What is the status of this entity? It is a complex social structure, consisting of an ensemble of production techniques and social relations. The concept is thus analogous to the familiar Marxist conception of the "mode of production." To describe the farming system, we must identify the characteristic ways in which agriculture was carried out in traditional China, including material features (techniques, seed types, irrigation devices, and tools) and the social structures through which farming took place. The phrase "Chinese farming system," then, refers to a relatively stable set of social practices and institutions whose typical features can be identified through historical inquiry. A description of the Chinese farming system would include accounts of traditional farming techniques, the social institutions surrounding agricultural activity, and typical units of cultivation— small peasant farms, some managerial farms, and some larger estates.

Any general description of the Chinese farming system, however, glosses over potentially relevant differences between regions and between sectors. Thus tenancy was more prominent in South China than North China; South China contained largely wet-rice cultivation, whereas North China was primarily involved in dry crops; managerial farming was subject to different economic constraints than peasant family farming; and so forth. So the concept of "the farming system" is unavoidably an abstraction; any account of the farming system at a given time—let alone over a long period—must select certain elements as most characteristic, even though variation across time and space is substantial. The historical reality encompasses an immense and diverse number of persons, institutional arrangements and variations, forms of labor practice, and the like.

It might be held that the Chinese rural economy cannot be discussed at any meaningful level of generalization beyond the particular local systems and that regional and sectoral variations make generalization impossible. Several circumstances mitigate this skepticism, however. First, all regional systems within China likely shared some important features. Second, all regional farming systems were probably subject to similar causal influences, so they tended to behave similarly. Finally, regional and sectoral systems, though different, were likely connected through trade, diffusion of techniques, and political influence. Generalizations about the farm economy of China as a whole, then, would seem legitimate, but they must be made with caution. Moreover, such generalizations will inspire the most confidence when they are grounded in careful studies of regional economies. Philip Huang and Ramon Myers analyze the rural economy of North China, Evelyn Rawski concentrates on the rural economy of South China, Peter Perdue provides a close study of the rural economy of Hunan, and so forth. Such studies permit a better idea both of the common features of agrarian life in traditional China and the ways in which regional differences are most pronounced.

The concept of the farming system, then, may legitimately be used as an ideal type: an articulated account of what the author judges the most characteristic features of Chinese farming over time. But the validity of this construct depends almost entirely on the explanatory results that may be reached when attention is directed along the lines suggested by the concept. If it should turn out, for example, that farming in South China was highly market sensitive, innovative, and managerial, whereas North China was largely subsistence oriented, technologically stagnant, and family managed, the concept of the Chinese farming system would be the wrong level at which to look for systemic regularities. The investigator should instead focus attention on the regional subsystems, since (on these hypotheses) these have distinct patterns of development.

Causal Reasoning

Both Chao and Lippit want to identify the *cause* of the pattern of agricultural development found in traditional China. And by this they mean the factors whose presence or absence leads to the presence or absence of agricultural breakthrough via law-governed processes. Chao identifies two important causal factors: a social system (peasant family farming) with its own economic laws, and a demographic-ecological influence (rising population and falling man–land ratio). (The demographic argument is itself an independent causal argument; Chao holds that population rises as a causal consequence of widespread cultural practices that regulate family formation.) The laws of change to which Chao refers are economic laws that derive from the assumption of economic rationality (essentially the laws of neoclassical economics); on the assumption that peasant farmers are rational, their behavior will be lawlike in response to changing economic circumstances. As population rises, individual cultivators are led to substitute surplus family labor for technical innovation, with the aggregate effect that farming techniques become more labor intensive.

Lippit's argument also works through a set of causal conditions. He describes a more complex social system than does Chao (peasant family farming within a class system through which agricultural surplus is siphoned off) and a schematic description of the distribution of power within this social system. Surplus extractors have more power than surplus creators (farmers), so surplus extractors successfully appropriate most of the surplus. This leaves peasants poor, with intensification of labor their only option for increasing income. And the elite—potentially able to make productive investment in agriculture—does not do so but instead consumes the surplus. In the aggregate, this pattern leads to intensification of the labor process, substitution of labor-intensive techniques, low levels of investment in production, and consequent technical stagnation. This account, then, depends on generalizations about the behavior of the various actors—farmers, landlords, officials. And it derives a set of conclusions about the process of economic development that emerges as the aggregate consequence of these behavioral regularities at the level of the individual agent.

Both Chao and Lippit offer a rational choice analysis of economic processes. Each assumes that the features of the farming system are determined largely by the aggregate result of rational individuals making choices in a given set of economic circumstances. Each assumes that the players are motivated to improve their individual welfare within given circumstances. And both agree that the proximate cause of technical stagnation is the lack of investment in the production process. Their central disagreement concerns the explanation of this lack of investment. Chao explains it as the consequence of a low land–man ratio, leading to a preference for labor-intensive techniques and a low absolute level of surpluses. Lippit, in contrast, identifies the consumption behavior of a surplus-extracting elite as the obstacle.

The model of causal relations at work in both cases appears to have several related components. Let us represent each claim as follows:

In circumstances C, A caused B.

First, each author attempts to show why stagnation was unavoidable, given the occurrence of the conditions each author identifies. To say that stagnation was unavoidable is to say that, given C and A, B follows from a set of laws that govern the pertinent system. So the claim of causal relation is a claim of lawlike connection between A and B. Second, this claim has a counterfactual aspect: if A had not occurred, then B would not have occurred. Thus Chao's analysis is committed to the assertion that if Chinese population had reached an equilibrium, stagnation would not have occurred, and Lippit is committed to the implication that if elites had devoted their rents, interest, and profits to productive investment, economic growth would have ensued. And third, each of these causal claims depends heavily on an account of the causal mechanism through which the cause produces its effect; thus Chao expends much effort to show how the condition of falling land–man ratio alters the decision-making environment of the farmer, inducing him to select labor-absorbing techniques of cultivation over labor-replacing innovations. The force of the causal hypothesis in these cases depends almost entirely on the force of the account each author gives of the causal mechanism.

Chao's and Lippit's claims to have provided a causal explanation of stagnation, then, may be represented schematically in this form:

The Chinese farming system arrived at P (a state of stagnation) because (a) individual behavior was regulated by laws L_i and (b) decision making within the system was subject to conditions C_i.

Each author provides a deductive analysis attempting to show that a description of P may be derived from L_i and C_i. The causal explanation, then, depends on identifying both the laws that regulate the behavior of individuals within a given system and the boundary conditions that, in the context of those laws, leads to the outcome P.

These explanations conform closely to the requirements of the deductive-nomological (D-N) model of explanation current in the philosophy of science.[45] Many objections have been raised to Hempel's formulation, particularly when applied to the social sciences. But here we appear to have a good example of a causal explanation in history that conforms closely to this model. These cases suggest two qualifications to the D-N model in application to social science, however. First, it is important to emphasize that the laws to which these authors appeal are not exceptionless natural regularities; rather, they are regularities of human behavior deriving ultimately from an account of rational decision making. Chao's application of marginalist economic theory illustrates this point clearly; the causal mechanism he identifies as leading to stagnation works through the adjustments to the production process that rational farmers would make in changing circumstances. If we had reason to doubt the rationality of farmers—for example, if we were to suppose that farmers chose techniques based on tradition rather than a calculation of costs and benefits—then this argument would collapse.

Second, it is important not to overemphasize the deductive completeness or rigor of these accounts. Hempel's ideal of a scientific explanation is something akin to a mathematical proof, whereas the arguments offered by Chao and Lippit are more akin to legal argumentation: a set of arguments intended to establish the plausibility of the links between premises in their extended arguments. None of these authors formally "derives" his conclusion from his premises; rather, each tries to show that the balance of evidence favors each step of his argument and that it is plausible to accept his conclusion given his arguments for the various premises.

Implications of This Debate for Classical Marxism

The debate over the causes of agricultural stagnation in China is a topic of intense interest to classical historical materialism: the problem of determining the "laws of motion" of a large, complex economy. To what degree are the categories and hypotheses of classical Marxist historical materialism suited to Chinese social and economic history? Classical Marxism may be represented as holding some or all of the following propositions:[46]

- There is a pervasive logic of development toward higher levels of productivity of the productive forces (technological determinism)
- There is a logic of development toward the emergence of property relations that unfetter the development of the productive forces (functionality of property relations)

- Class conflict and surplus-extraction systems are central variables in explaining large-scale patterns of social and economic development (primacy of class conflict)
- Socially necessary labor time determines the value of commodities in a market economy (labor theory of value)
- Population growth is a dependent variable, not a leading cause of social and economic change (anti-Malthusian doctrine)
- Modes of production contain within their social structures the seeds of their own supersession (internal process of development)

How do these propositions fare in light of our discussion of the process of economic development in China? Technological determinism, to begin with, fares badly in China. Dwight Perkins (1969) documents the development of agricultural productivity over six centuries, and this history shows modest growth in productivity coupled with more extensive growth of cultivable acreage, leading to a sixfold increase in agricultural output. This growth, however, just sufficed to keep the increased population at a roughly constant level of real income, and Perkins gives strong reasons for believing that the increase in output itself was the direct consequence of increase in population. So technological change was not dramatic; productivity increased only at the rate needed to support a growing population, and demography appears to have driven the whole process of development.

The thesis of the functional adaptedness of property relations to the needs of the productive forces also appears questionable in traditional China. Lippit makes a convincing case to the contrary, showing that the forms of property ownership—small peasant holdings and tenancy—persisted for many centuries and blocked the emergence of organizational and technical innovations that would have led ultimately to greatly expanded productive forces. Peasant farming and the associated property arrangements would appear to be dysfunctional from the point of view of facilitating the development of the productive forces.

By the same token, however, the primacy of surplus-extraction systems and class conflict appears to fare better in China's experience. Lippit shows how local property and surplus-extraction arrangements affected economic development. The forms of surplus extraction—land tenure arrangements, taxation, and credit arrangements—appear to play an important role in explaining local patterns of economic development and political activity by peasants and elites. Thus the class-conflict thesis appears to survive its test in the case of China. At the same time, however, we have seen that class factors are not the *only* causally relevant social features in explaining various aspects of rural society; this implies that the surplus-extraction framework will be only one important component of an adequate historical explanation.

The labor theory of value is subject to unexpected complications deriving from peasant self-exploitation and from extreme scarcity of land. The price of handicraft manufacture will reflect the low cost of peasant labor and the relatively high cost of traditional transport. The cost of grain, however, will reflect rents flowing to the owners of this scarce factor; this represents an extraction of surplus, but one that looms particularly large in the Chinese economy.

The anti-Malthusian strain of Marxism appears to fall by the way as well. Chao and others argue persuasively that population growth in traditional China was as much a function of Chinese family arrangements and other redistributive mechanisms as it was of existing property arrangements; more generally, population growth appears to be an independent variable that had important effects on economic development in China.

Finally, the notion that the Chinese mode of production (peasant farming and rural subsidiary production) contained its own dynamic of development toward a higher mode of production appears unsupported. Exogenous factors seem central to the actual course of economic development—Western commercial and imperialist contact, the Sino-Japanese war; and little suggests that these factors interrupted a powerful current of development in the traditional Chinese economy.

Where does this leave us in assessing the relevance of Marxism to understanding the development of Chinese economy and society? Some of the most general theses of historical materialism do not bear up well when applied to Chinese economic history. But this is perhaps as it ought to be; Marxism ought not to be understood as a template of historical change, to be applied mechanically to any and all social systems without empirical investigation. What survives from the Marxist program, and what still offers promise as a research strategy, is the framework of analysis in terms of property arrangements, surplus-extraction systems, class, and class conflict. This suggests, then, that historical materialism functions best as a research program, posing problems for research, rather than as a finished theory on the basis of which to predict the evolution of various modes of production.[47] I will next assess the political dimensions of this program more closely.

Chapter 5
Theories of Peasant Rebellion

In the nineteenth century a series of violent peasant rebellions erupted in China. The White Lotus rebellions, the Nian rebellion, the Moslem uprising, the Taiping rebellion, and the Boxer rebellion span the century and represent the resort to organized violence of tens of millions of Chinese peasants (see map 5.1). With the destruction of vast numbers of villages, market towns, and cities, these periods of unrest severely tested the military and bureaucratic resources of the Qing state and arguably laid the stage for the nationalist and communist revolutions of the twentieth century.[1] These uprisings have several noteworthy features. First, they were by and large *peasant* rebellions, originating in the countryside and drawing the vast majority of the participants from the village agricultural economy. Second, almost all had an important element of folk religion and sectarian organization; the White Lotus societies, the Moslem rebels of western China, and the religious ideology of the Taipings shared an intertwining of insurrectionary goals and religious eschatology. Third, most of these uprisings took place at times of severe ecological crisis: flood, drought, and famine. There is thus some basis for connecting the occurrence of rebellion with widespread economic hardship. Fourth, the declared and manifest goals of most of these rebellions were primarily political, not social or economic: the overthrow of the Qing dynasty and its symbols of power and (in the case of the Taipings, anyway) the creation of a new political order. In contrast to the revolutionary movements of the twentieth century, there was little direct attack on the system of landownership, gentry power, or social inequalities.[2] Finally, all these rebellions were ultimately crushed. Though the Qing dynasty was in decline, it marshaled the forces necessary to destroy its most powerful opponents and governed for another half-century.[3]

The theories considered here analyze peasant rebellion from several points of view: a millenarian theory, a neo-Marxist model, and a local politics model. Millenarian theories consider rebellions as manifestations of religious ideologies and movements that transform

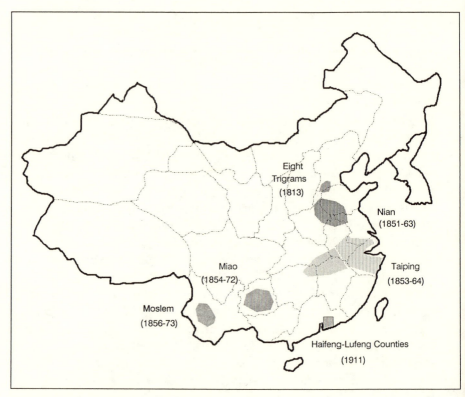

Source: Chesneaux, Bastid, and Bergere, 1976:109

Map 5.1. Peasant rebellions in Qing China

members of sects into rebels. Here the central problem is to identify the features of sect beliefs, organization, and practices that made certain groups in rural China particularly prone to rebel. Class-conflict theories consider rebellions as political responses to exploitation and conflicts of class interests between tenants and landlords, debtors and creditors, taxpayers and the state, and the like: rebellions are rational strategies of collective self-defense on the part of subordinate classes. Finally, local politics theories consider rebellion from the point of view of the motives of individual rebels and leaders: what makes peasants decide to support a budding rebellion, and what determines their level of support? Local politics theories are premised largely on the assumption of individual rationality at the level of the local decision maker and emphasize the local environment of choice: the institutional arrangements at the local level that condition the opportunities and risks constraining individual choice.

To perhaps oversimplify the contrasts among these theories, then, the millenarian approach identifies a culturally specific worldview and ideology as central to the explanation of rebellion; the class conflict theory singles out material class interests; and the local politics theory assigns a variety of local interests and organizational forms as the fundamental determinant of the occurrence and course of rebellion.

The study of peasant rebellions illuminates topics of individual and collective rationality in traditional societies. To what extent can peasant rebellion and political behavior be explained on the assumption that peasants make deliberative decisions about participation? What would induce a peasant to choose to join a band of rebels passing through his village? Is this an occasion for rational, deliberative choice or a moment of impulsive behavior? This raises in a new form some of the issues addressed in chapter 2 in connection with Popkin's *Rational Peasant* (1979). But it raises a complementary question as well: To what extent is it necessary to discern the workings of culturally specific values and worldviews—a political culture—to understand the choices and behavior of a given rural people?

Collective Action

Rebellion is an example of collective action; but this concept requires some analysis, for not all forms of mass behavior constitute collective action.[4] A collective action involves at least the idea of a collective goal (that is, a goal which participants in the event share as the aim of their actions), and it suggests some degree of coordination among individuals in pursuit of that goal.[5] Thus a mass demonstration against the government is a collective action, whereas the panicked retreat through the streets after troops have dispersed the demonstration is not. Both are forms of mass behavior, but only the demonstration has the features of collective intentionality and coordination that would constitute a collective action. We may define a collective action, then, as the aggregation of a number of individuals performing intentional, coordinated actions that are intended to help attain some shared goal or purpose. This account distinguishes collective action from other forms of mass behavior in which the individuals do not intend to contribute to a group effect—for example, a panicked stampede in a football stadium, a run on a bank, or a cycle of hoarding food during a famine.[6]

Collective actions can be classified according to the kind of shared goals that guide the individuals who participate in them—private interests and group interests. In some cases a collective action is inspired by the immediate gains available to each participant through coordinated action; in others, the action is inspired by the shared belief that the action will lead to an outcome that will benefit the group. An example of a collective action motivated by private interests would be a coordinated attack on a granary during a famine. No individual family has the strength to attack the granary by itself, but through coordinated efforts a group of fifty families may succeed. Each participant has the same goal—to acquire grain for subsistence—but the participants' aims are private. By contrast, a demonstration by Polish workers in support of the Solidarity movement would appear to be motivated by a perception of group interests—in this case, the interest that Polish workers have as a group in representation by an independent labor union.

Another important distinction concerns the immediacy of the goals of the action and the complexity of the strategies through which these goals are pursued. A tax riot has the immediate goal of intimidating the tax official and preventing tax collection; benefits are immediate and privately realized. By contrast, an armed attack on a colonial military outpost by peasant farmers may be inspired by the long-term aim of expelling the colonial power—a benefit that will only accrue, if at all, after many such efforts.

As we have seen in other contexts, the prospect of collective action raises the possibility of free riding: if the benefits of collective action are indivisible and undeniable to nonparticipants, it would be rational for the self-interested individual to not participate. To the extent that the potential benefits of a collective action are public rather than private, and to the extent that the action is designed to produce distant rather than immediate benefits, collective action theory predicts that it will be difficult to motivate rational individuals in support of the action.

Another important factor in the success or failure of collective action, besides the character and timing of benefits to members, is the idea of *assurance*: potential contributors' confidence in the probability of success of the joint enterprise. As Elster, Hardin, and others show, the level of assurance is critical to the decisions of potential contributors. If success is widely believed to be unlikely, potential contributors will be deterred from joining the collective action. An important dimension of assurance is the likelihood that other potential contributors will act. Each must judge the probability that enough people will support the action and so make success more likely. One central task of leadership and organization is to bolster the assurance of each member of the group in the likely support of other members.

How may this analysis of collective action be applied to rebellion? First, it should be noted that the term *rebellion* encompasses a spectrum of behaviors, ranging from a rash of individual attacks on landlords or officials to a large-scale revolutionary movement with complex organizational and military resources. (The term *rural disturbance* perhaps more accurately describes this range of forms of rural protest.) Thus a bread riot may or may not be a collective action in the sense described here. If the participants are engaged in uncoordinated, individual attacks on food stores, then the phenomena do *not* constitute a collective action, whereas if the participants coordinate their actions and aim at goals that can be achieved only through joint action, then the bread riot is a form of collective action.

This analysis provides us with a basis to analyze rebellion as a collective action. It forces us to consider the individuals' interests and goals in the action, the shared perceptions of group interests that participants hold, and the strategic views that individuals have of the relation between their participation and the attainment of individual and group goals through the action. As we saw in chapter 2, the theory of rational collective action requires that we explain group behavior on the basis of an analysis of the motives, interests, and calculations of the individual participants.[7] It was also argued there, however, that collective action theory interprets too narrowly the factors that may influence the individual's choices: private economic gain. Rather, an individual's beliefs about the collective interests of a group with which he associates himself may help motivate him to contribute to a collective project.

The framework of collective action theory suggests that we analyze a given rural disturbance around some of the following questions: What were the aims of the participants? What sorts of benefits did they expect—private or public? Were participants motivated by calculations of private gain, or were they also motivated by a perception of potential benefits for the groups to which they belonged? Did they expect immediate benefits over the course of the action—such as regular dispersals of captured grain—or were they motivated by benefits that would be realized only at the end of a successful political struggle?

The collective action framework also suggests that we consider whether the events described here—the Nian rebellion, the Eight Trigrams rebellion, and the disturbances in Haifeng county—display the characteristics of collective action that would be expected on the basis of an analysis of the individual interests of the participants. Are there symptoms of difficulties in mobilizing support that collective action theory would predict? Did rebel organizations provide incentives in the form of ongoing material benefits to its members? Did collective support rapidly diminish when the grounds of assurance began to disappear—for example, when the military forces of the Qing state effectively began to defeat rebel forces?

With these considerations in mind, let us now turn to three explanations of particular Chinese peasant rebellions.

Millenarian Theory

Current discussions of rebellions as millenarian uprisings originate in the writings of Eric Hobsbawm.[8] In his study of popular movements in traditional European societies, Hobsbawm (1959:57–59) distinguishes between "pure political" revolutionary movements and millenarian movements. Political revolutionary movements are organized around an explicit program of social, economic, and political reform, organize their followers around a set of shared interests, and pursue a developed strategy of revolutionary politics. Examples include the Chinese Communist party and the bourgeois political organizations of the French Revolution.[9] Millenarian movements, by contrast, are not primarily driven by a coherent program of economic or social change, are not held together by shared material interests, and typically do not have well-developed programs of revolutionary strategy. Instead, they are generated largely by a shared ideology— usually religious—based on an eschatology of historical change. Hobsbawm describes millenarianism in these terms.

> The essence of millenarianism, the hope of a complete and radical change in the world which will be reflected in the millennium, a world shorn of all its present deficiencies, is not confined to primitivism. . . . The typical old-fashioned millenarian movement in Europe has three main characteristics. First, a profound and total rejection of the present, evil world, and a passionate longing for another and better one; in a word, revolutionism.

Second, a fairly standardized "ideology" of the chiliastic type. . . . Third, millenarian movements share a fundamental vagueness about the actual ways in which the new society will be brought about. (57–58)

Hobsbawm's analysis of millenarian movements is founded chiefly on rural movements in southern Europe—Tuscany, Andalusia, and Sicily.[10] Particularly interesting are his account of typical features of millenarian ideologies and his analysis of individual motivation within the context of a millenarian movement. He shows that a shared vision of a future, better world (usually religious) can be a powerful motivator for members of such movements. And he emphasizes that a millenarian movement does not depend primarily on shared material interests and does not work through rational political calculations by its adherents.

Susan Naquin has provided the most developed analysis of millenarian rebellion in China through her treatment of several White Lotus rebellions.[11] The Eight Trigrams rebellion (1813), a revolt in North China by members of a number of loosely connected religious sects, attracted a cross-section of rural society, including peasants, storytellers, martial arts teachers, yamen runners, and palace eunuchs. The sects involved in the Eight Trigrams rebellion fell within the White Lotus tradition—a folk Buddhist religion that survived in China from the sixteenth into the early twentieth century. This religion was officially forbidden as a heterodox organization; consequently "the religion manifested itself as short-lived groups consisting of a senior teacher and all his pupils and their pupils" (Naquin 1976:7). The religious content of the rebellion manifested itself in banners, chants, secret rituals, charms, and the like proclaiming the religious beliefs of the adherents and in variations of a basic eight-character mantra recited by adherents: "Eternal Progenitor in Our Original Home in the World of True Emptiness" (Eastman 1987:219).

The Eight Trigrams rebellion comprised several loosely coordinated uprisings, including an abortive attack on the Forbidden City (the emperor's quarters in Beijing) and a more successful campaign through northern Henan province. Qing armies finally crushed the rebellion, which claimed nearly eighty thousand lives.

Naquin's explanation of the Eight Trigrams rebellion may be described schematically. It was fomented within a loose, extended community of White Lotus adherents scattered over many villages. White Lotus religious beliefs predisposed these adherents to respond to a call for uprising by their teachers. Lin Qing, a sect leader, had a personal incentive to foment rebellion to cement his own power and position. The hierarchical teacher-student organization of the White Lotus sect was well adapted to clandestine organization, permitting the spread of preparations for rebellion to other sect leaders. When circumstances developed in which Lin Qing was forced either to go ahead with the planned uprising or to face certain arrest, he chose to put his plans in motion. The Qing state was ill-prepared to crush a rebellion in its earliest stages, and rapid mobilization allowed the rebels to leapfrog over Qing countermeasures. Organizational short-comings of rebel forces eventually led to the military suppression of the rebellion by superior Qing military forces. Naquin summarizes her treatment of the Eight Trigrams rebellion: "It was in this way that the Eight Trigrams were created. Vigorous leaders had used ordinary sect ties to build a sect organization of extraordinary size and scope, and they had emphasized one dimension of the religion—its vision of apocalypse and millennium—to mobilize believers into rebellion. White Lotus sects had always contained the potential for such developments, but only with certain kinds of men and circumstances could this potential be realized" (1976:117). Thus Naquin holds that the key to understanding these White Lotus rebellions is to detail the religious ideology of adherents and the organizational forms the sects embodied.

The White Lotus sects worshiped a female deity, the Eternal Mother.[12] The Eternal Mother, the progenitor of all humanity, weeps at the sorry state her children have come to in the course of history and longs to return them to Paradise. She therefore intervenes in human history, sending buddhas and gods to help people find salvation. Her interventions occur at the end of three great periods of history (kalpas), and the end of a kalpa is marked by great disorders, natural and social. One kalpa has ended already, and the second is expected to end in the near future, at which time the Buddha Maitreya will be sent to earth to save humanity. The "turn of the kalpa" is thus a crucial period in human history—a time of great danger and great opportunity for the believer. Those who have been saved (that is, who belong to a sect whose teachings are correct) will live, but those who do not will die (1976:13). "Each sect group claimed that its own practices and predictions were more correct than the others and assured its members that theirs was the true path to salvation. . . . In more concrete terms, the turning of the kalpa meant the elimination of existing society and the coming to power of the followers of the

Eternal Mother" (13–14). The White Lotus religion was thus millenarian in that it predicted major, catastrophic changes in the near
future, held that its believers would survive and prosper through
these changes, whereas nonbelievers would not, and maintained that
its adherents could (and should) aid the turning of the kalpa by help-
ing to overthrow the old age.[13]

Any historical account must be organized around a set of research
topics and explanatory goals. Naquin's explanatory goals may be
summarized as follows: (1) provide a detailed and accurate narrative
of the Eight Trigrams rebellion; (2) explain why sect leaders were
disposed to foment and organize rebellion; (3) explain why ordinary
rural folk were prepared to respond to a call for rebellion; and (4)
explain how these groups had the physical and organizational capacity to use violence effectively against the state. Answering these questions, she believes, puts us in a position to say that we know what
happened and why. The events of the rebellion were thus-and-so, the
behavior of the participants can be understood in terms of their religious aims and beliefs, and the organizational resources available
permitted persons having those beliefs and aims to challenge the
military resources of the state effectively.

Naquin's chief analytical questions in considering the Eight Trigrams rebellion thus concern motivation and organization. These
issues may be subsumed under three questions: rank-and-file motivation, leadership motivation, and the organizational resources
available through the White Lotus sects.

What did rank-and-file rebels believe they were doing, and what
were their aims? Why did ordinary rural folk make the risky decision
to join these uprisings? Naquin's short answer is that believers joined
because their millenarian ideology led them to believe that the movement would succeed and that they would live or die depending on
their role in the catastrophes associated with the turn of the kalpa.
The religious beliefs of White Lotus teachings thus led adherents to
be prepared to participate in rebellion.

The religious interpretation of rebel motivation is insufficient,
however, when it is noted that the rebels were largely rural people
who were *not* members of the White Lotus sect. Naquin judges that
there was a core of 1,000 to 2,000 White Lotus adherents in the early
weeks of the rebellion, and during the course of the disturbance the
movement grew to roughly 100,000 participants (1976:194).[14]
Through what mechanisms, then, were local people recruited to
White Lotus sects and their rebellious plans? Naquin holds that

when the rebellion passed from the covert to the public phase, mass mobilization depended on a wider range of motives: coercion, opportunism, and sympathy for White Lotus teachings. Naquin emphasizes the rebels' use of threats and violence to secure support from nonadherents (1976:201–02) and refers to simple opportunism on the part of nonadherents. "Those who joined the Trigrams could participate in their roaming and freebooting and could share in the opportunity to eat, dress, travel, and behave publicly as important people. This opportunity for power and prestige was a strong magnet to many, even in the face of mounting Ch'ing opposition" (202–03). Perhaps more importantly, she notes that, since the rebellion occurred during a time of drought, the rebels were able to gain adherents by offering food supplies seized from various locales (203). "The Eight Trigram rebels . . . were from the start relatively rich in food supplies. They used violence with impunity to take what they pleased, and their occupied cities and villages became storehouses for grain provisions" (203).

These facts suggest a different orientation on this rebellion from the one Naquin advances. For these circumstances suggest that the stimulus of the disturbances was found in the White Lotus sects and religious beliefs but that the carrying power and force of the rebellion stemmed from more ordinary political motives—fear, hunger, opportunism, or the excitement of the moment. And in fact Naquin seems to concede this point, writing: "Although the great mass of followers of the Eight Trigrams were apparently motivated by combinations of fear, hope, greed, and hunger, there were also those who had previously belonged to a White Lotus sect and who dared commit themselves to rebellion only after others had taken the first step" (204).

What were the motives of the leaders of these rebellions—to further their religious beliefs, to build larger and more powerful movements, to acquire personal wealth and power, or some combination of these? And what resources for leadership were available to these men and women? Naquin offers two sorts of motivations for leaders: sincere religious motives of the kind just attributed to followers, and motives of political and economic self-interest. She shows that these leaders had a built-in incentive to foment rebellion to establish their credentials as interpreters of the signs of the turn of the kalpa. Sect leaders could enhance their power and wealth by mobilizing their followers, and they sometimes risked losing their privileged positions if they failed to provide a dramatic demonstration of their qualifications. These intertwined motives gave leaders a strong personal incentive to foment and organize rebellion.

White Lotus leaders used several means to establish their status as teacher. Some were healers, using charms, massage, and mantras to cure the sick. Others were boxing teachers, introducing their adherents to martial arts and charms that insured invulnerability. Almost all, however, taught the eight-character mantra that was used in conjunction with yogic meditation. Reciting this mantra was thought to bring the adherent many benefits; the mantra "had the magical power to 'encourage good things and protect against bad ones'" (1976:25). Naquin refers to benefits provided to the adept in the form of boxing and curing skills, as well as other material incentives (32–33). And she writes that, in order to increase contributions, followers were promised future gains through rebellion: "the Eight Trigrams promised that everyone who gave money or grain would later be given land or official position, the amount of land or degree of position depending on the size of the contribution" (50).[15]

This treatment is at least partly consistent with the framework of political entrepreneurship (Frohlich, Oppenheimer, and Young 1971). On the latter approach, one might hold that White Lotus leaders were political entrepreneurs, using their positions of power to advance their own interests, and that followers were drawn to the White Lotus cult for the benefits that organization was able to provide (such as status, training in martial arts, and access to healing services). This hypothesis finds some support in Naquin's own treatment of the sects; for example, she provides a biographical account of the central Eight Trigrams teacher, Lin Qing, whose career as a drifter, gambler, and quail-peddlar brought him finally into contact with a White Lotus sect (1976:72ff.). Lin eventually became the central teacher and leader within the sect; Naquin describes him as a bright, opportunistic man who pushed his way through the margins of society. Though Naquin does not draw this inference, it would seem natural to suppose that his position as a White Lotus teacher was only the most lucrative of Lin's many shady efforts to support himself and that the White Lotus religion was for Lin merely a convenient vehicle for pursuing power, money, and respect.[16]

Turn finally to the topic of organization. What explained the successes of mobilization and collective action of these groups? What organizational resources were available to White Lotus sects, and how could these resources be effectively deployed against the military power of the Qing state? Largely because the White Lotus religion was a proscribed heterodox tradition, its typical organization was a loose, sprawling collection of teacher-pupil hierarchies. A given sect could extend into a number of villages and towns if adherents traveled and acquired pupils of their own; in such a way a sect leader might come to have followers over an extended geographical area. Each such group constituted a separate sect, and communication was infrequent among sects within the same region (1976:55). This isolation obtained both because of the need for secrecy and the tendency of each leader to develop individual teachings and methods of securing respect.[17]

In extraordinary times, however (that is, times in which a turning of the kalpa was expected and rebellion was being planned), it was necessary to create higher-level organizations to coordinate plans. "In order to transform religious sects into revolutionary organizations, a higher level framework was necessary, one in which many dispersed and separate sects could be incorporated and coordinated. . . . A more common practice was to combine eight or nine groups on an equal basis by naming each one after either the eight trigrams or the nine mansions" (1976:17–18). This was the organizational form adopted by the Eight Trigrams rebels.[18]

These forms proved to be reasonably effective as military organizations, relative to the military capacities of the Qing state.[19] Naquin holds that the fundamental religious beliefs of the White Lotus sects explain the collective behavior of members. But it may be that more important is the organizational competence of the sects and their capacities for coordination, fund-raising, and planning. In this connection it is worth recalling Popkin's analysis of the grounds of success of religious movements in Vietnam—Catholicism, Caodaism, and the Hoa Hao sect. Popkin emphasizes the material benefits each organization was able to confer on its followers. He writes of the spread of Catholicism through poor villages in the nineteenth century, "The priest was the quintessential political entrepreneur. . . . Lacking village welfare systems, many peasants abandoned their overburdened villages for the better life the Church was promising on the earth" (1979:189, 191). Popkin cites such benefits as financial support, organizational resources to defend the poor villager against outside powers, and adjudication institutions that were less corrupt than state or elite institutions (188–93) as examples of the advantages Catholicism was able to offer rural Vietnam. Likewise, we might ask whether followers of the White Lotus sect—with the exceptional fanatic who acted wholly for religious reasons—were motivated by various benefits conferred by membership and participated because of their ties to the organization in more peaceful times.[20]

Naquin's approach has several noteworthy features. First, it is plainly historical and particularistic: Naquin wants to understand these events in the concrete circumstances in which they occurred. As a start, then, she does *not* aim to provide a general theory of peasant rebellions everywhere, about millenarian rebellions in other times and places, or even about Chinese rebellions of the nineteenth century. (Contrast her approach with that of Charles Tilly [1964] or Theda Skocpol [1979], for example, whose interest in particular occasions of popular unrest generally serves the theoretical aim of understanding collective action and class.)

Second, though Naquin is not content to simply narrate events to explain the rebellion, the narrative constitutes an extensive part of her work. She attempts to reconstruct the sequence of events from the conception of the uprising, to the coordination between sect leaders, to the instigating arrests, and to the military actions of the rebels and the state's armies. The details of the story occupy much of Naquin's attention, and (one suspects) she would be more distressed at the charge that her narrative is inaccurate than at criticism of her psychology of millenarian protest.

As noted above, Naquin concedes that the overwhelming number of participants in the Eight Trigrams rebellion were nonbelievers and that the leadership's actions may be understood as following from their political self-interests—not exclusively from their White Lotus ideology. Why then should we understand this as a millenarian rebellion at all rather than a subsistence-crisis disturbance? Naquin appears to have two reasons to regard the Eight Trigrams as a millenarian rebellion in spite of its important nonsectarian features: first, it was *precipitated* by events stemming from the development of White Lotus sects within the context of the Qing state, and second, it was *sustained* by the organizational forms spawned by the sects. This suggests a fairly complex causal hypothesis: millenarian sect beliefs created a predisposition toward rebellious motivations; material and ecological circumstances increased the volatility of rural people; and leaders and organizational forms within the White Lotus sects made rebellion possible. In these circumstances, when the spark fell—the arrest of a sect leader, for example—collective violence erupted.

This position is substantially weaker than initially promised. The millenarian theory appears to hold that millenarian revolts are characterized by a particular kind of mass motivation—one in which participants throw their material interests and concerns to the wind and act out the script of their millenarian beliefs. The Eight Trigrams revolt does not have this quality, however, even on Naquin's account. There would appear to be ample scope for a rational-choice analysis of political motivation, for both participants and leaders, even within this millenarian uprising.

Naquin's account apparently employs two rather different analytical approaches. Her attention to the religious ideas contained in the White Lotus tradition leads her in the direction of an interpretative social science—one that attempts to understand a historical or cultural event in terms of the distinctive worldview, values, and assumptions of the participants. This orientation leads to the hypothesis that the particulars of this cultural ensemble are critical to understanding the events. Her attention to organizational forms, in contrast—both those of the sects and of the Qing state—leads her to a political science approach. The critical things to understand here are the organizational resources available to both sides and the ways in which these resources enhanced or impeded the goals of the two sides. This element of Naquin's analysis brings her closer to that provided by Elizabeth Perry, discussed below.

It is also worthwhile noting what sorts of questions Naquin's approach *ignores*. The emphasis on millenarian beliefs leads Naquin to systematically overlook material and economic factors (for example, tenancy levels, ecological crisis, or rent levels). Naquin's approach emphasizes the ideological and institutional features of the White Lotus sects out of which these rebellions emerged, instead of trying to identify background material factors that might have prompted rebellion—rising rents, subsistence crisis, or dramatic assault on traditional rights. (She neglects these, of course, out of a judgment that they are not key explanatory variables.) Further, Naquin does not ask what factors trigger the transformation from quiet religious worship to violent rebellion (though she implies that the transformation is often provoked by state repression and the need of the sect leader to provide tangible signs of authority).

Second, Naquin is cautious in generalizing about the process of peasant rebellion in other times and places. She does assert that her accounts of these two White Lotus rebellions ought to help explain other peasant rebellions in late traditional China (1976:2). Naquin believes that the Eight Trigrams rebellion is a typical example of traditional peasant rebellions in China, in that it was "expressed through the organization of a religious sect and a millenarian ideology" (2). Study of this rebellion, then, is intended to shed light on other peasant rebellions in Qing China. However, Naquin does not provide the theoretical arguments needed to generalize from this case to other cases—whether in China or in other times and places. Naquin's explanation remains highly concrete, specific, and non-theoretical. She does not pose the more general question, what circumstances favor or inhibit the spread of millenarian sects in a traditional society?

Class Conflict Theory

Another model of peasant rebellions takes class conflict as its starting point.[21] Collective violence—food or tax riots, social banditry, rebellion—is interpreted as an expression of social tensions created by an exploitative economic system and the conflicts engendered between landlord, tax collector, and peasant. This model has loomed large in analysis of twentieth-century peasant politics; peasant movements in China, Central America, the Philippines, and elsewhere have been analyzed as expressions of the conflict of material interests between peasants and the rural property arrangements that exploit them. Schematically, the class conflict model holds that rural property relations define an objective set of class relations among landlords, tenants, laborers, and the state. The property relations establish a surplus-extraction relation between the elite and the producers, permitting the elite to exploit the producers through rent, interest, corvée labor, taxation, or tribute; they thus constitute a coercive system of exploitation. Members of the exploited segment of rural society have an implicit capacity to perceive the exploitative nature of their situation and are disposed to alter that system—that is, they are able to arrive at a state of class consciousness. When a revolutionary party appears on the scene with sufficient organization and power to be a plausible political force, peasants are disposed to adhere to it. Thus rebellions occur when the mass of producers acquire both the political resources and the advantageous circumstances needed to mount a potentially successful rebellion.[22]

Central to this program of explanation is analysis of (1) the social relations of production that define objective material interests for affected groups; (2) the political and social arrangements that shape the political consciousness and motivations of participants; and (3) the political resources that are available for deployment in collective political action.[23] The class conflict model offers a program of explanation: to explain peasant rebellions on the basis of the social tensions contained in peasant society and the class consciousness of the peasant rebels. This framework combines objective material factors (for example, levels of exploitation, particulars of the production process, characteristic forms of technology) with a model of political motivation (individuals act out of consideration of their class interests). The class conflict model attempts to establish a close link between the objective material factors and patterns of political behavior: the economic system creates an objective set of interests for the various classes (landlord, official, peasant), and members of classes come to recognize their material interests and act accordingly.

In application to traditional agrarian China, this model might be filled in along these lines: The primary rural producers are rent-paying peasants engaged in farming and rural handicrafts. Peasant production gives rise to a small but real surplus; this surplus is extracted from the peasant in the form of rent, merchant profits (on handicraft products), interest, and taxation. Victor Lippit estimates that 25 percent of the rural product in early twentieth-century China was available as surplus and that the vast majority of this surplus made its way into the hands of landlords, moneylenders, and the state (1987:89–91). Peasants are thus *exploited* by landlords, merchants, tax farmers, and moneylenders and are predisposed to support popular movements aimed at reducing or eliminating the power of exploiting agencies. Peasants, finally, are capable of recognizing their objective conflicts of interest with local elites and the state and are disposed to participate in forms of collective action aimed at overturning these relations of exploitation. When rebellious organizations appear—for example, the Taipings or the Nian—peasants are disposed to support these movements as a social protest.

Jean Chesneaux (1973) applies this framework to the Taiping rebellion: "The Taiping movement was fundamentally an agrarian one, a revolt of the peasants against their 'natural' enemies within Chinese society, against landlords, gentry and officials" (25). Chesneaux credits the Taipings with a social program based on a perception of class conflict (27). In its early stages, Chesneaux writes, "this was a real people's war, and the peasants rose in response" (30). Likewise, Chesneaux interprets the Nian rebellions as organized around class struggle. "In the tradition of brigand justice they distributed goods to the poor and inscribed on their banners the words,

'Kill the officials, kill the rich, spare the poor!'" (33). Applying Hobsbawm's (1965) influential construct, Chesneaux interprets the Nian as "social bandits" (35).

The class conflict model is plausible in this context for several reasons. First, property arrangements and relations of exploitation are relatively transparent; the class structure of traditional rural China is easily discerned. Moreover, these property relations work effectively to extract a significant surplus from small farmers into the hands of landlords, officials, moneylenders, and the like. And second, the success of the class conflict-inspired Communist Revolution of the twentieth century makes it plausible to suppose that class conflict politics were latent in nineteenth-century China as well. For these reasons we would expect that historians within a broadly Marxist framework would select the nineteenth-century rebellions for close research. This expectation is borne out; books by Robert Marks and Jean Chesneaux represent full-scale studies, and works by Eric Wolf, Theda Skocpol, and Robert Paige offer less thorough treatments. However, unanticipated difficulties confront the class conflict model. When we examine these rebellions in detail, nonclass factors emerge that seem to play a critical role in the occurrence of the uprising; and in each case it is difficult to document peasant class consciousness.

Robert Marks extensively analyzes rural collective action within the class conflict framework in *Rural Revolution in South China* (1984). Marks studies collective action in Haifeng county in South China in the nineteenth and twentieth centuries, leading up to peasant support for the revolution of 1911 (See map 5.1.) Several features of Marks's analytical framework are characteristic of class conflict analysis generally. First, Marks pays particular attention to the social and economic structure within the context of which collective action takes place. This refers particularly to the property arrangements, land tenancy arrangements, and instruments of taxation that exist at a given time. These arrangements structure peasant life by defining the terms of their access to the land (and hence to subsistence). They also define the apparatus of surplus extraction: the means by which local elites and the state confiscate part of the surplus generated through peasant labor. And they define the material interests peasants share as a class.

Second, Marks analyzes peasant behavior in terms of their perceived class interests. He holds that class consciousness (more or less articulate) is a central variable in peasant political behavior. Marks writes, "While the authorities may have perceived events in Haifeng as symptomatic of general disorder, those who were causing disorder simply were trying to fashion a *new* order in which the main issue was control of the land. Peasants won important victories, and it was from this position of strength that the new land tenure system was put together" (19). Like Chesneaux, Marks employs Hobsbawm's concept of the social bandit in interpreting banditry and pirate activity in the eighteenth century (28ff.). He holds that there was what approached a parallel bandit society with villages organized along egalitarian lines (26).

A third characteristic feature of Marks's approach is his emphasis on mass politics rather than elite leadership or party organization (xvi). Marks maintains that indigenous peasant movements and political traditions—not the presence or absence of outside political leadership and organization—are the primary factors in the occurrence of rebellion and revolution. "The central conclusion that emerges from this approach is that the peasants of Haifeng made their own history: they were not the passive objects of someone else's history. Peasants made the more visible history chronicled in the documentary record—the riots, uprisings, or other types of collective action evident in the 1920s; moreover, through these actions, peasants had a hand in making the very structures that patterned subsequent action as well" (282). Marks describes this as a bottom-up approach rather than a top-down approach, but it is more distinctive than that. Local politics theories are also bottom-up; Marks adds to the emphasis on local factors a premise about the capacity of peasants to formulate and carry out a political agenda that serves their class interests.

Finally, Marks emphasizes imperialism and the intrusion of the global capitalist economy into Haifeng county. He maintains that the increased tempo of commercialization in Haifeng that resulted from Western economic intervention substantially and rapidly harshened class relations—raising the level of class consciousness among peasants and workers.[24]

Marks's account may be represented as follows: Over several hundred years the property relations governing land tenure in Haifeng county evolved as a struggle between peasants and landowners. Peasants effectively defended their interests and secured rights that protected their subsistence interests. Under pressure of increasing commercialization and imperialism in the mid- and late nineteenth century, these gains began to unravel, leading to increasing poverty and exploitation. Peasant unrest began to increase; peasants became more radical and were readily mobilized into People's Armies in the days before the 1911 Revolution.

The class conflict framework could be challenged in at least two ways: first, by maintaining that traditional China did not embody classes or exploitation, and second, by conceding that agrarian China was a class order but holding that class relations were a distant second to other political or cultural factors in motivating political behavior in traditional China—either because ideology conceals objective material interests or because participants perceive other factors as more important than objective material interests.

Ramon Myers defends the first possibility; he maintains that the peasant economy of Qing China was so extensively commercialized, with economic power so broadly distributed, that elites could not significantly exploit peasant cultivators. A free market, according to Myers, is incompatible with exploitation, and the rural economy of Qing China was such a market. Writing of the North China rural economy in the late nineteenth century, Myers concludes:

> There is scarcely any evidence that exploitation of one group by another was either severe or a consistent practice commensurate with the operation of a rural market. Various economic groups acted in their own best interests through the market, and the highly competitive nature of the market reduced to a minimum the monopoly power any group could exert over another. The price of land, cost of credit, and value of commodity exchange involved the peasant in a continual series of economic transactions with other households or the market towns. (1970:288)

According to Myers, all producers—including peasant cultivators—derived incomes equal to the marginal product of their contributions.[25]

As a general proposition, however, Myers's position is unpersuasive. On theoretical grounds John Roemer (1982) has demonstrated that exploitation and surplus-extraction are fully compatible with smoothly functioning factor markets: exploitation depends on differential ownership of land and capital, not on monopoly pricing. Highly commercialized markets are thus compatible with exploitation. And on empirical grounds such diverse economic historians of traditional China as Dwight Perkins, Philip Huang, and Victor Lippit agree that a substantial rural surplus was available in the traditional economy and was extracted from peasants through rent, interest, and taxation.[26] Moreover, various authors argue that local elites and lineages dominated market arrangements—contradicting Myers's assumption that the commercialized rural economy embodied free markets.[27] If we define exploitation as coercive surplus extraction from the immediate producers, then these points show that the rural economy represented a system of exploitation of peasants. Thus the "no-exploitation" view appears untenable.[28]

The second objection of the class-conflict theory is the view that these rebellions are largely motivated by factors other than class. Lucien Bianco (1986) argues this position in his study of spontaneous peasant uprisings in Republican China.

> The spontaneous peasant movements analyzed above show three main characteristics. The first is the weakness of class consciousness among the peasantry, a weakness illustrated by the comparative rarity and traditional nature of the social movements directed against the wealthy. . . . The second main characteristic of spontaneous peasant movements is their parochialism. In default of class consciousness, there was a sense of belonging to a local community, which overrode distinctions of class. . . . The need to limit themselves to survival strategies, which dictated these attitudes, also explains the third characteristic of peasant agitation, namely its almost invariably defensive nature. (301–2)

In many cases of social conflict in rural China, nonclass factors seem of prime importance: religion, intervillage conflict, vertical social organizations (kinship organizations, religious organizations, flags).[29]

As we have seen, Susan Naquin provides substantial evidence that the core of the Eight Trigrams movement was highly heterogeneous in class and that rebel motives were largely a combination of White Lotus millenarian beliefs and fears for subsistence—*not* an expression of class consciousness and antilandlord sentiment. Similarly, Robert Marks himself emphasizes the cross-class nature of conflict between the Red Flags and the Black Flags in Haifeng county; powerful lineages centered in competing market towns instigated violent conflict between localities rather than between classes. And Lucien Bianco comes to similar conclusions. The social composition of the rebellions themselves thus poses an obstacle to a class-conflict analysis of the major rebellions of the nineteenth century. A second problem matches this difficulty: direct evidence of explicit class consciousness among followers or leaders in the nineteenth-century rebellions is scant. Neither in manifestos that aim at class issues nor in movements with a rough-and-ready social program (land redistribution, tax reform, forgiveness of indebtedness) do we find unambiguous expression of class-oriented political activity.

Class conflict theories also confront a serious difficulty in arriving at an analytically justifiable level at which to characterize group interests and identity, which must be done if we are to speak meaningfully of class and class conflict. When Robert Marks writes that the peasants of Haifeng county began to conceive of themselves as a class in the middle and late nineteenth century, does he mean that poor peasants of a given *village* came to recognize their joint interests or that poor peasants throughout the region came to recognize their joint interests with other peasants beyond their own acquaintance and social intercourse? At the local level it is possible to imagine the social mechanisms through which such group identity might emerge through normal social contact (though it is also possible to identify mechanisms working in the opposite direction—for example, competition for the right to rent a piece of land or cross-class allegiances based on lineage or patron-client relations). But it is more difficult to conceive of mechanisms at work in local society that would lead to a broader sense of group identity, in which poor peasants of many lineages, villages, market systems, and ethnic groups should come to regard themselves as a cohesive class, sharing important interests and disposed to engage in political activity to support those interests.

The class conflict model thus encounters problems of the proper level of aggregation. Class interests may be viewed from perspectives that range from the local to the global. For example, tenants in a given village or marketing community share certain interests in common (water rights, gathering firewood, and so on), which give them a basis for engaging in collective action. Moreover, they have concrete opportunities to develop political activity together through shared organizations and acquaintances. But class interests may be defined at a larger scale as well: tenant farmers throughout North China share certain material interests—economic and political—with one another. A concrete example is imperial tax policy—should taxes be remitted in times of crop crisis, should taxes be assessed to land or to farmer, and so forth.

Class conflict theories tend, however, to consider class interests on too high a level—regional or national rather than local. But vertical local interests may loom larger in the material welfare of villagers than horizontal regional interests, making it difficult to secure collective action around regional class interests. A policy or strategy may be rational at one level of interests and counterproductive at higher or lower levels. A strategy of demanding tax relief in Henan may thus impose greater tax burdens on farmers in Sichuan. This point makes it plausible to suppose that local nonclass interests might mask extralocal class interests—local elites and peasants may join in violent action against neighboring villages in conflict over water rights, disputed land rights, and so on. In this connection Lucien Bianco (1986:270) argues that peasant material interests were invariably localistic, often cutting across class. He concludes that Chinese peasants could not have achieved—or even aimed at—social revolution without the intervention of the CCP.

Marks acknowledges this point when he refers to extensive intervillage conflict over access to water and wood resources, for example, that have a cross-class character (62). Lineages vied for power over these resources, and control of a market town was a common cause of intervillage and interlineage feuding. "By the late nineteenth century, the Flags had polarized Haifeng and Lufeng counties into two great camps—the Red Flags and the Black Flags. And since neighbors were enemies (or at least competitors for resources), the countryside had taken on the appearance of a giant checkerboard with neighboring marketing systems (or emerging systems) under opposing flags" (67). This point suggests, however, that class factors were eclipsed by economic interests shared across village society as a whole—a point Marks appears to accept for pre-twentieth-century rural violence.[30]

Turn finally to the problem of political motivation. The class-conflict model assumes a straightforward link between material interest of a group and political motivation. But political behavior is undeniably mediated by culture, religion, morality, and ideology, so political behavior may be largely independent from, or even contrary to, objective material interests. Establishing that peasants have an objective interest in land reform or rent reduction thus establishes nothing directly about their political behavior; we need to know more about the immediate determinants of political behavior. A serious worsening of exploitation may turn out to have a demoralizing rather than incendiary effect on an exploited group.

These points suggest that the class conflict model makes revolutionary politics too easy. First, exploitative relationships are not as visible as the class conflict account presupposes. A tenant may also be kin to the landlord; relations of friendship and obligation may exist between tenant and landlord; and local cultural values may seem to justify the unequal relations between classes.[31] Second, as we have seen, a gap generally lies between local material interests and regional or national class interests. The peasants of Haifeng county share some interests with peasants everywhere in China, but they also share some local interests with local landlords in opposition to peasants elsewhere in China (for example, over water rights and irrigation systems). And third, problems of motivation arise even if we assume that peasants generally endorse the social program of the organization in principle; for rebellion is a risky business, with benefits available to supporters and nonsupporters alike. In general, then, the class conflict theory tends to give insufficient attention to the problems of local politics.

None of the rebellions surveyed here would seem to favor an interpretation of the political behavior and intentions of the participants grounded primarily in class conflict. Many of these movements cross classes, with village elites often providing leadership.[32] Second, none of these movements had a prominent social agenda, such as land tenure reform or tax reform, and many had highly localistic aims. This suggests that the class conflict model does not provide the resources to analyze the political behavior that these movements represented. But two qualifications are needed here. First, though class consciousness appears to have played little role in these movements, the social tensions created by the land tenure system, the system of taxation, corvée labor, and the like clearly constituted important elements of the social environment. These structural factors may well emerge as crucial to explain why a given group supported rebellion at one time and not another. Though these were not rebellions of class conflict, the structures defining class conflict were present and were important variables in the occurrence of these rebellions. The structural conditions created by the class system of rural China may have been salient, even if class consciousness was not an important causal variable.

Second, though the class conflict model does not appear to fit the nineteenth-century rebellions well, it seems to fit twentieth-century movements substantially better. The communist movement in China, through which the party worked long and hard to mobilize poor peasants in support of their program of revolutionary change, appears to be a particularly clear example of a popular movement based on class issues.[33] Likewise, other communist movements in Asia, such as the New People's Army in the Philippines or similar militant organizations in South Asia evidence the power of class-oriented social movements. (See essays on this topic in J. Lewis 1974.)

How are we to account for this difference between nineteenth- and twentieth-century peasant movements in China? Three elements appear particularly significant: the advent of an explicit theory of class conflict and revolutionary politics (Marxism); the extension of modern communication and transportation facilities; and the development of modern forms of political organization. Class conflict-oriented social movements require leadership; articulate communicators must be able to bring a localistic peasantry to an awareness of its class interests and away from its lineage, village, patron-client, and other loyalties. But this requires an educated and politically sophisticated population of potential leaders. Significantly, the May Fourth movement shows the emergence of such a group in China, with substantial influence from classical Marxism, Marxist-Leninism, and the early experience of the Russian communist movement.[34] Next, we saw that traditional peasant movements were highly localistic; but more tightly knit urban-rural systems and their road, rail, and telegraph sinews brought the resources to break down this localism.[35] Finally, the twentieth century made available to peasant revolutionaries a panoply of new organizational devices. The Guomindang and the Chinese Communist party could knit complex national organizations that were by and large capable of creating and implementing policies, raising revenues, and arranging military resources. This ability stands in striking contrast to the low level of organization present in any of the rebellions surveyed here.

Local Politics Theory

One family of theories pays close attention to the local politics of rural disturbances. The guiding thread of these theories is that rebellion is a form of deliberate collective action that originates in the local interests of the individuals who participate and is facilitated by the local political resources (organizational forms, militias, kinship organizations, and so on) available to potential rebels. These theories may employ factors studied by either millenarian or class conflict theories, but they seek primarily to uncover the local processes through which these general factors come into play. A distinctive feature of these theories is the observation that large-scale rebellions are often only unintended, unforeseen consequences of essentially local processes. The local political process is intentional and rational, whereas the global process is unintentional. Theda Skocpol describes such an approach when she writes of the French, Russian, and Chinese revolutions, "Peasants participated in these Revolutions without being converted to radical visions of a desired new national society, and without becoming a nationally organized class-for-themselves. Instead they struggled for concrete goals—typically involving access to more land, or freedom from claims on their surpluses. Such goals were entirely understandable in terms of the existing local economic and political circumstances in which peasants found themselves" (1979:114).

In *Rebels and Revolutionaries in North China, 1845–1945* (1980a) Elizabeth Perry takes this approach.[36] She analyzes the Nian rebellion (1851–63) and the Red Spears uprisings (1911–49), both in the Huaibei region on the North China plain (several hundred kilometers south of the region in which the Eight Trigrams rebellion of 1813 occurred). (See map 5.2.) The Nian rebellion represented the gradual transformation of local bandit gangs into loosely coordinated regional forces capable of defeating regular Qing armies. By 1856 small Nian groups had come together in a loose confederation of five "banners" under the nominal leadership of the bandit Zhang Luoxing; leadership and power within the Nian, however, remained at the community rather than regional level. Nian groups were generally adept at cavalry warfare and practiced mobile strategies that the more static Qing military forces had difficulty in countering. The Nian groups retained close connections with their local communities, which often took the form of walled villages and towns; these villages provided both an economic base and a defensible retreat for Nian groups. At its peak the Nian may have had as many as 100,000 men under arms and held sway over large parts of Huaibei. Manchu and Mongol cavalry supplemented and finally replaced regular Qing forces and after years of inconclusive fighting destroyed the Nian armies in 1868.[37]

Perry's account of rebellion in Huaibei emphasizes the ecological circumstances that surrounded peasant life in North China. Unlike Naquin, Perry is concerned to identify the standing conditions and processes of change that stimulated rural disturbance. She notes that the North China plain had an extremely harsh ecology, enduring regular flooding, drought, and famine. The region's low agricultural productivity resulted in a low level of commercialization. As a result, peasants were both poor and insecure, and they had precariously

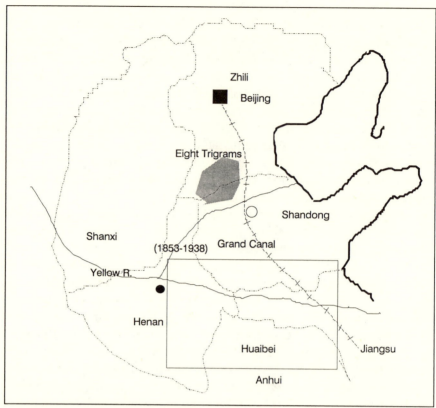

Source: Perry, 1980:16

Map 5.2. North China

little surplus to tide them over periods of disaster.[38] Perry puts the point this way: "In sum, interactions between people and nature rendered Huai-pei [Huaibei] a highly precarious ecosystem. During the century under consideration (1845–1945), nature wielded the upper hand" (16).

Perry thus puts the problem of survival at the center of peasant behavior in this region and time and explains the extensive rebellions that occurred during the period as the result of several peasant survival strategies, both individual and collective. She distinguishes broadly between predatory and protective strategies. Predatory strategies include smuggling, robbery, and banditry, whereas protective strategies include crop-watching societies, local militia, fortification, and tax resistance (58–95). She holds that each type of strategy (predatory and protective) gave rise to distinctive forms of collective action. Further, the forms of collective action inspired by each strategy influenced the subsequent development of collective action inspired by the other. The Nian rebellion grew out of the formation of increasingly powerful bandit gangs (predatory strategy), whereas the Red Spears period reflected the autonomous power of local militias directed by local notables (protective strategy).[39]

Several points should be emphasized. First, Perry contends that these examples of rebellion reflect rational choices by participants; they result from rational strategies of survival, not mere jacqueries. "This book takes issue with such a view of rural rebellion [as anomic irrational protest] and proposes an alternative interpretation of traditional peasant insurrection as a sustained, structured, and sensible form of collective action. The analysis focuses upon the rural inhabitants themselves, emphasizing the adaptive value of peasant violence for coping with the local environment they inhabit" (2).

Second, though, Perry argues that these rebellions need to be understood in terms of their local circumstances and the local aims and opportunities of participants—not national or regional goals and politics. Unlike the CCP's twentieth-century mobilization efforts, which encompassed a national program and a set of revolutionary goals, Nian leaders did not set out to overthrow the Qing state; rather, they were brought into opposition to state power inadvertently while pursuing local concerns. Local interests and opportunities led to these rebellions, not a shared revolutionary ideology or program.[40] As Perry writes, "If it is recognized that peasant insurgency originated and persisted more as a response to local conditions than as a direct challenge to state authority, regional variations assume central importance. For the argument is that any lasting pattern of collective violence was quite likely an adaptation to the parochial setting—one which could be variously hostile or adaptive to revolution depending upon its particular content" (8). Further, "Competition [between predators and protectors] might have remained at this parochial level had it not been for the involvement of outside actors: the central government and the Taiping rebels. These external forces merged predators and protectors in a common antagonism toward the state. What began as simple predation was pushed into a rebellious posture" (96).

Third, and related to the localism of these rebellions, Perry emphasizes the individual opportunism that these periods of uprisings represent. She describes the evolution of the Nian rebellion in these terms: "For most participants, the Nien presented a concrete opportunity to garner one's livelihood in a situation of extreme insecurity. The movement began as a series of familiar efforts by impoverished

peasants to seize scarce resources from others. The later Nien reflected these origins: plundering forays followed the routes of salt
smugglers, community feuds continued to be conducted along previous lines" (148).

This opportunism characterized both followers and leaders; Perry
analyzes the behavior of the bandit chieftain in the same opportunistic terms. "What complicates the picture somewhat is the pivotal role of the bandit chief. This individual, we must recall, was
largely interested in expanding his own power. The scope of the
chieftain's control depended upon the kinds of outside coalitions he
was able to forge" (71). Thus Perry urges that we analyze these processes of collective action in terms of the fairly narrow interests of
the participants (noting, of course, that different Nian chieftains and
followers may have had significantly different interests).

Fourth, Perry emphasizes the influence of unintended consequences on the emergence and evolution of these rebellions. Some
strategies of survival for peasants were individual, not collective; and
yet some of these strategies created a new social environment in
which rebellion was more likely. An example of this process is the
occurrence of female infanticide (51ff.). Families adopted this practice to increase family income and security, but the long-term aggregate result was a skewed demography in which there was a large
surplus of young men. These young men (bare sticks) became natural
recruits for bandit gangs and local militia—thus providing resources
for the emergence of collective strategies of predation and protection.

Another type of unintended consequence is the regional or national
effects of a local disturbance. The Nian uprising showed remarkable
staying power and might well have forced dynastic change at the
national level, but this was never an explicit goal of the rebels. These
rebellions were not consciously designed as assaults on the state; the
rebellion was largely the unintended consequence of an individual
strategy of survival.

These features of Perry's analysis put her position within the "political economy" paradigm (already described in the treatment of
Popkin in chapter 2); the collective event or action is analyzed in
terms of the interests and opportunities of the participants, on the
assumption that all actors make self-interested rational decisions
about their behavior. And the localism of this approach is also consistent with the political economy approach; in most cases, the interests and opportunities that define the position of the individual
participants have a fairly narrow horizon. The exception is the

emergence of the national leader, whether of a millenarian sect (see Tai's [1983] analysis of the Hoa Hao movement in Vietnam) or of a national political party (such as Ho Chi Minh). The political interests of leaders at this level will transcend local interests and may confer a broader horizon on the political movements they lead.

In line with her proximity to rational choice analyses of collective action, Perry is concerned with two additional sets of problems: organization and free riding. She believes that the success or failure of a given effort at collective violence will be heavily influenced by the effectiveness of existing organizations; she thus devotes significant attention to uncovering the organizational resources and forms available to the Nian. "Much of the following discussion of peasant survival strategies will therefore be concerned with identifying the levels of social organization at which particular strategies were employed. Collective action implies organization, but this may be variously based upon kinship, settlement, class, friendship, occupation, or a number of other ties. Only after having clarified the underlying structures of action can we proceed to the central issue: the relationship of these strategies to peasant rebellion" (49).

Perry also treats religious ideology and organization. The rebellions she considers are in the same region as the White Lotus rebellions, which Naquin describes, and the Red Spears case shows significant evidence of White Lotus presence (charms, incantations, belief in invulnerability). But Perry does not believe that religious factors were significant in the Nian rebellion. "Although scattered hints of White Lotus influence can indeed be found, these do not add up to a compelling case in favor of secret-society direction. White Lotus sects constituted simply one of many allies to whom the Nien were drawn in their continual search for support. The origins of the uprising lie not in anti-Manchu millenarianism, but rather in a highly pragmatic effort by vast numbers of Huai-pei [Huaibei] inhabitants to seize and sustain a livelihood" (97). (The Red Spears, by contrast, did have a significant religious dimension.)

Perry thus analyzes the Nian rebellions as the result of different survival strategies, some directed explicitly toward collective action, others primarily individual with unintended consequences for collective action. The participants are largely motivated by rational self-interest, attempting to choose a strategy that best assures family welfare and security. These strategies are strictly localistic, even when they erupt in regional or national rebellion. Organizational resources available to rebels play a key role in the success or failure of these rebellions, because the organizational forms permit the leadership to mobilize and control large numbers of followers by appealing to their private rational calculations. Perry examines the mechanisms through which these organizations handle collective action problems (free riding). And she assigns little importance to religious motivation, emphasizing instead perceptions of self-interest defined in terms of welfare and security.

Perry's analysis thus differs sharply both from Naquin's and from the class-conflict model. Against Naquin, she doubts the importance of religious motivation in these rebellions. Against the class conflict model, she doubts the importance of class consciousness (since this concept implies a broader horizon than the village), and she doubts the existence of a larger revolutionary program in these rebellions. Rather, she treats these rebellions as the aggregate and largely unintended consequence of a number of interlocking, local strategies of survival, which, in the context of the political and economic environment of Huaibei, erupted into major regional rebellion.

Rationality and Rebellion

These cases all concern the proper explanation of a particular form of mass behavior, organized violent collective action by rural folk. Each theory is concerned to identify the motives of the participants and the organizational forms through which their protests ensued; two (Perry and Marks) emphasize the material and ecological circumstances in which rebellion occurred; one (Naquin) places a religious worldview at center stage; and one (Marks) places the social-economic environment, and the forms of class consciousness generated by that environment, at the center of the account.

A central axis of each of these theories is the question of political rationality in the context of traditional political behavior. To what extent does the explanation of traditional rural rebellion require referring to the culturally specific worldview and values of the participants, and to what extent can these rebellions be explained as rational political movements in which leaders and followers each have a clear view of their demands and the mechanisms through which they pursue them? To what extent, that is, can we understand these rebellions using the ordinary tools of political analysis—material interests, organizational resources, political entrepreneurship, mobilization strategies, goals and programs, tactical planning—and to what extent do distinctive cultural beliefs and motives underlie these disturbances?

The rational-intentional model of individual action interprets individual behavior in terms of the conscious intentions, goals, and beliefs of the agent. To be rational is to be deliberative about goals and to choose strategies that are well designed to attain those goals. This conception of rationality is neutral concerning the nature of the goals that the individual chooses to pursue. It is useful to distinguish between an individual's immediate private interests and goals, and the broader range of political and group interests that may also motivate the individual. In considering the rational decision making of participants, we must thus consider both the immediate private interests that are affected by their decision to support a collective action *and* their commitments and values concerning the interests of the groups with which they associate themselves. Individuals, when joining in political activity with others, sometimes have goals that they hope will be achieved for the group, and this element is an important aspect of their motivation in supporting the activity.[41] In this context we may ask whether an individual's decision to support a given collective action is rational, given both private interests and commitments to various group interests and individual beliefs about the probability of success of the strategies underlying the collective action.

Let us turn now to the problem of collective rationality. In what senses could a collective action—for example, a walkout, boycott, or rebellion—be considered rational? One answer to this question is couched in terms of the choices and behavior of individuals. A given rebellion is rational insofar as it is the intentional result of the coordinated actions of a large number of actors who have a clear view of their goals and of the way in which collective action is designed to achieve those goals. The rebellion is the result of deliberate political behavior. This approach construes rebellion along the lines of other forms of political behavior, such as election campaigns, boycotts, or industrial strikes. It defines the rationality of the event in terms of the rationality of the actors and the judgment that the event is the intended result of their actions.

Some forms of collective behavior are, in a metaphorical sense, at least, collectively rational. The shortcoming of the idea of collective rationality, however, is the absence of a collective agent. So to propose that some forms of collective behavior may be collectively intentional, one must provide an interpretation of this view that works through the intentions and goals of the individuals whose actions constitute the collective action. This view of collective rationality focuses on group interests rather than the rationality of the participants. This model holds that rebellion is rational insofar as it objectively forwards the interests—economic or political—of the rebellious group. It does not consider whether the actors have designed the rebellion to have this result but considers only how well collective strategy fits collective interests. This conception of collective rationality is parasitic on that of individual rationality: the action (rebellion) is rational if it is an appropriate means of pursuing the collective interests of the rebels. It is an extension of the idea of individual rationality to collective or group rationality (an action is rational if it is an appropriate means of pursuing the individual's goals, given the individual's beliefs). To make this account of collective rationality credible, however, it is necessary to show how group interests can be disaggregated into individual interests through appropriate organizational and ideological institutions.

These two conceptions of collective rationality may join or conflict in various cases. In particular, a collective action may be rational in the first sense and irrational in the second sense; it may result from the intentional, rational political decisions made by participants, and yet the aggregate results may be both unintended and contrary to the participants' objective or perceived interests.

The strongest sense in which a rebellion might be rational combines individual and collective rationality. In such a case we postulate that (1) the participants have formulated a clear conception of their goals and interests and have formulated a coherent strategy of collective action to achieve those goals; (2) their goals explicitly include large-scale social and political changes that would enhance their shared interests at the regional or national level; (3) the rebellion unfolds as planned by participants and leads to the intended global changes that actually serve the collective interests that had motivated participants. On this set of assumptions the collective action is rational all the way down: the outcome of the rebellion was intended by participants and conforms to their objective collective interests, and participants joined in the rebellion on the basis of a rational process of decision in which they formulated their goals and chose appropriate means to pursue these goals. The action is then both collectively and individually intentional and rational.

Let us classify the theories we have considered along these lines. Naquin takes us away from the "political rationality" model in several ways. First, she maintains that the motives for action of the participants differed greatly from the material interests that are typically postulated by political scientists; instead, participants were motivated out of a religious impulse. Second, the participants had few long-term strategic concerns; they did not aim to bring about specific changes in policy but rather to contribute to a wholesale change of worlds. Third, the participants were not guided or even much constrained by prudence; they appear to have joined, initially at least, with little regard for the riskiness of the activity. Finally, the participants acted on the basis of a body of magical beliefs—the protective powers of charms and incantations, the likelihood of the Eternal Mother's imminent intervention. Thus Naquin holds that participant behavior is not primarily goal directed, and she is not concerned with the question of the rationality of the collective outcome either.

Both local politics and class conflict theories treat rebellion as the outcome of deliberative rational choice on the part of participants and differ chiefly concerning the character of the goals toward which individuals aim. The local politics framework holds that the goals that drive individual contributions are almost always local interests, working through opportunistic local coalitions. For the class conflict theory, by contrast, members of a class come to recognize their shared interests and struggle for a global change of institutions and regime. They are thus both rational-action explanations. The class conflict theory picks one set of factors within the environment of action as decisive—property relations and exploitation—and asserts that they determine the forms of political alliance and the goals of political action that should be expected from a peasant movement.

Perry's analysis falls in the local rationality, collective unintentionality category: participants generally lacked global intentions, but locally rational calculations guided their behavior. Popkin's analysis (described in chapter 2) also falls in the local rationality, global unintentionality category, with a twist: national political movements can seize local resources and deploy them intentionally toward global goals. Localism distinguishes Perry's analysis from the class conflict model. Like the class conflict model, the local politics theory assumes that peasant political behavior is strategic. But it leaves open the question of the goals of peasant political action and concentrates on the process of collective action and the political and institutional factors that lead the process to escalate into large-scale rebellion. Perry explains the Nian rebellion as the aggregate and largely unintended consequence of interlocking, local strategies of survival which, in the context of the political and economic environment of Huaibei, erupted into major regional rebellion.

Finally, class conflict models postulate the strongest kind of collective rationality: participants have both local and global aims, they design collective action toward achieving global aims, the chosen strategy serves those aims, and the eventual outcome objectively favors those aims.

Of what explanatory use is the category of "collectively rational but locally unintended" actions—that is, rebellions and the like that objectively further the interests of participants but through a process that was unforeseen and unintended by participants? This might be described as the "cunning of reason," and some Marxists are prepared to describe the process of socialist revolution in these terms. Further, there is a functionalist impulse toward thinking that this circumstance in some sense helps to explain the occurrence of the event. But is this a reasonable assumption? I think not. The rationality of collective action must be disaggregated into the intentions and political behavior of the participants; unintended collective benefits cannot be directly relevant to the course taken by a given collective action.

Let us turn to a different problem of collective rationality: public goods and free riding. As we saw in chapter 2, the gap between a shared group interest (for example, in successful collective defense) and the individual interests of the members of the group (for example, in avoiding the risks of militia service) implies the likelihood of free rider problems in many potential collective action opportunities. Group interests do not always disaggregate into supporting individual interests. Rebellion would appear to pose problems of free riding with a vengeance, since the benefits of a successful rebellion are generally not excludable to noncontributors.[42] Therefore rational agents ought to be expected to become free riders and not contribute to rebellion. To make out a rationalist theory, then, particular attention must be paid to the circumstances that permit peasant movements to overcome free rider problems, or an alternative model of rationality in which contributions to collective projects are directly rational must be provided.[43]

Perry's treatment is attentive to collective action problems (without specific reference to the collective action literature). Collective defense is particularly relevant in this context. In many cases a local militia organization could feasibly protect a village from attack by bandits. (This does not necessarily mean that the local militia could withstand concerted bandit attack, only that militia organization could induce bandits to turn their attention to less well organized villages.) However, collective defense is a clear example of a nonexcludable public good: every villager is protected from bandits if any is. Individual villagers therefore have a rational incentive to shirk militia service. Perry highlights this problem and tries to identify mechanisms through which local militias were able to overcome the free rider impulse. In the case of village militia, for example, nonmembers were charged double rates—"a powerful incentive for participation. Where participation . . . was compulsory, absences were punishable by fines levied upon the families of the absentees" (1980:198). "Like crop-watching associations, Red Spear societies were a cooperative response to a degree of threat too severe for solution by individual households" (199). "The prevalence of large-scale banditry meant that villagers found it necessary to organize from among themselves groups of armed guards, or militia, to provide the requisite protection. Leadership and funding for these defense forces came from the wealthier inhabitants—gentry, landlords, or rich peasants." (84)

Another salient example of a public good is fortification. The labor expended on constructing a fortification is a contribution to a public good. "In areas of poor, freeholding villages . . . *yu-chai* [fortified retreats] were usually temporary refuges managed cooperatively by all members of the community. However, in places where landholding was severely concentrated, such that one or two families controlled great tracts of property, the construction of forts was likely to be considerably more lavish" (92). Plainly, the former case represents a clear example of cooperative collective action, whereas the latter represents a case of the sort described by Hardin (1982) in his discussion of group size. In this case, protection from bandits is a public good with steeply stratified benefits; so the few great families can afford to fund and organize the whole project and still benefit. These families thus constitute a k-group for this good. (See chapter 2 above for further discussion of this analysis.)

Local politics theories must pay attention to public goods problems; for the core of this approach is the effort to explain local individual political behavior on the basis of the individual's perceived interests. To the extent that such calculation leads to extensive free riding, local political behavior should be expected to be much weaker than it might potentially be—unless other local factors are available to discourage free riding. We surveyed some of these factors in chapter 2—reciprocity, community sanctions, conventional behavior, and local political resources—and these factors are equally relevant in the context of rebellion. Particularly important, however, are local political organization and leadership. To the extent that organizations—Triads, bandit gangs, White Lotus sects, or Communist party groups—provide leadership and other resources to mobilize and coordinate local contributions, the prospects for successful collective action are substantially increased.

The issue of collective action leads naturally to the question of the institutional forms through which successful rebellions have been fomented and carried out. Rebellion generally requires the coordination of large numbers of participants, as in the simultaneous attack on several towns; it requires fund-raising, sometimes on a large scale; it requires some system of discipline through which lower-level leaders or generals can be induced to accept guidance or commands from higher-level leaders; and so forth. Movements that fail to construct such institutional or organizational forms may be expected to fail in the face of concerted attack by the authorities; consequently, we need to ask how different peasant movements have solved the problem of organization. What political and institutional arrangements facilitated or inhibited rebellion? Did deficiencies in Qing military or administrative arrangements make rural rebellion easier? Did Chinese rural society possess distinctive organizational resources of its own (for example, heterodox organizations, lineages, Triads) that could be used to facilitate rebellion?

The elements of leadership and organization provide the sinews through which local political activism or unrest can be knit into a regional or national movement. There is a long-standing dispute in the analysis of the Communist Revolution in China over the relative roles of widespread but local peasant activism, on the one hand, and the national organization of the CCP, on the other.[44] But it now appears clear that effective organization and leadership are essential if local unrest is to be successfully aggregated into an effective political movement. This is true for several reasons. First, we have seen in the studies considered here that a high level of localism is inevitably implicit in spontaneous political unrest; this localism implies that collective action will tend to collapse as the stimulus for unrest leaves the locality. Thus local resistance to the Japanese in China during the Sino-Japanese War had much this characteristic except when an effective national organization, such as the Guomindang or the Chinese Communist party, was capable of sustaining local efforts in support of more distant anti-Japanese goals.

Second, we have surveyed some of the daunting problems of coordination and assurance that must be met if local activism is to be transformed into a national movement. Local activists must be satisfied, first that other groups in other areas will respond to the call for more regional political actions and second that the actions of separate groups will be coordinated so as to have a reasonable prospect for success. An effective centralized organization, capable of gathering information and developing effective strategies, appears to be an unavoidable ingredient of such coordination.

Finally, regional or national political efforts can succeed only if a high level of political education has been put into place, so as to raise political awareness of local activists from local concerns to regional or national political interests. One prominent example of this sort of political education may be found in the efforts of the CCP to extend a sense of class consciousness among poor and landless peasants, leading them to identify their fortunes with other poor peasants in other regions of China.[45]

Political Culture

To this point we have explained collective behavior fairly narrowly in terms of participants' interests and calculations about the effects of potential collective actions. But Naquin and Scott doubt whether an explanation of rebellion based on rational self-interest is adequate. Naquin shows that cultural and religious beliefs are relevant to political behavior. Scott shows that political behavior is mediated by a culturally specific moral system defining just and unjust social arrangements. Both imply that a narrow analysis of material interests will not suffice to explain political behavior. These points are supported by criticisms raised against the rational peasant theory in chapter 2. There it was argued that the conception of economic rationality as self-interested calculation is too narrow to serve as the basis for explanation of social action. In the context of peasant collective action, the point may be put in these terms: most political action involves a normative component that cannot be reduced to narrow self-interest. So the conception of political rationality must be extended to include such factors as local religious beliefs, kinship loyalties, moral and political commitments, ideology, and the like. We may refer to the ensemble of such factors as a local *political culture.* These factors affect the process of individual decision making on the part of potential participants; and several authors above—Naquin, Marks, and Scott—hold that variations in these factors in specific communities lead to significant differences in political behavior.

A political culture is a shared tradition defining the moral and social worldview within which individuals locate themselves. Such a tradition might include some or all of the following elements: a popular conception of justice in economic, political, and social matters; a popular vision of group solidarity; shared models of how popular protest should be organized (for example, the traditional bread riot or the eat-in); shared recollections of past moments of solidarity (1848 for French workers, the Nghe An-Ha Tinh rebellion for Vietnamese revolutionaries); and a shared body of songs, sayings, aphorisms, and folk heros embodying shared values. (No doubt one could add other elements as well.) These features of social consciousness may bind the members of a group—loyalty to other members of the group, solidarity with one's partners in a political struggle, and commitment to a future social order in which the interests of one's group are better served.[46]

Different societies—and distinct segments within one society—may have very different political cultures.[47] French workers, for example, had a shared tradition of violent popular demonstrations that English workers lacked; this contrast led, in general, to a pattern of peaceful assembly in England and violent street fighting in France in the nineteenth century. Various authors have suggested (Marx among them) that the material conditions of life of a group—patterns of settlement, forms of cooperation involved in agriculture, and the history of shared political activity—produce distinctive features of social consciousness—moral commitments, an experience of solidarity, and a moral vision of the social world. Thus Marc Bloch held that the French peasantry had developed a strong political tradition and a high level of solidarity through the joint influences of communal control over agriculture and ongoing political struggles against the seigneurial system. This political tradition, Robert Brenner maintains, permitted French peasants to develop the resources necessary to defend traditional rights in land ownership at a time when English peasants were losing those rights. The analytical point is, then, that groups with different historical experiences and different material circumstances may possess very different political cultures and may react to changing circumstances in divergent ways—rebelliousness, resignation, emigration. From this it follows that an adequate explanation of political behavior must take account of the particulars of the political culture of the group whose behavior is at issue.[48]

A particularly important contribution of the moral economy literature is the detail it provides concerning the specifics of the moral and political culture of various peasant societies and some of the material determinants of these elements. A significant example is E. P. Thompson's classic work, *The Making of the English Working Class* (1963), in which Thompson attempts to discover how various groups within the English working class were able to develop over time the intragroup strands of commitment that engendered loyalty and solidarity. And James Scott (1985), writing about a very different historical experience (rural Malaysia in the 1970s) likewise attempts to discover the complex fabric of moral values, religious ideas, jokes, and sneers through which the underclass of Malaysian rural society articulated its experience and its relations to other strata. Scott urges quite plausibly that we cannot understand the political behavior of a group until we understand the moral worldview of its members— how they regard their relations to landlords, the state, the religious authorities, and the like and how they conceive of legitimate political activity.

Marxists have sometimes noted this element of social movements; Miliband, Gramsci, and Thompson have sought to work out details of the political cultures of working peoples. One implication from this chapter, however, is that both local politics and class conflict theories must pay more attention to this variable. Each implicitly assumes a direct connection between material interests and collective action; Popkin's rational peasant is a particularly clear example of this assumption. As Scott, Tai, and others emphasize, however, political action unavoidably proceeds through the prism of local political culture. (When Peng Pai approached poor villagers with the best of Marxist intentions and categories, he was shunned as a dangerous madman. It was only when he adapted his appeals to the political visions and vocabulary of the poor peasant that he met with success [Galbiati 1985].)

The concept of political culture, then, bridges individual and collective interests in explaining collective behavior. A local political culture can (but need not) motivate individuals to undertake actions and strategies that favor their group interests, and to persist in these strategies even in the face of risk and deprivation (that is, in circumstances where the political strategy imposes extensive costs on the individual's interests). This treatment of political culture leads to a sensitivity to the point that political behavior is often driven by a set of motives that are richer than a narrow calculus of self-interest.

This leads us back to some of the conclusions of chapter 2. There it was argued that a theory of individual behavior that takes a narrow view of individual interests is insufficient; it is rather necessary somehow to take into account the values and worldview through which deliberation takes place. In this chapter that conclusion is amplified. In order to explain the political behavior of a group it is insufficient to know what the group's interests are, whether local or class. Even if we supplement a class and interest analysis with an account of organizational resources, we will still be unable to predict political behavior. Rather, it is necessary to have a fairly specific account of the moral values, religious beliefs, and cultural worldview within the context of which material conflicts are played out.[49]

The Role of Material Factors in Explanation

We have focused on explaining collective action through reference to individual motivation and agency. But several of these theories have also referred to another important explanatory category—material and ecological factors. Philip Kuhn notes, for example, that the geography of North China is favorable for banditry, rebellion, and other forms of social violence: "Here the boundaries of Shensi, Szechwan, and Hupeh meet to form a border area, a sanctuary for rebels and a barrier to government troops" (1980:39). Geography contributes to rebellion in several ways. Rugged terrain—mountains, marshes, forests—gives the advantage to local irregular forces over the state forces. By making military operations more difficult and slow, bandits and rebels are able to elude the forces dispatched against them. In addition, the relatively low productivity and economic development of peripheral regions lead to lower population density and relatively poor communication and transportation resources—again favoring the irregular force over the state. Finally, the low level of economic development suggests that the state's administrative resources will be fairly thin in such regions, given the correspondence between administrative density and revenue extraction. (Skinner [1977b:307–08] makes a similar point in his analysis of the organization of the Qing bureaucracy.) This means that when rebellion occurs in regions of this sort, the state will have fewer local resources with which to make an immediate response, and will have to mobilize officials and military forces from other regions.

Examples of material factors particularly relevant in the context of peasant rebellion include ecology, agriculture, demographic trends, and such economic variables as commercialization. How should these diverse factors figure into explanations of collective action? Two mechanisms of influence appear particularly important. First, these factors constitute portions of the environment within which collective action occurs; as such, they influence the decision-making process. If, for example, rebellions tend to occur in periods of climate instability, this may be because climate instability leads to subsistence crisis, which induces agents to seek out strategies of collective action that will provide greater security. Population increase can play a similar role: as population rises in a given economy, pressure on available sources of income will increase, which may make such strategies as banditry more attractive to individuals. Finally, if rebellion and rural unrest is more common in areas of high tenancy than low tenancy, it may be that tenants have a shared interest that leads them to rebel which nontenants lack.

Material factors may also impose constraints and opportunities on participants. Remote, rugged areas hamper the state's military forces, permitting bandits, who might be deterred by the certainty of capture in the core of a region, to practice their craft on the periphery. In contrast, the establishment of a national rail network may make large-scale rebellion substantially less likely because it permits the state to respond quickly in force to local disturbances. Material and ecological factors are relevant to explanation of collective behavior, but they all work through their influence on the political behavior of participants; and this means, generally, that they influence the incentives, constraints, and opportunities available to agents in given times and places.

Relations among These Theories

The theories surveyed here all share common threads: local politics and the roles of ideology, class interest, normative schemes, social perceptions, and rational calculation. Are these competing hypotheses about a single set of law-governed phenomena, or are they instead complementary analyses of factors that often coexist in a given period of social unrest? My judgment is that each illuminates problems insufficiently examined by the others. The local politics framework is particularly sensitive to the local processes of collective action: the institutional forms and organizational resources that are often available in rural society, the importance of identifying local material interests as a source of motivation, and the often unintended consequences of local politics at the regional or national level. The class conflict model, by contrast, possesses a substantial range of analytical tools in terms of which to analyze one important feature of rural society: the relations of class and exploitation through which rural production is performed. These property relations largely constitute the material interests of all local agents—landlords, tenants, smallholders, officials, and merchants—and thereby provide substantial insight into the springs of rural political behavior as well. The class conflict model can benefit, however, by borrowing from the local politics framework—in particular, its sensitivity to the local processes of rural collective action. Finally, the millenarian theory (and the moral economy theory discussed in chapter 2) provides analytical resources in terms of which to describe the forms of consciousness—beliefs, norms, values, religious commitments—that mediate political behavior. The problem before historians of China, then, is not to determine which of these frameworks is the ultimate truth but to appreciate and absorb the important insights each has provided into the multistranded fabric of rural collective violence.

Chapter 6
Generalization and Theory

I have now completed my treatment of a range of controversies drawn from current studies of agrarian societies. In this chapter and the next two I turn to a more general perspective and draw out the more comprehensive themes that are suggested by the cases. For the goal of this book is to shed light on problems in the philosophy of social science. Accordingly, it is appropriate to consider whether these controversies share philosophical or methodological issues that may be usefully addressed in greater detail. Many of the issues are familiar from the philosophical literature, but careful consideration of the previous controversies should permit us to explore them in greater detail and with greater insight.

An important goal of scientific research is to arrive at generalizations about empirical phenomena and to discover their underlying causal processes. In social science such a goal sometimes takes the form of an account of processes through which important social phenomena develop—for example, urbanization, social unrest, or population change. This aim is problematic, however. For some social scientists and philosophers maintain that each society is a unique particular, defined by distinctive cultural features; it is thus impossible to assert generalizations that go beyond cultural boundaries. Is it possible or desirable, then, to find a basis for generalizations about social phenomena that can be validly applied across cultures?

Generalizations in Social Science

A generalization is a statement of law-governed regularity among classes of events, entities, or processes. Generalizations typically involve an inferential leap from a limited range of phenomena to a more comprehensive range. Examples drawn from the cases considered here include the following:

- Peasant cultures embody a subsistence ethic
- The Nian were successful because they had close ties to villages

- Large-scale collective action requires competent organizations
- Rapid population rise in traditional societies impedes economic growth
- Local marketing systems tend to conform to the hexagonal geometry postulated by central-place theory

Generalizations serve a number of purposes in social science. One aim is to discern, within the jumble of specific features of a historical event, common social factors that may be identified in a variety of social environments and play an important causal role in the particular case. Many researchers, for example, have postulated that certain structural features of rural social unrest recur in many places and times. Examples include land tenure relations, the technology of production and cultivation, the mechanics of the exercise of state power, and the role of local elites.[1] By identifying the role of such factors in the particular case—for example, the Eight Trigrams rebellion—it is possible to illuminate the dynamics and causal background of this particular event, as well as to add to a richer understanding of the social processes that lead to rebellion in other social and cultural contexts. On this approach, the discovery of cross-temporal or cross-cultural generalizations is itself an aim of social science: to add to our understanding of some of the common influences and processes of social organization and change in many contexts.

Generalizations are also explanatory. They may help explain social events by subsuming these events under general laws, reducing the chaos of the social given to an analysis that exposes an underlying order. A goal of generalizing when treating a historical particular is to show how this event is similar, either in its structure, process of development, or causes, to other historical events. It is a significant discovery (if true) that the Taiping rebellion, like most nineteenth-century Chinese rebellions, depended for its mobilization success on the sense of injustice experienced by its lower-class followers; this would illuminate both the specific case and the general pattern of rural disturbances in traditional China.

It might be held, finally, that middle- and high-level generalizations are best viewed as research hypotheses that permit social scientists to formulate an organized analysis of their domains of phenomena. Such research hypotheses might take this form: "land tenure relations make a difference to political behavior through thus-

and-so a process"; "electoral politics are disproportionately dominated by local elites because . . ."; "the level of local militarization
influences the probability of rebellion"; and so forth. Such hypotheses constitute a range of potentially relevant causal factors that the
local investigator should consider, along with a compressed account
of the factors that secure this sort of causal connection. (This appears
to be Stinchcombe's view of the role of theory and generalization
[1978:1–3].)

On this approach, the aim of generalizations is to raise questions
for research, which may be investigated in the context of a particular
range of social phenomena—not to provide answers to these questions. The social historian of rural India, for example, may consider
the significance of land tenure arrangements in explaining the incidence of rural violence. He or she may find, first, that the land tenure
arrangements of rural India are substantially more complex and diverse than other agrarian societies, so that close attention must be
paid to local arrangements to see if land tenure arrangements are an
important causal factor. This historian may then determine that
other factors, such as caste and ethnic differences, eclipse the causal
significance of the land tenure system in rural India.

Several types of generalizations have recurred in the cases discussed here: generalizations across space (for example, from one region of China to another); generalizations across time (from one Chinese dynasty to another); generalizations about a class of events on
the basis of a small sample; and generalizations across cultures (from
the experience of Chinese peasants to the experience of peasants in
other regions of the world). Each raises difficulties.

Consider first cross-cultural generalizations—assertions that a
class of social events, states, or processes is to be found in a variety of
cultures and that all (or most) such events conform to similar law-
governed regularities or possess similar causal structures. Skocpol's
(1979) claim that France, Russia, and China all experienced a revolution that had the same sorts of structural causes is one example.[2] The
controversial claim that all cultures have religions, or even that all
religions satisfy certain functions (Geertz 1971b), is another. Such
claims are contestable for at least three reasons. First, a conceptual
problem exists: Are there social concepts that succeed in identifying
classes or kinds of social phenomena in a culture-neutral way? Why
should we suppose, for example, that there is a suitable concept of
"religion" that fits all cultures? Second, a "cultural specificity" problem exists: because the search for cross-cultural generalizations ab-

stracts from the specifics of the local culture, it seems to deprecate the significance of local culture. But many authors, including particularly Geertz, hold that the cultural specifics are the essence; abstract from them and social inquiry abandons what is crucial. Finally, a serious epistemic problem exists: How should we gather appropriate data to evaluate the claim?

All generalization involves the application of abstract concepts to concrete social phenomena. I begin, therefore, by discussing some of the logical features of concept formation in social science.

Concept Formation in Social Science

All social analysis and description involves the application of general concepts to concrete social phenomena. To refer to an ensemble of violent actions as a "riot" is to apply a concept to an extended body of social behavior. Let us briefly consider, then, the relation between the concrete particular and the abstract universal in social theory. Though this way of formulating the problem may sound excessively abstract, it is a familiar distinction to the social scientist. The concrete particular is the specific complex event that is the immediate object of investigation: the Eight Trigrams rebellion of 1813, the city of Hankou in the 1840s, the normative attitudes of Malay villagers in one village at one time. A great many events occurred in North China in 1813: several groups of White Lotus adherents assembled and attacked a series of market towns, imperial authorities marshaled their military forces, city dwellers made various accommodations with both rebel and government forces, and so forth. Various kinds of evidence are available to the researcher through which to investigate the concrete particular: government reports on the affair, contemporary accounts by participants and observers, confessions by leaders, and so on. The social historian uses data to discover the specifics of the concrete particular.[3]

To describe this set of events as a "rebellion" is to prepare the way for conceptualization and generalization. It is to presuppose, first, that the events are connected and may be treated as aspects of one complex event. It is also to characterize these events as organized, defiant assaults on the state—rather than as a set of spontaneous uncoordinated violent outbursts. To characterize this event as a "millenarian rebellion" offers a yet more specific hypothesis about its character—that its course depended in some important way on the religious beliefs and organizations of the participants—while at the same time assimilating the event to an abstract ideal type or model.

Several possible sources of error arise in the application of an abstract concept to a concrete phenomenon. The most straightforward is the possibility of simple misapplication of the concept—for example, classifying as a "rebellion" a series of events that were merely a series of ordinary private quarrels. Perhaps more seriously, it is possible to draw invalid inferences from an ascription of a concept. If, for example, the typical range of phenomena encompassed in our conception of "rebellion" have been political movements motivated by the political interests of the participants, the historian may implicitly assume that the current example of "rebellion" should have this character as well. This assumption may lead him or her to seek for the hidden political agenda in a series of disturbances that are really largely religious in inspiration. This error may be described as the fallacy of *reification:* the assumption that all phenomena ranged under a given abstract concept must share a common set of essential properties.

The application of concepts to historical events is thus itself a generalizing, abstracting activity; it is to classify *this* event within a conceptual space that points up its similarities to some events and its differences from others. Conceptualization unavoidably requires abstraction: the deliberate disregard of some of the specifics of one empirical situation to emphasize the features the situation has in common with other situations in other times, places, or cultures. Thus description of a concrete event—or ensemble of events—as a "thus-and-so" depends on the construction of abstract categories, concepts, or "ideal types" under which to subsume specific empirical situations.

Consider some examples of abstract social concepts employed in this study: revolution, millenarian rebellion, state, economic growth, agricultural involution, contract, religion, high-level equilibrium trap, bureaucracy, marginal product of labor, community, class, feudalism, mode of production.

These concepts represent rather different logical types. Several appear to be cluster terms—concepts encompassing a variety of phenomena that share some among a cluster of properties (Putnam 1975a:50–54), without there being a core set of essential properties. The concept of state is a good example; a wide variety of political institutions, from the rationalized French absolutist state to the theater state of Bali, may properly be included under this term. Some of the descriptions associated with the concept of a state—elements of the cluster—include these: an institution of governance, an institution possessing a monopoly of force, an institution possessing legitimacy, an institution providing for centralized conflict resolution and law enforcement, an institution with exclusive rights to collect taxes, an institution charged with arranging military affairs. None of these descriptions is essential to "state-ness," however, and in various societies nonstate organizations serve one or more of these functions. Here Wittgenstein's discussion of the concept of a game is pertinent (1953:paragraphs 69–71). Wittgenstein shows that no set of necessary and sufficient conditions delineates the concept of a game; rather, a set of properties links various practices under the concept of a game through a series of family resemblances. It would appear that the concept of state is logically quite similar to that of a game; the concept is open-ended, defined in terms of a cluster of properties typically possessed by the organizations referred to as "states," without any of these properties being essential to the concept. The concepts of riot, strike, and religion appear to have this same open-textured quality; a diverse range of social practices and economic and political systems may be classified under these terms.

Generalizations about the phenomena characterized by cluster terms must be advanced with caution. This point is important because there is a tendency to reify concepts—to suppose that, because the concept of riot can be applied to social disturbances in medieval France, Qing China, and contemporary Sri Lanka, these incidents must have something in common (the essence of a riot). Once we recognize that such terms lack a set of necessary and sufficient conditions to define the phenomena they cover, this inference is entirely unjustified, and it may well emerge that the phenomena themselves, as well as their typical causes and courses of development, exhibit sufficient diversity that no interesting generalizations whatsoever can be constructed about riots.

Other concepts on this list appear to have a tighter semantic structure. A second type of concept—symptom concepts—has a simple definition in terms of the observable features of the intended class of phenomena. Examples include revolution, famine, civil war, local elite, and electoral democracy. Thus a revolution is a mass movement against an existing political regime, leading to a successful overthrow of that regime; a famine is a period of time, in a significant geographical region, in which large numbers of people have insufficient food to satisfy subsistence needs. Because this sort of concept is deliberately blind to the causal history of the events so classified, it is apparent that the class of phenomena encompassed by such a concept may have diverse causal properties. Thus it is quite possible that the processes that led to the Islamic overthrow of the shah of Iran (the Iranian revolution) had little or nothing in common with the processes that led to the Chinese Communist revolution; and famines caused by the devastation of war may have very different dynamic properties from those caused by crop failure or entitlement shift. This finding suggests that it may be difficult or impossible to make true generalizations for all members of a class identified by such a criterion; a concept defined by the superficial features of a class of social phenomena may group together a number of subclasses, each of which shares causal properties with other subclasses but not with the more comprehensive class. (That is, a symptom concept may fail to identify a "social kind.")

A third type of concept found here may be referred to as a theoretical construct: a concept defined fairly precisely in terms of a larger theoretical framework. Consider the concept of class. In Marxian terms, this refers to a group of persons who share a common position within the relations of production—the property relations through which economic activity takes place (G. Cohen 1978:63–77). To apply the concept of class to a novel case, it is necessary to analyze the local economy and discern the ways that participants gain access to the means of production and finished commodities. Subsequent analysis of the local population into classes is straightforward—wage laborers, managerial farmers, small peasant proprietors, leaseholding farmers, landlords, merchants, officials, and so on. On this treatment, the concept of class is *not* a cluster term; instead, it is part of a larger theoretical construction, with clear and specific criteria of application.[4] Other examples on the list above that have much the same logical form include economic growth and marginal product of labor. Each is defined with respect to a developed economic theory and can be applied relatively straightforwardly on the basis of the assumptions of the theory.

A particularly important type of theoretical concept in social science is that which characterizes a collection of events or occurrences in terms of a hypothesized common causal mechanism. The term *crater* illustrates this type of theoretical construct in natural science. A crater is not merely a circular formation on the surface of a planet; rather, it is a circular formation with a particular causal etiology (having resulted from the impact of a large object). Classifying a given formation as a crater, therefore, brings with it a hypothesis about the causal history of the formation; if that hypothesis is falsified, then the attribution of the concept to the formation must be withdrawn. Examples of causal etiology concepts in the social sciences include Marx's conception of a crisis of underconsumption and Naquin's concept of a millenarian rebellion. Each involves a hypothesis about the causal antecedents of the crisis or rebellion to which the concept is applied.

The category of theoretical construct also embraces most "measure" concepts: those defined through some set of procedures to represent some variable quantity. Examples include the rate of profit, cropping ratio, nuptiality rate, and the real wage. In all but the most primitive cases, such concepts can be applied only within the context of a set of theoretical assumptions about the character of the variables to be measured, the mathematical relations among them, and the properties of the method of measurement.

A final logical type to be found among these examples is what Weber referred to as an "ideal type": a complex description of a group of social phenomena that emphasizes some features and abstracts from others. To Weber, an ideal type is a "conceptual pattern [that] brings together certain relationships and events of historical life into a complex, which is conceived as an internally consistent system" (1949:90). An ideal type is concrete in the sense that it is designed to refer to a specific type of social phenomenon—capitalism, the feudal manor. It is abstract, however, in that it provides an idealized theoretical description of that phenomenon. Weber writes of his conception of urban life: "We construct the concept 'city economy' not as an average of the economic structures actually existing in all the cities observed but as an *ideal-type*. An ideal type is formed by the one-sided *accentuation* of one or more points of view and by the synthesis of a great many diffuse, discrete, more or less present and occasionally absent *concrete individual* phenomena, which are arranged according to those one-sidedly emphasized viewpoints into a unified *analytical* construct" (90).

Examples of such constructs include Geertz's concept of agricultural involution, Hobsbawm's concept of a millenarian revolt, Popkin's concept of the rational peasant, Kuhn's concept of local militarization, and Frohlich and Young's concept of the political entrepreneur. In each case the researcher posits a structured representation of a social category that singles out certain features and abstracts from others. The resulting representation has no full embodiment in history but may be attributed to diverse historical contexts. Finally, the characteristics attributed to the type permit the researcher to reason about the developmental tendencies of the system or individual so characterized.

Consider the concept of a bureaucracy. Here the central idea is that of an administrative hierarchy of officials organized to implement and enforce a set of rules or procedures. We are further invited to conceive of the internal properties of such an organization: record keeping, extensive internal communications, an internal system of discipline, and a norm of rule-applying rationality. When details of specific bureaucracies are abstracted, the eventual specification of the concept may fail to describe accurately any particular social organization. Thus no existing social organization is fully rational; none has a fully effective system of hierarchical control; none fully separates between the organization's declared purposes and the private interests of officials; and so forth. But the value of the ideal type is that it provides an abstract model that may be applied to a range of social phenomena, and to the extent that the model fits existing social organizations, predictions based on the model will have some relevance to the behavior of the existing organization. Among the concepts listed above, millenarian rebellion, feudalism, and commodity market appear to have the character of ideal-typical concepts.

Most of the concepts used in social research can be assimilated to one of these types: cluster concepts, symptom concepts, theoretical constructs, measure concepts, and ideal types. All are cross-cultural: they pick out classes of social events, structures, or processes in a range of cultures. One may take several views of the significance of general concepts. One might hold that social concepts are merely convenient cubbyholes in terms of which to classify and describe social phenomena. By contrast, one might say that social concepts sometimes identify a social kind—a class of social structures or entities that share important causal features and are found in many social contexts. On the former approach, it is conceded that description requires concepts, but it is held that many conceptual frameworks would do equally well and that the framework in use is not distinctive. It is a pragmatic question rather than one of truth or falsity whether one framework or another should be used. At the opposite extreme, however, it is held that a good set of social concepts have the potential to identify *real* categories of social phenomena—to divide the social world at the joints, as it were. (Skinner's stance toward functional regionalization illustrates the latter view; he maintains that his macroregions analysis of China corresponds to the real functional organization of Chinese society and economy [1977b:217–19]). And the best interpretation of this claim is that good concepts segment social phenomena into groups or types that share strong causal relations.

The Realism of Social Science Concepts

Are There "Social Kinds"?

We may approach the problem of the realism of social concepts by considering the notion of a natural kind, for a persuasive interpretation of realism in natural science is the view that good scientific concepts refer to natural entities, structures, or systems. The concept of a natural kind refers to a class of entities, characterized by some description, that share similar causal properties and are governed by the same causal laws. (Hilary Putnam summarizes these criteria with the requirement that the entities possess the same "hidden structure" [1975e:241].) "Water" refers to a natural kind, whereas "air" does not; for (as we now know) "water" refers to the molecule H_2O, whereas "air" refers to a mixture of oxygen, nitrogen, and trace gases. Pure air does not exist, but pure water does.[5] And—most importantly for scientific explanation—research can identify the common causal properties of the entities within a natural kind and then provide a scientific explanation of the behavior of those entities in a variety of environments.[6]

What, then, is a social kind? Without presuming that there are any such kinds, we can provide a strictly parallel account to that of a natural kind. A social kind is a class of social phenomena, entities, or processes that possess similar internal structures and that consequently possess similar causal properties and are subject to the same causal laws. The entities that fall under a social kind, then, are similar in their causal or dynamic properties.

This provides a formal specification of the concept of a social kind; the harder question is whether there are any such kinds. Do any of the concepts considered above refer to classes of social events, states, or processes that are highly similar in their causal properties? Neither cluster concepts nor symptom concepts hold much promise of identifying social types. We have seen that "states" and "revolutions" both

encompass classes of social phenomena that are sufficiently heterogeneous as to make it highly dubious that they share a hidden structure; and we have little reason to suppose that the phenomena
grouped together according to these criteria are likely to share underlying causal properties or dynamic patterns.

More promising, however, are the other two types of concepts
surveyed here: theoretical constructs and ideal-typical concepts.
Each of these is constructed with a background causal or explanatory
hypothesis in mind; in each, the investigator attempts to define a
concept that identifies a recurring hidden structure—an ensemble of
causal properties or structures that hang together and that may plausibly be held to give rise to a recurring dynamic pattern.

This analysis leads to a conclusion: the plausibility of the existence of social kinds depends on the existence of credible causal laws
or processes governing social phenomena. If such processes exist,
then theoretical concepts that identify classes of phenomena with
similar causal properties may plausibly be said to identify social
kinds. Candidates include "millenarian rebellion," "class system,"
and "commodity market"; these cases have developed theoretical
frameworks that purport to identify a set of causal processes that
determine a common structure for the indicated set of social
phenomena.

Causal Regularities

Do causal processes or other regularities underlie social phenomena?
In the next chapter we will consider the nature of social regularities
in greater detail, but, briefly, reasoning about the motivations and
behavior of intentional persons in the context of specific social arrangements gives us a basis for arriving at conclusions about the
causal properties of certain types of social institutions. Particularly
prominent among these causal laws are regularities that derive from
economic decision making, rational political behavior, and other
forms of rational action within specific social arrangements.

Consider an example: Charles Tilly's (1964) argument that the
various cropping regimes of eighteenth-century western France produced dramatically different political psychologies in subregions.
(Tilly goes on to explain the occurrence and spread of counterrevolution in 1793 on the basis of these differences.) To simplify Tilly's
analysis somewhat, western France contained regions that were devoted primarily to subsistence agriculture (rye), to market grain pro-

duction (wheat), and to viticulture (grapes). The economic circumstances of these three rural populations led them into different
patterns of life. Subsistence cultivators were uninvolved in market
relations, and they had little contact with the expanding urban networks in the region. The village clergy had sparse competition for
leadership—from either local merchants or local officials, since there
were few of either. These peasant proprietors and leaseholders thus
tended to have conservative political attitudes and did not sympathize with the Revolution. By contrast, winegrowers depended
heavily on markets; they were attuned to economic circumstances in
regional cities and even the international market; they were more
exposed—and more receptive—to modern ideas through their urban
contacts; and they were intensely aware of the harmful effects of
internal tariff barriers on their own material interests. This population, Tilly holds, heartily supported the Revolution and was *not*
disposed to join the counterrevolutionary movement.

Whatever its merits, Tilly's account illustrates both the way in
which causal connections are established in social science and the
basis of our confidence in expecting that similar factors will be pertinent to the process of social change in other environments. Once we
observe that human actors are concerned about their immediate family welfare and can discern the import of various local factors on that
welfare, we can see why we should expect a connection between the
rustic economy—the specific arrangements through which rural people pursue their livelihoods—and their political attitudes and
behavior.

This sort of generalization presupposes that law-governed social
processes recur across cultures. One of the chief functions of social
theory is to analyze the specifics of these processes; when Mancur
Olson or Russell Hardin provide an abstract description of the logic of
collective action, they give the empirical investigator a detailed analysis of one cross-cultural regularity. The researcher can then employ
such an analysis in an attempt to discern the workings of such mechanisms in a specific case. This approach postulates that there are
objective social laws and processes that theoretical models may accurately describe and that may be found in many social contexts. (Of
course, the construction of an explanation of a concrete historical
event depends on investigating the circumstances that surround the
event. Social theory does not replace close empirical investigation.)

This account requires that an assertion of causal regularity be supported by correct theoretical analysis—an analysis that shows what it is in the circumstances guiding and constraining the behavior of the relevant human actors such that *these* social arrangements lead to *that* social outcome. Theories thus justify generalizations by identifying the underlying processes that distinct social phenomena may share.

Is the search for underlying social processes, structures, and laws credible? Is it reasonable in the domain of social phenomena to suppose that underlying processes and mechanisms can explain the range of observable social phenomena? And through what sorts of mechanisms do underlying processes fix, influence, or determine observable phenomena?

The general question can be disposed of quickly. Too wide a variety of successful analysis exists to take the implied skepticism seriously. Examples include theories of the logic of collective action, which have been deployed to explain strikes, rebellions, and fund-raising drives in many cultures and times; the theory of cooperative games, which explains a variety of kinds of social coordination; central place theory in geography, which explains the placement of towns in an economic landscape; and the theory of agricultural involution, which holds that peasant societies when subjected to subsistence pressure from the outside will subdivide economic tasks so as to secure a living for each villager. In each case the theory provides an account of underlying structures and individual motivations that is then used to explain concrete social phenomena. These examples show that the assumption that social science should explain social phenomena by analyzing a set of unobservable social structures or processes is reasonable.

This analysis suggests that it is reasonable to suppose that law-governed causal processes are at work among social phenomena and that these processes may be discerned in a variety of cultures. This formulation may lead the reader to conclude that there are "laws of social development" that are analogous to laws of nature and that such laws will eventually permit social scientists to make large-scale, precise predictions about the development of various social forms (capitalism, military dictatorship, Oriental despotism). It is important to see that this conclusion is unjustified. Causal processes are at work among social phenomena, but they are limited in their scope and predictive value. Social laws are best expressed as laws of tendency rather than laws of strict necessity; they interact in unpredictable ways with other processes within existing social environments—making it extremely difficult to draw confident predictions from them; and they concern fairly low-level social structures—specific economic arrangements, patterns of individual political behavior—so that it is rarely possible to derive high-level laws of development on the basis of such regularities.

To illustrate the last point, consider the role of causal laws in classical Marxism. At one extreme, Marxism offers generalizations about the sequence of modes of production and the dynamic of development to be expected from each mode. These function as highly general assertions about the social process within feudalism, capitalism, the peasant mode of production, and the like. At the other extreme, however, Marxism rests on a range of hypotheses about the causal processes at work within a class society—hypotheses about the circumstances that affect the organization of the firm, the political behavior of the proletariat, the economic choices of the peasant, and the like. These hypotheses are couched at the level not of the mode of production but of the local-level processes through which individual behavior and social institutions interact. My suggestion here is that the social scientist is on the surest ground when providing analysis of the latter process and is also in the best position to offer cross-cultural generalizations at this level. When the social scientist turns to higher-level claims about the social system as a whole—for example, the pattern of development to be expected of any capitalist economy—both the basis of the generalization itself and its projectability to other social contexts is most shaky.

In another context, I have argued (1986) that the aim of discovering strict social laws, similar in form and predictive power to laws of nature, is deeply flawed in social science; it depends on an unsupportable analogy between natural and social science. In natural science it is reasonable to suppose—exotic counterexamples notwithstanding—that the behavior of natural objects and systems are subject to strict causal laws.[7] This confidence stems from the essential similarity of natural objects within the same taxa—all helium molecules are identical and are subject to the same causal laws. Social phenomena, by contrast, are radically heterogeneous. Human behavior conforms to generalizations, but it also shows a wide range of individual differences. And no two social institutions or practices are identical. Thus the institutions of revenue collection in France, Britain, and the United States have enough in common to classify them as national revenue collection agencies, but differences between these concrete institutions are substantial and causally significant. It would be quixotic to expect each institution to give rise to the same causal regularities.

Most important, social causal regularities stem ultimately from the behavior of human beings within specific social environments. Because humans are intentional decision makers capable of perceiving their environments and shaping their actions to suit their aims, some regularities do arise, but the behavior of an intentional actor is quite different from the behavior of a natural object subject to determinate causal laws. Human beings make perceptual errors, they act out of a diversity of motives, they miscalculate. As a result, human behavior can be interpreted and predicted, but it will frequently diverge from the predictions offered by an idealized theory of intentional action. At best, social regularities must be laws of tendency rather than exceptionless laws. (Further discussion of laws of tendency in Marx's social science may be found in Little 1986:24–29.)

Finally, the density and complexity of social causation narrowly limits the hope for comprehensive generalizations about social development. The specifics of land tenure relations are causally relevant to the political behavior of a group of people, but so are a vast number of other factors: the specifics of local religious beliefs, the status and visibility of local elites, the degree of commercialization of agriculture, the presence or absence of foreigners in local society, the degree of literacy, the level of urban-rural integration; the list is lengthy. Moreover, the causal factors relevant to the formation of political attitudes may interact in unpredictable ways; thus it may emerge that sharecropping arrangements promote conservative attitudes when coupled with low rural-urban integration but radicalize peasants when linked with high rural-urban integration.

These considerations suggest that the search for causal generalizations in social science might be best aimed at middle-level causal processes rather than high-level generalizations about social types; the researcher in a particular domain could then attempt to sort out the effects of various causal influences and arrive at an analysis of their relative weights in the particular case. What seems unlikely, on the whole, is that social theory will ever be able to provide useful causal generalizations about high-level structures (modes of production, types of political regime, and the like).[8]

The search for generalizations about common causal factors among social phenomena is fruitful and desirable, and depends heavily on cross-cultural studies. It seems likely that common forms of

social process, working through stereotyped forms of individual behavior, may be hypothesized to recur across cultures. There are two
goals in arriving at such generalizations. Some, like Popkin and Skocpol, are interested in the generalizations for their own sake, for the
light they shed on human social life generally. Perhaps more important, however, such generalizations, when applied thoughtfully and
flexibly, provide a basis for the investigator of local arrangements to
formulate causal hypotheses about processes in a particular region.

Second, it has emerged that generalization and the existence of
law-governed social processes are closely connected. Valid generalizations depend on discovery of a set of causal factors and environmental constants, the joint product of which is the generalized regularity. We might call this sort of generalization a theoretically
grounded generalization.

We have every reason to be cautious about generalizations,
whether across cultures or across time and space. Two similar historical events (for example, the Eight Trigrams and Nian rebellions) *may*
share an underlying cause and can thus be analyzed in the same
terms. But they may also embody fundamentally different processes,
in which case generalization would be illegitimate. And the only way
we may confidently extend such a generalization is through appropriate empirical and historical research at both ends; theory cannot
determine what sort of rebellion the Nian was without detailed research into the circumstances, organizations, leadership, and
motives of participants.

The Case against Social Kinds

Let us briefly consider the case *against* the utility of general concepts
or cross-cultural "social kinds" in social science. In his comparative
study of Islam in Morocco and Java (1968), Clifford Geertz argues
against the quest for a description of social kinds that transcend
particular social and cultural contexts. He asks to what extent a
comparative study of a religion in two contexts ought to seek out a
level of description that renders both the same and to what extent the
investigator should look rather for distinguishing features of the two
embodiments of the religion. Geertz believes that even such social
constructs as Christianity or Islam require cultural interpretation in
distinct cultural environments. He maintains that the religious beliefs, practices, and values of Islam differ radically between Morocco
and Java and that the only possible entry into these symbolic systems

is through careful ethnographic interpretation of the two cultures. "'Mysticism,' 'piety,' 'worship,' 'belief,' 'faith,' 'sacredness,' 'tradition,' 'virtue,' 'spirituality,' even 'religion' itself—all these words we use . . .—thus turn out, when we compare the way in which each of our peoples came, on the whole, to develop a characteristic conception of what life was all about, a conception they called Islamic, to mean rather different things in the two cases [Javanese and Moroccan]" (54). Geertz's arguments here appear flatly inconsistent with the idea that abstract types of social entities or processes can recur across cultures. Geertz appears to endorse the view that each culture is involved in a process of self-definition, so that the "reality" of Islam as a religion and a set of social practices is fundamentally different in Morocco and Java. The meanings of such key concepts as charity, piety, and equality have evolved differently in the two contexts and have contributed to substantially distinct cultural systems and ways of living.

> Both these styles [Moroccan and Javanese] strongly marked by beliefs and practices one can only call . . . "mystical." But what "mystical" means in the two cases turns out to be very far from the same thing. To overcome this difficulty by generalizing the notion of mysticism so as to obscure these contrasts in the hope of finding broader, more abstract resemblances seems a most unpromising strategy, for to move away from the concrete details of the two cases is also to move away from the place where any general truth we might discover must necessarily lie. If, however, we use a concept like "mysticism"—or "mystic" or "mystical"—not to formulate an underlying uniformity behind superficially diverse phenomena, but to analyze the nature of that diversity as we find it, then pursuing the different meanings the concept takes in different contexts does not dissolve its value as an ordering idea but enriches it. (24)

Charles Taylor and Alasdair MacIntyre make similar points in connection with the possibility of cross-cultural political science. Thus in "Understanding and Ethnocentricity" (1985) Taylor writes of politics in India: "Politics exist in contemporary India. There are practices by which people contribute to shape the incidence of power, whatever inequalities and exclusions may mar the democratic process. Contemporary India thus does need a concept of this kind. But if I am right, this is one thing that cannot be provided ready-made from outside. An appropriate concept—or concepts—of politics in India will only arise through an articulation of the self-definitions of people engaged in the practices of politics in India" (133). On Taylor's view, then, a "science" of politics for India must extract its categories, concepts, and causal hypotheses from the concrete experience of politics in India—not from abstract political theories based on the experience of modern Europe. The concepts to be employed must be specific to the terrain, and the Indian terrain is radically different from modern Europe.[9]

Consider, finally, Alasdair MacIntyre's discussion of the possibility of comparative theories of politics. "I shall be solely interested in the project of a political *science*, of the formulation of cross-cultural, law-like causal generalizations which may in turn be explained by theories" (1973:172–73). MacIntyre, like Geertz and Taylor, emphasizes the densely interlinked quality of local concepts, social practices, norms, and self-ascriptions—with the implication that each practice or attitude depends inextricably on an ensemble of practices, beliefs, norms, and concepts that are culturally specific and, in their combination, unique. MacIntyre thus holds that as simple a question as "Do Britons and Italians differ in the level of pride they take in civic institutions?" is unanswerable because of cultural differences in the concepts of pride contained in the two European cultures (172–73). "Hence we cannot hope to compare an Italian's attitude to his government's acts with an Englishman's in respect of the pride each takes; any comparison would have to begin from the different range of virtues and emotions incorporated in the different social institutions. Once again the project of comparing attitudes independently of institutions and practices encounters difficulties" (173–74).

These points pertain to difficulties in identifying political attitudes cross-culturally. Could it be said, though, that political institutions and practices are less problematic? MacIntyre argues a position already familiar from Taylor's views explored above: that political practices in turn depend heavily on local political attitudes. "It is an obvious truism that no institution or practice is what it is, or does what it does, independently of what anyone whatsoever thinks or feels about it. For institutions and practices are always partially, even if to differing degrees, constituted by what certain people think and feel about them" (174).

These points raise problems concerning the identification of social phenomena themselves. Taylor and Geertz suggest that we cannot refer to social practices and institutions except through the specific complex of meanings and understandings found within the culture itself. Taylor's example of bargaining is a clear example of this point (1985:32–36), and Geertz's discussion of the unsuitability of the ensemble of European political concepts (state, power, personal advantage) in application to traditional Bali makes the point as well (1980:121–22). Each case displays an underlying skepticism about the existence of cross-cultural social entities or types. Rather, each prospective such entity (contract, state) on closer analysis turns out to depend so closely on the specific values and meanings of the local culture that it is inappropriate to use the same concept in referring to these practices.

These arguments suggest that it is *not* possible to formulate general concepts that adequately embrace the specifics of social phenomena in diverse cultures. However, this conclusion does not follow. Geertz, Taylor, and MacIntyre have chosen their examples carefully. In each case the argument depends on the circumstance that the phenomenon in question is partially constituted by the symbol system, moral values, or magical beliefs of the local culture (Italian pride, the role of charity). If the causal properties of a type of institution depend on a culturally specific fact, then it is tautological that it is impossible to abstract from that fact and still adequately explain the workings of that institution. This point shows the validity of the interpretation theory approach to social inquiry. But it does not establish the stronger point that *all* social inquiry requires interpretation. And in the present context, Geertz, Taylor, and MacIntyre fail to establish that *all* social phenomena are culture specific. Consider one example: the concept of sharecropping land tenure arrangements. This economic structure is found in many agrarian societies. And it imposes a distinctive set of incentives, opportunities, and constraints on the farmer and landlord. For example, both lord and farmer have depressed incentives to introduce productive innovations, since each will receive only half of the benefits produced. Sharecropping also provides the farmer with a strong incentive to cheat during the harvest—harvesting early or at night. And it gives the lord an incentive to push the tenant toward cash cropping rather than subsistence farming, since the lord typically prefers cash income to a large store of grain. These are tendencies implicit in sharecropping and have been observed in a variety of cultural milieus.

It is also true that land tenure relations may acquire cultural incrustations of meaning in a particular cultural environment—and even that these incrustations may affect the workings of the economic arrangements. It seems wholly implausible to insist, however, that local land tenure relations can be understood *only* in terms of the local meaning attached to them; sharecropping creates similar economic tendencies in varied social environments. These tendencies follow from its economic characteristics—the arrangements through which the tenant acquires access to the land and the amount and character of rent collection—and from the goal-directed behavior of lord and tenant within the context of these arrangements.

A similar story could be told about many other social, economic, and political structures—for example, electoral politics, slavery, and collective action. In each case analysis permits us to identify a social structure whose chief causal properties work through simple prudence rather than any more culturally specific feature of individual psychology; and prudence itself is a widespread human trait. These considerations suggest that common processes are at work in many social contexts; if that is the case, then it is plausible to suppose that institutions and structures that possess similar causal properties will result. And this in turn suggests that the aim of identifying "social kinds" of phenomena across cultures is not hopeless.

Microstudies, Macroconclusions

A central type of generalization encountered among the theories examined here is that through which a researcher establishes a range of results for a limited time and place (for example, Hankou in the mid-nineteenth century) and then attempts to determine the degree to which these results may also describe a more comprehensive domain (for example, the Chinese commercial city of the late Qing). Local studies are the microscope of social research; they permit social science to arrive at the most detailed and accurate understanding of historical processes. But rarely are we satisfied with a local study that is so narrowly defined that it supports no more general hypotheses or explanations. So the problem before us is this: What are the inferential relations between detailed local studies and more comprehensive generalizations about the world within which the locality is situated?

We have surveyed a number of local studies in the preceding chapters. Thus Robert Marks confines his research to Haifeng and Lufeng counties, drawing exclusively on archival materials pertaining to those counties; Elizabeth Perry is concerned only with the Huaibei region of North China; and Susan Naquin considers a small region of the North China plain. Some of these authors attempt to support more comprehensive generalizations on the basis of such studies— generalizations about larger regions or longer time frames. Such a generalization might, for example, attempt to characterize pertinent patterns in North China as a whole, rural China as a whole (Marks), or the long tradition of peasant rebellions in North China (Perry). Are such generalizations legitimate? If so, what principles justify them, and what cautions should govern their construction?

The question before us has two parts. Why are local studies important in the methodology of historical research? And what types of inferences should be expected between the findings of local studies and the more general questions that arise about larger stretches of time and place? Two answers to the first question, one methodological and one substantive, are suggested by the theories surveyed here. The methodological concern has to do with defining standards of rigor of scholarship in historical inquiry, whereas the substantive point has to do with the localism of political processes. Historians may aim to answer rather general questions, but the substance and objectivity of their research depends heavily on their study of historical processes at the local level because that is where evidence is available. This is an epistemic point; it has to do with the character of the evidence available to support historical conclusions.

A consideration stemming from the nature of social phenomena also suggests the importance of local studies. One may hold that general processes (for example, the pattern of increased rebelliousness) are composed of local processes, and it is impossible to understand the higher level without understanding the local level. To know why so many rebellions took place in nineteenth-century China, we must first know (roughly and approximately) why the Taiping rebellion, the Nian, the Eight Trigrams, and others occurred; and to arrive at convincing answers to these questions we must know a good deal about the social, cultural, and economic context of these rebellions.

Political processes, moreover, particularly in traditional societies, are commonly driven by local interests. This is the heart of Brenner's theory of agrarian change: that change within European feudalism was driven largely by the local balance of power between lords and peasants. Yung-fa Chen's (1986) analysis of the Chinese Communist party's success during the Sino-Japanese war likewise depends on a hypothesis of localism: it is necessary to understand the local en-

vironment of choice, political power, and circumstances of life to
know whether a given strategy of mobilization is likely to succeed.[10]
Chen (1986:2–6) holds that explanations based at the national
level—whether Chalmers Johnson's thesis of anti-Japanese nationalism or Mark Selden's populism—are unsatisfactory because
they fail to give an adequate account of the CCP's local successes and
failures. This line of thought leads to the conclusion that historical
generalizations and inferences must be grounded in a wide range of
local studies.

Though the local studies approach has undeniable virtues, it also
has pitfalls. It may lead researchers away from attempting to arrive at
appropriate generalizations at all. The blinkered historian whose
knowledge of a particular area is exhaustive but who studiously re-
frains from posing more general questions is familiar to all. More
seriously, the local studies method may make it difficult or impossible to investigate certain kinds of systemic causes of historical
change. Long-term demographic change, for example, may affect a
locality (as through slowly rising prices) without manifesting itself
locally (local population size is stable). Emmanuel Le Roy Ladurie
(1974) provides a useful example; his research is organized around a
local study (Languedoc), but he addresses global factors as well (long
waves of demographic change).[11]

Let us turn now to some specific issues pertaining to generalizations based on local studies. Any generalization from a limited set of
events to a larger set must confront the likelihood of exceptions.
When Perry concludes that the Nian bands were largely successful
because of their strong ties to isolated fortified communities, she
generalizes over the experiences of dozens or hundreds of bandit
groups. It is plain that any generalization over such a set is unlikely to
be without exception. So it may turn out that some bandit groups
succeeded for other reasons—perhaps protection by corrupt local officials—in spite of little popular support. Does this invalidate the
generalization? No; if it did, then all social or historical generalizations are invalid. Instead, we should understand a historian's generalization about a diverse set of experiences as a statement about the
most common, most causally important, or most representative type
of experience. A more precise generalization might be preferable—
one that indicates the main body of exceptions, for example—but it
is unreasonable to require that historical generalizations be without
exception.

Within the literature on China, a common complaint against generalizations is that the author draws data from a region with one set of patterns or practices and projects this pattern to other regions of China. The criticism is often made that China is heterogeneous and that efforts to provide one explanatory scheme for diverse regions or times is unlikely to succeed. Instead, the critic urges that explanation be sensitive to local variations and that generalizations be limited to saliently homogeneous regions and times.

Robert Marks's work is relevant in this context. Marks attempts to arrive at generalizations about rural unrest in nineteenth-century China as a whole, but all his data are drawn from two counties in South China. These counties are unique in many ways: they are coastal, they were subject to considerable Western contact, their agricultural systems are distinct from those of North China, they are highly commercialized, they are ethnically distinct from North China or West China, and so forth. Each of these factors, moreover, is demonstrably relevant to the occurrence of social unrest. So the argument can be made that generalizations for China as a whole—or even for all of South China—cannot be drawn from these data. These observations suggest a problem: What would justify drawing generalizations about a region as a whole over an extended time on the basis of a study of a locality within that region for a shorter time?

Consider a hypothetical example. Suppose a local study of Haifeng county leads to the finding that smallholders are the most politically militant and volatile class in the countryside. Suppose, further, that the investigator explains this fact as the consequence of the subsistence vulnerability of the smallholder coupled with the smallholder's access to effective political traditions and organizations. Other classes (for example, landless workers), the investigator finds, have objective reason to be militant but lack the political resources necessary to transform this motivation into political activity.

Now suppose that the investigator attempts to extend this finding to other regions of rural China to predict that smallholders generally will be the most ready supporters of rebellion. To justify any projection of findings in one domain onto another, it would appear necessary to defend the following assumptions: (1) the phenomena described by the original finding are not accidental or artifacts of the investigation; (2) a background set of social processes in the local environment leads to the phenomena described by the finding; (3) these processes are also at work in the larger region; (4) the environment of the larger region is not so different as to defeat the workings of these social processes; and (5) no countertendencies in the larger region are sufficiently powerful to offset these processes.

These assumptions embody the idea that identifiable causal processes recur in different social environments and that different environments may be sufficiently similar that these processes will engender similar outcomes in the various environments. The investigator must examine available knowledge about the larger region to judge the similarity or dissimilarity of the two regions. Generalization from local studies is thus best understood as the extension of a theoretical analysis in the local context to its application in the larger context; and to make this extension it is necessary to demonstrate that the same processes are at work, in a sufficiently similar environment, as to lead to the same outcome.

This analysis suggests some important cautions over the formulation of generalizations. Most important, the assumption of the approximate similarity of the two environments is usually questionable. Regions of China (let alone East Asia, Asia, or the world) differ in a multitude of ways, any of which *might* be causally relevant for the processes under investigation. Consider some of the following variations across regions of China: ethnicity and religion, land tenure systems, soil fertility, subordination to central state power, cohesion of local elites, market integration, literacy, contact with the West, urbanization, vulnerability to bandits and invading armies, and so on. It would appear rash to suppose that two regions are sufficiently similar as to give rise to the same outcomes as a result of a common process of development or change. Thus, even granted the assumption that a common process of change is at work, the generalization from one region to another is highly questionable. This suggests that such generalizations must be based on careful macrostudies, drawing pertinent information from throughout the larger region—not simply on a mechanical projection of results from one area to another.

This point about the wide variation in social environments over space can also be argued for temporal periods. Ramon Myers, for example, employs a great volume of data from the republican period (1930s) to establish some of the economic variables of the North China economy. He then generalizes from this data by projecting it backwards, holding that similar patterns were probably to be found in North China throughout the previous century. Here again, however, it is important to recall the many changes wrought during this period; once we recognize this variation, it becomes less plausible that we can simply project backwards the economic patterns of the early twentieth century onto the late eighteenth century.

Both temporal and regional generalizations within China appear to require great caution; the range of social environments over both time and space makes it quite possible that factors will be present in one time and place that interact with social processes in such a way as to produce outcomes that are not to be found in other times and places. This conclusion would appear to be even more pressing if we attempt to move from China to Asia as a whole; the differences between the social environments of Java, North India, and South China are vast and plainly relevant to the causal arguments that underlie social and economic generalizations.

A second caution stems from the importance of diversity itself within the social realm. Some researchers have taken variation rather than regularity to be most characteristic of social phenomena; on this approach, it is diversity rather than homogeneity that the social investigator needs to analyze and characterize. This approach leads to a preference for more concrete rather than more general investigations. Thus Skinner emphasizes that social scientists should pay attention to the differentiating features of the phenomena they study: the city, rebellion, or village society. Skinner puts the problem this way in his discussion of the Chinese city as a social type: "But are generalizations the sole or even the most important objective of the intellectual quest? Is the point to categorize the Chinese case so that it can be placed unambiguously in the proper cell of particular cross-cultural contingency tables? Should we aim here at a set of conclusions in the form of generalizations about *the* Chinese city—statements that by their very nature can reflect only the lowest common denominator of all empirical cases?" (Skinner, ed. 1977:5). By implication, his answer is negative; it is more important and useful to identify those features that distinguish the Chinese city from the European city and those that distinguish some Chinese cities from others. Beijing, for example, was a very different urban agglomeration than Hankou in the nineteenth century; Skinner would presumably hold that we can gain insight into the differences only if we study each as a system with its own functional organization, history, and economic and political systems. "The 'Chinese' city is no less a constructed ideal type than the 'preindustrial' or the 'Oriental' city. And when we survey the range of premodern Chinese cities . . . when we comprehend this varied array, we run into the same difficulties that beset generalizations about more inclusive constructed types" (5).

Clifford Geertz often offers a similar stricture on social research, maintaining that variation rather than homogeneity is central for understanding social phenomena. Thus Geertz, in his study of Islam in Java and Morocco, favors concreteness over generalization: "In this area of study, at least, the interest of facts lies in their variety, and the power of ideas rests not on the degree to which they can dissolve that variety but the degree to which they can order it" (1968:24).

Skinner and Geertz argue that—in some cases, at any rate—differentiation rather than generalization is most useful for social science. There is a distinct trade-off between more comprehensive generalizations and more detailed knowledge of the forms of variation found among the phenomena over which the generalizations range.

These qualifications suggest, however, not that generalizing is an improper activity within social science but that *both* generalization and concrete description are important within social research. Social phenomena are diverse, and they do embody patterns and causal processes that support generalizations. So the researcher is forced to make thoughtful decisions, in the conduct of research and the formulation of research goals, about the proper level of concreteness and generality in terms of which to treat the subject. It is perfectly credible, moreover, that the balance will be different in different areas of social science. Perhaps, for example, the study of religion demands concreteness because of the great variation common in institutions and beliefs, whereas the study of urbanization properly supports broader and more comprehensive generalization.

These cautions should not be taken to imply that generalization is improper or unjustified in area studies. On the contrary, a village study that concludes, "This is the way it was in the village—idiosyncratic, unrepresentative, and unusual," is of only the most arcane interest. Rather, the research community should expect a narrowly defined study to produce hypotheses about patterns or causal processes that were also found in other places and times and that the local study thus illuminates the larger context.[12] The cautions indicated here are just that: reminders that generalizations must be carefully drawn with close attention to regional or temporal variations that might invalidate them when projected too broadly.

The Role of Theory in Area Studies

Many of the issues discussed in preceding chapters fall within what one might call the "logic of theoretical inference" in social science. I have tried to illustrate the importance of attention to background assumptions and inferences through scrutiny of several theoretical arguments. Some might hold that these criticisms discredit the role of theoretical models in historical explanation quite generally. My own view is the reverse: that theoretical constructs are an essential part of social and historical explanations and that their application to a concrete social phenomenon may be given an objective evaluation.

Should historians and area specialists employ theoretical models in attempting to understand and explain such concrete historical phenomena as the occurrence of peasant rebellions, the pace of technical innovation in traditional China, or the organization of the Qing bureaucracy? Many theoretical models come to mind: the moral economy framework in application to rebellion, Elvin's analysis of high-level equilibrium traps, or Skinner's analysis of the system of imperial postings. A skeptic might hold, however, that social phenomena are always sui generis and therefore that theoretical models merely distort the phenomena and mislead the investigator. Instead, this skeptic might maintain, the investigator should become immersed in the data available concerning *this* historical phenomenon and extract an analysis directly from the given. On this account, theoretical models are pernicious.

Against this skeptic I would argue that it is necessary to look more closely at the claim that social phenomena are sui generis. True, the particular conjunction of circumstances present in that event is unique. But it is reasonable to suppose that social processes are at work in this event that are *not* unique and instead underlie social phenomena in many times, places, and cultures. Theory construction depends on the assumption that social phenomena are somehow law-governed and systemic; the goal of theory formation is to arrive at an account of the laws, mechanisms, and processes that engender this regularity. (An example of such a process might be the free rider problem in collective action, which may be predicted in any situation in which individuals make decisions based on rational self-interest.) It is the task of social theory to formulate hypotheses about such processes and the task of the area specialist to try to see which of the potential influences or processes are present. A theoretical model, then, is a legitimate effort to formulate a hypothesis about an underlying structure, process, or law that may be identified in a variety of circumstances.

This view (that there are underlying social processes which are law-governed and which recur through different times and places) suggests that theorizing is appropriate in area studies and indeed necessary if we are to explain social phenomena rather than merely describe events. But this raises a new question: Is there any sense in which theoretical beliefs may be said to be objective and true? A skeptic might maintain what philosophers refer to as "conceptual relativism." On this view, the researcher must employ some set of explanatory categories to impose order on the diverse phenomena, but many schemes would do equally well and no objective basis exists for favoring one scheme over another. This means that the theoretical order the scientist "discovers" in the data is an artifact of the particular but arbitrary features of the theoretical presuppositions the scientist brings to the investigation. Consider an example: Elizabeth Perry's analysis of the Red Spears rebellion in contrast to Susan Naquin's analysis of the Eight Trigrams rebellion. Both Perry and Naquin are concerned with peasant rebellions that have a strong component of White Lotus activity in circumstances of ecological crisis. However, the two authors offer radically different explanations of these phenomena. Perry analyzes the Red Spears rebellion in terms that emphasize peasant rationality, survival strategies, ecological constraints and opportunities, and the like, whereas Naquin emphasizes the importance of the millenarian worldview, the religious motivations of the adherent, and particulars of White Lotus organizational resources. Naquin pays relatively little attention to material factors or rational decision making. Our conceptual relativist might maintain that this shows that there is no "true" analysis of either rebellion; the data can be organized according to either framework.

Against this view I would hold that this overstates the indeterminacy of such disputes. The dispute between two such theories as Naquin's and Perry's can be minimized. Empirical and explanatory requirements significantly constrain the correctness of a given interpretation. The applicability of a theoretical construct to a historical phenomenon can be evaluated with some objectivity. Consider the moral economy approach to peasant rebellions: the investigator looks for shared moral ideas, a sense of injustice, and relatively wide group identity. In the hands of an uncritical researcher the available data could be forced into these categories. But the investigator could conclude that this theoretical framework fits the data badly; that is, it is possible to arrive at a fairly objective conclusion that a given theory does not accurately describe the underlying social processes.

These considerations suggest that the formulation of theoretical models has an important role within applied social science. A number of cautions concerning the use of social theory have emerged from these studies, however. First, the grand concepts of social theory—capitalism, feudalism, Oriental despotism—have created problems through their extreme generality. When the investigator comes to the study of traditional China with the question "Was this a protocapitalist system?", he or she risks overlooking the distinctive features of the Chinese economy in an eagerness to assimilate it to a preconceived model. This suggests not that the investigator should put aside conceptual equipment when approaching the study of China but that he or she should bring middle-level concepts in terms of which to analyze the specifics of the Chinese economy instead of a comprehensive model. The concepts of class, bureaucracy, local elites, marketing systems, and many others are social science concepts developed in a variety of contexts, and they are of enormous value in making sense of the Chinese phenomena. But the particular constellation of factors in China cannot be predicted.

Second, much contemporary social theory has been constructed on the basis of acquaintance with European examples. The models of feudal and capitalist economies, the process of economic development based on Britain, the conception of the state as a rational center of power that dominates civil society, the concepts of imperialism and colonialism—all these derive more or less directly from the historical experience of Western Europe. In many ways, however, that was exceptional, and models based on it may export badly to the social, political, and economic arrangements of Asia and other non-European societies. It is particularly important in this context to cast doubt on certain stereotyped contrasts and models of development: traditional-modern, feudal-capitalist, and stagnant-dynamic—a point Paul Cohen (1984) emphasizes in his recommendations for a "China-centered" approach to the study of China.

This caution suggests not that the social scientific study of Asian societies requires new concepts and models tailored to the historical experience of Asia but that the investigator be self-consciously aware of the distinctiveness of the European experience and select and modify theoretical models according to the particulars of the Asian examples being examined. It was argued above that cross-cultural causal processes derive from common material circumstances and some particulars of human nature; these processes justify some confidence that the experience of Europe will have some bearing on understanding the experience of Asia as well. But it must be remembered that diversity is as much the rule as homogeneity, and the researcher must insure that concepts and theories mesh with the local phenomena.

These cautions point up what is perhaps a chief task of social theory: the careful formulation and articulation of concepts and schemes of classification in terms of which to analyze diverse social phenomena. In this book we have seen points at which poor concept formation led to bad social science. The reification of the concept of riot, the uncritical projection of the model of capitalism to traditional China, the carelessness sometimes associated with the concept of class, and the vagueness of the concept of subsistence—in each case the explanations and analysis of the local phenomena could be enhanced by a more developed and articulated discussion of the pertinent concepts and theories.

I will raise a final qualification concerning the scope of scientific social theory. Is it possible to construct a science of history (for example, as a sequence of modes of production) or a science of society in general (universal laws of social organization and change) or a science of a given society as a whole (such as British society in the nineteenth century)? The treatment of causal laws and regularities above entails negative answers to each question. The problem with each task is the comprehensiveness of its ambitions; each aims at a full explanation of a dense range of social phenomena. The implicit assumption must be that there is a short list of "social causes" to which all historical and social phenomena are reducible. But this is enormously implausible.

Social science should be approached in an unabashedly pluralistic way: any given social theory identifies one type of social cause or mechanism, but there exists no a priori way to identify the factors relevant to a given process, and certainly no ultimate, monocausal theory to which all types of social change can be reduced. This view does not entail conceptual relativism, and it does not reduce scientific objectivity. Rather, it reflects the idea (advanced by Weber, among others) that there can be no finite list of potentially relevant social causes and influences; consequently, there can be no final social science. This recognition, though, would invalidate the idea that Marxism, semiotics, or general equilibrium theory contain the general solution for all problems of social explanation.

Chapter 7
Explanation

A central aim of every case considered in this book is to provide a scientific *explanation* of a range of social phenomena. What features do these explanations have in common? Two elements are especially important: the assumption that social phenomena can be explained as the aggregate result of rational individual behavior, and the assumption that social phenomena admit of causal explanation. It will emerge that these two claims are in fact compatible with one another; the first provides a general account of some of the main types of social mechanism that underlie the second.

An Explanatory Paradigm

Studies of rural Asia reveal a wide and complex range of putative explanations: narrative accounts of historical events (Naquin's treatment of the Eight Trigrams rebellion), rational choice explanations of large-scale political phenomena (Perry's explanation of the Nian rebellion), causal explanations of social phenomena based on material factors (Perry) or normative factors (Scott), and explanations of large-scale historical patterns based on general equilibrium models (Skinner's central-place theory). The underlying assumptions about explanation on which the authors rely, however, have much in common. Their diversity concerns distinctions in emphasis within a core model of explanation rather than different assumptions about social explanation.

These are some of the main explanations we have surveyed (and a few that we have only mentioned):

- The low level of successful collective action in Vietnamese village society is best explained as the result of individually rational decision making on the part of villagers (Popkin 1979:24–25)
- The Saya San rebellion occurred because local elites and the state were unresponsive to peasant subsistence rights during a period of subsistence crisis (Scott 1976:149–56)

- Peasants revolt out of a sense of moral outrage (Scott 1976:3)
- Marketing systems (networks of market towns and surrounding villages) in rural China had a roughly hexagonal structure because this arrangement minimizes transport cost (Skinner 1964–65:22–28)
- The Eight Trigrams rebellion occurred as a result of the millenarian beliefs of White Lotus sectaries in North China (Naquin 1976)
- Chinese agriculture stagnated because it was trapped in rising man–land ratios (Chao 1986)
- The Shandong rebellion occurred because the authorities arrested Wang Lun (Naquin 1981)
- The Taiping rebellion succeeded in the first year because it leapfrogged the ability of the Qing state to organize a coherent military response (Kuhn 1980)
- English agriculture experienced a breakthrough to sustained economic growth because English property relations and political powers enabled capitalist landlords to earn profits in farming (Brenner 1976)

Can we make any generalizations about these examples? First, it seems clear that causal analysis is prominent among these examples, with different explanations singling out varying aspects of a causal relation. Thus Brenner, Kuhn, and Naquin (1976) identify *background causal conditions* (persistent institutional or cultural arrangements) of the explanandum; Scott and Popkin refer to the *process* through which the explanandum comes about; and Naquin (1981) refers to an instigating *event* within a large causal field. Many of these examples implicitly conform to the following conception of explanation:

> To explain an event or standing condition, it is necessary to identify the causal field within which that event or condition is located: the background conditions that influence it, the laws or processes that bring it about, and the particular events or circumstances that instigate it.

This condition expresses the idea that explanation of an event centrally involves knowing why the event came about: what the relevant background conditions and events were and what the processes were through which those events gave rise to the explanandum. (This principle also suggests a comparative study of comparable circumstances in which various elements of the causal field are missing; does the explanandum occur or not? This approach is central to Skocpol's [1979] treatment of revolution and Brenner's [1976] analysis of agrarian change in England and France.)

Second, assumptions about individual motivation and the process of individual decision making are central to virtually all of these explanations. Scott and Naquin refer to normative sources of action; Popkin, Skinner, and Chao to calculations of rational self-interest; Marks, Brenner, and Lippit to material class interests. In most cases the author explains the explanandum as the aggregate of many individuals acting deliberately within a social and natural environment. This feature is subordinate to the causal point, however, in that it describes a chief mechanism through which social changes occur (in the judgment of these investigators, in any case). This view may be put in terms of a view about the nature of social processes of development or change:

A social event, occurrence, or condition is best explained as the aggregate consequence, intended or unintended, of many individuals acting on the basis of specific motives within a particular environment of action.

This proposition describes the typical social *mechanism* through which causal links are established among social phenomena. Social structures, institutions, practices, and the like have causal powers only insofar as they influence the behavior of the individuals who operate and act within them. The problem for the social investigator, then, is to discover the main forms of motivation and deliberation present in a given social context and the salient features of the natural and social environment within which individuals are forced to act. Each case discussed here makes such assumptions; the chief dichotomy among them is between those that emphasize rational self-interest and those that stress extra-rational factors (normative, religious, magical influences on action). This model may be described as an "aggregative" model of explanation; it holds that social phenomena should be explained as the aggregate consequence of individual behavior.

Third, several of these examples employ social structures, institutions, and systems to explain the explanandum. Chao and Skinner, for example, explain features of the Chinese rural economy as a manifestation of a form of economic equilibrium; they conceive of the economy as an abstract system of transactions regulated by prices and work out the equilibrium conditions of this system given its initial conditions. Brenner and Lippit refer to a set of social institutions—property and land tenure arrangements—as the background condition that explains the process of change he is concerned with. And Kuhn refers to the comparative efficiency of two organizational forms (the Qing military bureaucracy and the Taiping organization). This feature of these explanations involves attention to the social environment of individual action. Thus a set of land tenure relations constitutes a regulative system that constrains individual choices. They are enforced coercively—either by the landlord or by the state. And they define both opportunities and limits on the strategies that individuals may use to further their interests.

The organization of the Qing military bureaucracy is a different sort of example. The best explanation for the particulars of this organization is that the central imperial government was determined to prevent concentration of armed force in the hands of provincial military authorities; to avoid this undesirable outcome, strict rules for the distribution of forces in the countryside were created. Once this system of military control was put into place, however, the friction of distance and administrative procedures entailed that forming a large military force in response to rebellion would be a slow process—leaving open the possibility that rebel organization might leapfrog the state's preparations.[1]

These points may be formulated as another thesis about social explanation:

Social institutions and practices are regulative systems that define opportunities and constraints that guide, limit, and inspire individual action.

Explanations in terms of social institutions and systems, then, may also be assimilated to the basic causal model described above; they constitute part of the social environment of action within which individuals act and thus constitute background causal conditions. Institutions work only through the individuals who constitute them, and they themselves are to be explained in terms of the incentives and constraints that define the environment of action of the individuals who created them.

A fourth observation is that several of these explanations are put forward as *historical* explanations: explanations of particular events or changes in terms of the conditions and events in the context of which the explanandum occurred. Naquin and Kuhn are concerned with particular historical developments; their explanations depend on canvassing the circumstances surrounding these events and discovering the influences—some highly contingent and some discernibly law governed—that gave rise to the event in the way that it occurred. This appears to be a pragmatic feature of explanation; what distinguishes Kuhn or Naquin from Popkin or Perry, primarily, is a concern for the details of the historical process. Popkin and Perry are more interested in the general processes and background conditions that lead to rebellion, while Kuhn and Naquin emphasize the particular and contingent circumstances that led to the unique features of *these* rebellions.[2]

These observations suggest that it is possible to construct a model of explanation that fits all these cases relatively well, with different emphases in different cases. To explain a social event it is necessary to show why the event occurred, to discover its causal antecedents. In the social world the chief mechanism of change is individual action within a specific social and natural environment. On this model, an explanation of a social phenomenon E (event, change of state, chronic pattern) requires the following elements: (1) An account of the institutions and practices (C) at the local level within the context of which persons act; (2) An account of the motives, beliefs, and process of deliberation (I) through which persons act; and (3) An account of the means by which individuals acting within these circumstances leads to the observed outcome. Such an explanation, then, would ideally be an explicit deductive argument linking antecedent conditions with the explanandum:

> A derivation of a description of E as the aggregate consequence of the actions of a group of persons with motives and beliefs I within circumstances C.

Different authors emphasize different parts of this explanatory model; some stress institutional background conditions, others the pathways of individual decision making and action, and still others the contingent events that influence the process.

This account suggests an important difference between typical social science explanations and typical natural science explanations: the character of the law-governed processes through which change is thought to occur. Causal systems among natural phenomena are thought to be governed by strict laws of nature (putting aside quantum phenomena). Causal relations are mediated by *mechanisms* in the strict sense, so that whenever the same set of antecedent conditions obtains, the consequent occurs as well. This strict necessity of physical causation is interpreted as deriving from the real physical properties of the entities involved in the causal system.[3] Whatever the adequacy of the idea of strict causal necessity in natural science, however, the idea has no application to the processes identified in this model of social explanation. Rather than exceptionless laws of nature mediating antecedent conditions and outcome, this model postulates that the behavior of large numbers of individuals mediates antecedent conditions and outcome. And individual behavior is postulated to be deliberate (and thus rule-governed) but not causally determined by factors outside the agent's intentional control. Regularities of behavior will arise because individuals are making rational decisions, but these regularities are not strict, exceptionless, or mechanical.

If the regularities that derive from rational action are not mechanical, neither are they merely statistical generalizations. That peasants tend to revert to food crops in place of commercial crops in times of rapidly fluctuating prices is not a mere description of a statistical regularity; it can be interpreted in terms of simple hypotheses about the peasant farmer's goals and beliefs about the near-term economic environment. The observed substitution is rational, and the resulting regularity is the predictable consequence of many peasants making this rational decision.[4]

Generalizations can be made about the explanatory practices of all these cases, then. Each depends on a fairly simple model of causal explanation of an event or process in terms of standing conditions and instigating conditions, and each postulates a mechanism of social causation that works through the intentional behavior of human beings. In contrast to the view that the social sciences are radically distinct from the natural sciences, in this regard natural and social science share an important element. The chief distinction between a causal explanation in natural science (for example, of weather phenomena) and one in social science (for example, of peasant rebellion) concerns the mechanism of causation and the regularities that govern that mechanism. In the social science examples considered here, the mechanism is the intentional behavior of human beings rather than the law-governed properties of nonhuman entities.

Rational Choice Explanations

The rational choice model of explanation stresses participant motivations and rational decision making, attempting to explain social phenomena as the aggregate of rational individual decision making within structured circumstances of choice. And in fact, many of the explanations considered above depend on a framework of rational choice explanation. Recall some of the cases that assume individual rationality in constructing explanations of diverse phenomena. Two authors, Popkin and Perry, employ the concept of individual self-interest to explain political behavior. Two others, Skinner and Chao, use the tools of microeconomics to explain aggregate patterns of economic development (patterns of settlement, technological stagnation)—thus presupposing economic rationality on the part of participants. And Lippit, Brenner, and Marks employ a Marxist variant of rational choice analysis, an analysis that attempts to explain collective political behavior in terms of individuals' efforts to further their class interests. Even Scott's formulation of the moral economy framework has an important rational choice component; his peasants act on a risk-averse principle rather than a "greatest expected utility" principle but are equally deliberative and purposeful.

What these stories share is an explanatory strategy. To explain a given social phenomenon, it is sufficient to account for: (1) the circumstances of choice that constitute the environment of action; (2) the strategies that rational, prudent persons would pursue in those circumstances; and (3) the aggregate effects of those strategies. A rational choice framework holds that a social pattern or development may be explained as the aggregate consequence of the rational actions of many participants, given their social and natural environment. Perry explains the emergence of Nian armies as the result of local predatorial strategies of survival; Popkin explains the failure of collective action in village societies as the effect of free rider choices; and Lippit explains the stagnation of Chinese agriculture as the absence of incentives and opportunities toward technological innovation by landlords and peasants.

Aggregative Explanation

The central assumptions of rational choice models are these: (1) human beings are deliberative; (2) human beings are capable of forming true beliefs about their natural and social environment; and (3) human beings are concerned about individual and family material welfare and are disposed to act in such a way as to protect and, if possible, enhance their future welfare. The central goal of rational choice models is: (4) to explain aggregate social patterns or events as the consequence (intended or unintended) of processes of rational individual decision making within a specific social and natural environment. Each feature of this model requires comment.

Premise (1) refers to the individual's capacity to deliberate among alternative actions.[5] The assumption of deliberativeness amounts to the view that humans act on the basis of reasons and means-end calculation. It assumes that persons are capable of surveying a range of choices at a given moment and of predicting the probable consequences of each choice; that is, they are aware of how their environment influences their welfare. They then choose an action from the possible choices. This account is deliberately vague concerning the principle of choice. We may imagine that the decision is influenced by the probable consequences of the chosen action, the consistency between a given action and an accepted moral rule, the consistency between a given action and one's model of the exemplary person, and so forth. The assumption of deliberativeness thus does not entail that the process involves maximizing good consequences (welfare, utility, income); it is consistent both with satisficing behavior (Simon 1979) and with risk-aversive rules of choice like the minimax rule. And this assumption is offered as a capacity of human beings, not an invariable and pure feature of action. Plainly, persons sometimes act impulsively, without deliberation.

Premise (2) represents a hypothesis about causal knowledge: human beings can arrive at veridical beliefs about the gross causal properties of their immediate environment and can act prudently on the basis of these beliefs. Thus early agriculture depended on humans' ability to somehow understand the causal relations among water, soil, and seed; and the history of any system of farming, in any part of the world, illustrates the ability of "primitive" farmers to arrive at subtle and accurate beliefs about the technique and circumstances of farming. But similar points may be made about the social environment; peasants can assess the fluctuating strength of the central authorities, for example, in determining whether to participate in a rice riot.

Once again, this assumption is intended to be modest. It does not assert that individuals have accurate beliefs about the whole of their environment or that magical thinking plays no role in belief formation. Rather, persons have the capacity to form factual beliefs about those aspects of the environment of greatest practical import to their material welfare and security.

Premise (3) represents a theory of the core interests that underlie most human activity. Let us understand the term *welfare* to refer to the individual's means of satisfying basic subsistence and consumption needs—food, clothing, shelter, education, and entertainment—and the conditions of security that permit the individual to rely on the ability to continue to satisfy those needs. (In addition, one might include autonomy and basic liberties.)[6] Premise (3) holds that the goal of satisfying minimal welfare needs is central to all human environments. It asserts *not* that material interests are the only relevant motivation but rather that welfare concerns are motivationally important, whatever else may influence choice.

This assumption does not equate with egoism, for several reasons: it is narrower, referring only to material interests; and it is broader, allowing that individuals may be directly motivated by family welfare interests. Most important, however, this premise does not postulate that welfare concerns exhaust the motivational arsenal; it leaves it open that individuals may have nonwelfare motives as well.

These assumptions about rationality, then, are fairly weak. But they are enough to permit an important inference. In circumstances where welfare factors are the sole relevant motivation, we would expect deliberative individuals to pursue a maximizing rule of choice. Suppose that possible actions a and b each increase family welfare with the same probability; the welfare (W) produced by a is greater than that produced by b—that is, $W(a) > W(b)$—and no other relevant difference exists between a and b. (That is, neither a nor b offends local moral sensibilities, neither involves betraying a friend, neither involves having to look ridiculous in front of one's peers.) Unavoidably, then, a deliberative reasoner concerned with family welfare will prefer a over b. But note that maximizing behavior has emerged from this framework rather than being built into it.

These premises constitute a version of the foundations of applied rational choice models; let us now turn to their goal. The goal is to attempt to explain large-scale social, economic, and political phenomena as the aggregate, often unintended outcome of individual rational decision making. Here the formal tools of rational choice theory are of value; for this family of disciplines offers a variety of analytical techniques for deriving the aggregate effects of the actions of many rational decision makers. Game theory, collective action theory, and marginalist economic theory each provide aggregation techniques for a range of situations within which rational decision makers act: strategic conflict and cooperation, public goods problems, and markets.

Examples of such explanations drawn from the cases above include Popkin's account of collective action problems in village society, Perry's account of the emergence of rebellion as the unintended consequence of individual strategies of survival, and Skinner's account of the topology of the placement of villages, towns, and cities. In each case the author identifies a pattern of rational individual behavior responding to a set of incentives and constraints, and then attempts to show how this pattern of individual behavior aggregates into the observed macropattern.

Social Constraints on Choice

Rational choice theories of social phenomena stress the natural and social environment within which persons act. Particularly important is that some features of the social environment may be described abstractly in terms that permit cross-cultural application. To the extent that these abstract characterizations capture the salient elements of the institutions—the elements that motivate and constrain individuals—consequences can be drawn about the effects of these structures in a variety of societies without needing detailed information about the cultural specifics.

Paradigm examples of institutions, structures, or practices that are applied cross-culturally in these studies include these:

- Forms of labor organization: family farming, wage labor, cooperative labor
- Surplus extraction systems and property: taxation, interest, rent, corvée labor
- Institutions of village governance: elites, village council
- Commercialization: exchange, markets, prices, subsistence cash crops, and systems of transportation and communication
- Organized social violence: banditry, piracy, local militias
- Extralocal political organizations: court, military, taxation, law

These represent institutions, practices, organizations, and social forms that may be found in various social contexts—China, Vietnam, Indonesia, medieval France, contemporary Iowa. They constitute part of the social and material environment in the context of which rural people (peasants) live their lives and to which these folk adapt their behavior. And some of these authors show that some features of various rural societies can be explained by analyzing the effects of such institutions on the decision-making processes of the participants—with no more specific information about local cultural variations.

Does this mean that these are "value-neutral" descriptions of institutions? No. Rather, these institutions and practices must be understood in the context of the core conception of rationality described above. Peasants, on this approach, are presumed to consider existing circumstances of commercialization and choose farming strategies accordingly. They attribute the appropriate economic significance to markets, prices, cash incomes, and so on. Likewise, they are presumed to know the implications of various land-tenancy arrangements, credit arrangements, and tax-distribution schemes and to prefer those that minimize obligation and risk; once again, we assume that they take a calculating stance toward these arrangements. In short, the core conception of deliberative rationality permits us to put forth a core conception of material and social institutions and practices and to postulate that peasants orient their behavior toward these practices accordingly.

Scope and Limits of Rational Choice Explanations

The rational choice approach in applied social research does have limitations. The above assumptions about rational action and belief provide a schematic conception of at least one important dimension of human action in varying natural and social circumstances; they imply, ceteris paribus, that individuals will act to protect and further their material interests. However, this set of assumptions is not advanced as a complete theory of motivation, psychology, or value for human beings everywhere; it is intended instead to describe one central, and relatively fixed, element of individual action.

It is thus necessary to define fairly precisely what rational choice explanations are intended to accomplish. If they are advanced as concrete descriptions of all forms of behavior, then the ethnographic response is decisive: the rational choice description is too abstract to be accepted. But rational choice explanations can be (and should be) limited in several ways. First, they ought not be assumed to be relevant to every type of socially significant behavior. Thus religious or familial behavior *may* reflect motives that are quite uncalculating and independent of material interests. On the other hand, farmers' agricultural decisions may reasonably be treated using the rational choice model. Second, rational choice explanations are based on an assumption of normal or typical forms of behavior. Even though each individual's action may diverge from the purely rational for various reasons, the assumption is that rational calculation influences individual behavior and that the contrary influences tend to counter-balance one another in a reasonably large group.

Third, the level of description appropriate to rational choice explanations has important limits. Consider Geertz's analysis of agricultural involution. If our only concern is to know why involution occurs, it is sufficient to identify the links between involution and the material interests of the persons involved. But if we want to know how the involuted institutions came into being, how they function in Java, and what concrete beliefs and values the Javanese villager brings to involution—we must revert to the level of ethnographic inquiry.

Note, finally, what the rational choice model does *not* assume: it does not assume that peasants are rational calculators in all spheres of life (for example, sport, love, or friendship) or that they are welfarist in relation to all their social institutions (for example, religion). Consequently it does not assume that all aspects of social life can be explained as the aggregate outcome of rational individual decision making. To describe fully the psychology and motivations of persons within a given culture, it would be necessary to go beyond a sparse rational choice model—to understand the symbolic systems, the cultural and religious commitments, the jokes and irrational aversions that comprise action in concrete specificity. We would need, that is, a full ethnographic study of this people. The attraction of a rational choice model is simply that it offers to explain *certain* structural facts about traditional societies without such information. And its confidence in this program derives from a cluster of supposed facts about the circumstances of human life and the nature of human deliberativeness.

Throughout this book we have been concerned with the problem of explaining agrarian societies. How well or poorly does the rational choice model fit this range of phenomena? There seem to be good reasons to believe that this framework is illuminating in this context. For the social and technical circumstances of traditional agriculture plainly affect the material welfare of the individuals and families who abide within them. And many of the concrete choices that confront the peasant are relatively free of other influences—religious, political, ideological. Cropping decisions (what crop to cultivate), investment behavior, purchase and sale of land, work-sharing arrangements with other poor peasants, patron-client relations—all of these situations (and many others) pose problems of choice for peasants that manifestly affect their material interests. The central structural factors of peasant social life are thus germane to the rational choice model. If we now apply our two assumptions, deliberativeness and welfare orientation, and we assume further that other motivational factors are absent, we may then infer that peasants will behave in ways most advantageous to their perceived individual and family interests. They will choose to maximize family welfare (which may, of course, involve minimizing risk rather than maximizing income).

If these fairly innocuous assumptions are accepted, then there is a good a priori justification for applying rational choice analysis to important aspects of traditional social life. In particular, given the close connection between the institutions that define traditional agriculture and the material needs of peasants, this model would lead us to expect that peasants will act in a calculated and rational way about those institutions. Likewise, given the proximity of surplus extraction systems—taxation, credit, rent, corvée labor—to the material needs of peasants, this hypothesis would lead us to expect that peasant behavior in relation to these institutions will be calculated and prudent.

The assumptions of deliberativeness and welfare orientation thus satisfy some contexts of traditional life particularly well. This suggests that individuals in those circumstances will, on average, behave rationally and in turn that the aggregate features of those parts of social life should be explainable on the basis of a rational choice analysis.

If we assume further that traditional agriculture is organized through competitive markets in labor, land, and capital, then this conclusion permits us to apply the tools of microeconomics to peasant agriculture.[7] We saw in chapter 4 that Kang Chao (1986) analyzes the traditional Chinese agricultural sector in terms of the concept of the marginal product of labor and land and argues that this analysis explains important features of traditional Chinese society—for example, the tendencies toward higher rates of tenancy and agricultural stagnation.

The rational-choice framework would appear to provide a credible basis to analyze and explain many features of agrarian life. The same limits discussed here hold when applying this approach to peasant societies, of course; for even rational peasants have a diverse set of motives, a range of social practices, only some of which appear to evoke the calculating rationality presupposed by the model of rational decision making, and so forth. Yet the rational choice and materialist models survive the criticisms addressed to them by interpretation theory.

Applied rational choice theory as developed here offers the basis for a rapprochement between rational choice theory and interpretation theory. The two represent different levels of description of the motives and actions of concrete individuals. Rational choice theory abstracts from the richness of human experience and singles out material welfare as the central goal of action; it abstracts from the complex, many-sided character of decision making and describes a logically structured process of predicting consequences, assessing probability and risk, and choosing among definite alternatives. For some purposes this level of detail suffices to permit us to understand individual action and explain aggregate patterns; for other purposes, it is necessary to detail more fully the individual's values, meanings, jokes, and worldview.

Cultural Relativity and Agency

The rational choice framework encounters strenuous criticism from some social scientists and philosophers. An important strand of thought in the philosophy of social science holds that social science unavoidably depends on the interpretation of meaningful human behavior and social practices and that those meanings and practices are highly culture-specific. As a result, a cross-cultural concept of rationality that might provide a basis for explanation of social phenomena cannot be constructed. Wilhelm Dilthey's hermeneutics sociology represents an early formulation of this approach, and the writings of Clifford Geertz and Marshall Sahlins have developed and refined the view. This approach—which may be broadly described as interpretive social science—is distinctly unsympathetic to rational choice social science. Significantly, virtually all of the theories surveyed here fall within a broadly materialist, rational choice framework. If the interpretive social science framework offers telling arguments, our cases should be affected.

The philosopher Charles Taylor has written extensively on the interpretive character of social explanation. He holds that the distinctive feature of the human sciences is that they involve the interpretation of the self-understandings of human beings. In the opening sentence of "Interpretation and the Sciences of Man" he asks rhetorically, "Is there a sense in which interpretation is essential to explanation in the sciences of man?" (1985b:15), and throughout a series of essays he argues for an affirmative answer to the question. The social sciences are unavoidably "hermeneutical": they involve the effort "to make clear, to make sense of, an object of study" (15). Taylor argues that it is impossible to characterize human behavior properly except in terms of the meanings and intentions that behavior represents: "To be a full human agent, to be a person or a self in the ordinary meaning, is to exist in a space defined by distinctions of worth. . . . My claim is that this is not just a contingent fact about human agents, but is essential to what we would understand and recognize as full, normal human agency" (1985a:3). Good social science is therefore forced to confront social phenomena as a meaningful "text" that can be decoded only through interpreting the meanings, values, beliefs, and reasons of the persons who constitute that social order, and those meanings and values are highly culture specific.

The interpretive paradigm insists on the fundamental cultural variability of human meanings, with the result that frameworks that abstract from the cultural particulars will unavoidably disregard the essential. Thus Clifford Geertz maintains that systematic unpacking of local meanings is mandatory for social inquiry because few, if any, transcultural universals exist in either society or individual.[8] Even the concept of the person is culturally specific; so it is impossible to make generalizations about even the most basic features of human aspiration and self-conception. Geertz writes: "The Western conception of the person as a bounded, unique, more or less integrated motivational and cognitive universe, a dynamic center of awareness, emotion, judgment, and action organized into a distinctive whole and set contrastively both against other such wholes and against its social and natural background, is, however incorrigible it may seem to us, a rather peculiar idea within the context of the world's cultures" (1983:59). In light of this radical diversity of human selfhood across cultures, the anthropologist is strictly obliged to attempt to work out the *local* system of values, conceptions, beliefs, and the like through which local people conceive themselves and constitute their social world. It would appear to follow, however, that social science inquiries premised on some set of core characteristics of human motivation—for example, self-interest—are radically misguided.

A related complaint against rational choice theory is that this framework places narrowly defined economic interests at the center of the theory of individual motivation and economic institutions at the center of the theory of social change. Some critics hold that both assumptions are radically unsupportable. It is not possible to define economic interests independent from the culturally specific norms and values through which individuals construe their social environment; and it is unacceptably reductionist to suppose that material economic institutions "underlie" other social institutions. Thus Geertz writes in the following terms: "[Economism] is the view that the moving forces in individual behaviour (and thus in society, which is taken to be an aggregate of individual behaviours or some stratificational arrangement of them) are those of a need-driven utility seeker manoeuvring for advantage within the context of material possibilities and normative constraints" (1984:516). Geertz holds that the rational choice enterprise cannot even begin because the concept of need is itself a cultural particular; there is no culture-independent way to characterize the needs that persons are postulated to seek to satisfy. This claim may be put in the following terms:

> Needs and interests are always culturally defined, so to apply the core conception to a particular society we must engage in the hermeneutic project in order to discover what local standards of need are.

Against "economism" Geertz calls for inquiry into the complex cultural context of a given social phenomenon, and he insists that we can understand a given society only within a framework of analysis that fully emphasizes the distinctive *cultural* features of that society—its religious views, its moral and normative context, and the categories of the worldviews of its members.[9]

The criticisms considered above converge on a methodological maxim:

> To explain a social phenomenon, it is necessary to have detailed, culturally specific understanding of the complex worldview—

beliefs, values, norms—within the context of which individuals in that culture act.

This position thus expresses fundamental skepticism about the project of explaining social phenomena on the basis of an abstract analysis of means-end rationality and an abstract, materialistic account of goals and beliefs.

Geertz presents a negative methodological maxim here: that a certain kind of social science is wrong-headed or impossible and that culture must be brought back into social science. However, the scope of Geertz's complaints needs to be clarified. What sort of methodological advice is Geertz intending to provide: advice for all social scientists and all research questions or advice for ethnographers? For some purposes, the highly particularistic investigation that Geertz recommends is clearly unavoidable. Thus the cultural anthropologist who attempts merely to assimilate the subjects' behavior to a utility-maximizing model has no doubt left out much of critical interest for an ethnographer. We want to know, paraphrasing Geertz in a different context, what it is like to be Balinese, and this requires reference to symbolic systems, religious practices, and meaningful patterns of social behavior.

But Geertz's view is more general; he appears to hold that no social inquiry concerning Bali that does not employ a fine-grained account of Balinese culture is possible. This claim is less obvious than the former; it is not clear that *every* program of research into things Balinese is equally tied to the features of Balinese culture. Balinese peasants are as likely as anyone else to do their marketing in the market town that is easiest to get to; they are as likely to prefer a shorter working day to a longer; and they are as likely to calculate the probability of success before deciding to join a tax riot. This suggests, however, that a rational choice framework has traction on these aspects of Balinese social behavior and that predictable aggregate patterns should ensue—for example, concerning the placement of villages or towns in the countryside.

Consider Geertz's point about the cultural specificity of needs. Some needs obviously are culturally specific, such as the medieval lord's need for martial skills, the Confucian scholar's need for tranquility, or the American teenager's need for loud music. But it is less clear that all needs vary this much, and the needs identified in the core conception appear to be human rather than cultural. Food, shelter, clothing, personal security, medical services—these are practical needs that all humans have and recognize and that much practical activity is directed to satisfy.

Evans-Pritchard's observations about the centrality of practical pursuits in traditional and primitive societies is a useful corrective to the cultural relativism implicit in these criticisms:

> Most specialists who are also fieldworkers are agreed that primitive peoples are predominantly interested in practical economic pursuits: gardening, hunting, fishing, care of cattle, and the manufacture of weapons, utensils and ornaments, and in their social contacts; the life of household, family and kin, relations with friends and neighbours, with superiors and inferiors, dance and feasts, legal disputes, feuds and warfare. Behaviour of a mystical type in the main is restricted to certain situations in social life. (Evans-Pritchard 1934:9)

Against the view that each culture is radically incommensurate with all others, Evans-Pritchard maintains that a large core of practical activities may be found among diverse cultures and that these activities are oriented toward satisfying core needs.

Geertz's case for radical cultural relativity, then, would appear to be overdrawn. Some features of Balinese culture are wholly singular and unique, and the explanation and analysis of these features will require reference to the cultural matrix of Bali. But it follows neither that *all* features of Balinese life are unique and particular nor that there is not a range of social behavior in which Balinese peasants behave much like peasants elsewhere—with a prudent regard for their welfare and security interests.

A more general reply is also available to the rational choice framework. For the interpretive framework insists primarily on the centrality of human *agency* in social phenomena. But it is noteworthy that all the cases considered here accept the basic point that social phenomena depend on human action, which requires that we understand human agency.[10] Unlike the behaviorist theories that are the primary target of Charles Taylor's criticisms, the theories considered here do not attempt to abstract away the features of agency that underlie social processes. These authors accept, with Taylor and Geertz, that human beings are not causally determined systems but act on the basis of wants, desires, beliefs, norms, values, and worldviews. The question is, at what level should these components of agency be described?

Here we find sharp disagreement between most of our authors and the interpretive program. The interpretive framework holds that it is impossible to arrive at an abstract, supracultural conception of human agency; rather, the particulars of human agency must be constructed for each specific culture. The Balinese notable, the French Catholic peasant, and the American businessperson have radically different conceptions of themselves and their relations to other persons; they have radically different goals and aspirations; they embody strikingly different moral and religious worldviews; so in general, to understand their actions, this vast, complex, and culturally specific set of representations must be decoded.

For the rational choice theories considered here, by contrast, it is *not* held necessary to engage in this sort of detailed cultural excavation—for many explanatory purposes. (It goes without saying that such cultural investigation *is* necessary for some purposes.) These theories hold instead that an abstract characterization of agency that is cross-cultural and universal can be provided. The premises about agency go something like this:

> All persons in every culture are agents whose actions reflect a core of instrumental rationality on the basis of which they make decisions about their practical lives.

> The sphere of practical life includes those activities through which agents satisfy their material needs and those social and political arrangements that either facilitate or threaten those needs.

These propositions have a specific standing: they are high-level empirical generalizations and are intended to describe only a part of the person's agency. The claim is, then, that important cultural differences may exist among persons at the level of agency but that these differences are superimposed over a structure of practical rationality that has an environmental and biological base; it is through this faculty of practical reasoning that human beings have solved problems of subsistence. And once having identified this core of practical rationality, several of these theorists believe that important social phenomena can be explained by postulating nothing more than this core. Other social phenomena, however, may be more recalcitrant, and perhaps we may have to provide culturally specific interpretations of agency in these cases.

Thus many of the theories discussed above finesse the interpretive problem by postulating a core conception of the agent—whether Chinese peasant, Vietnamese notable, medieval lord, or modern European farmer—in which a process of means-end rationality centrally influences action. It is assumed, first, that we can identify a set of universal core goals or values (among, no doubt, a larger set of culturally specific goals). These include individual and family welfare and security. Second, it is assumed that all persons are capable of deliberating about the causal order in which they find themselves and assessing the potential means available to them in pursuit of their goals. Finally, it is assumed that the person is disposed to choose a strategy from among the possible range of actions that is likely to achieve the goal. These assumptions are put forward as empirical hypotheses about human motivation and action—*not* as an a priori requirement or action.

To the extent that this schematic account of human motivation is plausible, however, the interpretive imperative will be less compelling in application to some research problems in social science than in others. For in some cases a social regularity could be explained as the consequence of rational individual decision making, with no culturally specific interpretation. Many of the explanations surveyed above are premised only on a description of the material circumstances of life—the technical requirements of agriculture, the incentives and disincentives posed to individuals through various institutions, and so on. Such explanations do not require that the researcher provide a thick description of the significance of various elements of the social world from the participant's point of view; instead, they purport to explain important social and demographic changes as the result of rational adjustments to a new environment of choice. The rational choice framework can be described as sharing central assumptions with the interpretive paradigm; the difference between the two has rather to do with secondary assumptions about the universality of certain forms of human intentionality (means-end rationality).

Does this position imply that *no* important cultural particulars can be understood only in terms of the significance that peasants attribute to these practices and institutions? No; tenant-client relations may be embedded in moral or religious understanding, as well as economic-political calculations of advantage. What this view is committed to, however, is that the economic-political aspects of land tenancy systems are universally salient and play some important role in explaining peasant behavior of the peasant and that in some cases a fuller and culturally informed interpretation of the self-interpretation of these social relations is unnecessary.

Let us assess the interpretive challenge to the rational choice approach. Is it reasonable to hold that all social sciences must employ a hermeneutical approach? The interpretive framework is a legitimate approach to some problems in social science but is not a legitimate requirement for all social science. In substantial areas of social science and explanation, problems of significance and interpretation do not arise and objective factors—material interests, social structures, coercive institutions—play the central explanatory roles. None of the cases considered here require hermeneutic analysis. In particular, the concept of rational self-interest, or prudence, can legitimately be applied cross-culturally, and social scientists may reasonably postulate that much social history can be understood as the aggregate consequence of individuals acting out of a prudent regard for self or family welfare. This rational choice framework is not suited for every topic of social inquiry, but for the problems at the heart of these cases—technological change, rebellion, social cooperation, and economic decision making—the rational choice framework is defensible. It follows that these constitute important areas of social science where the central problem is to discover *not* culturally specific meanings and values but rather the specific social arrangements and institutions that channel individual activity and result in a given pattern of social life.

Rational choice theory, materialism, and culture science are competing research programs, each founded on a valid insight into one aspect of human behavior and society. Both deliberative reason and cultural meanings influence behavior, social practice, and history. The question is, to what extent and in what circumstances is the influence of practical reason sufficiently strong to permit us to explain and predict outcomes without extensive interpretation of cultural factors? And the premise of Popkin, Perry, Skinner, Marks, Brenner, and (partly) Scott, is that such areas exist, particularly those involving the social arrangements of agriculture, the political behavior of persons when political outcomes substantially affect interests described in the core, and the economic structures that result from commercialization.

The interpretation theory assault fails to discredit the rational choice framework. Does this mean that the interpretive approach is itself misconceived? Or are hermeneutic social science, interpretive social inquiry, and cultural investigation of meanings themselves legitimate programs for social science? Of course they are, and they provide answers to questions that other approaches cannot. Are there convincing reasons to suppose that all social inquiry must be interpretive and culturally specific? No; rather, substantial areas of social science are premised on a sophisticated set of assumptions about rationality and the material circumstances of life that are theoretically legitimate and empirically fruitful. Finally, are these areas unrelated to interpretive social theory? No; they share the assumption, implicitly or explicitly, that social science must flow through an understanding of human agency—choice, belief, reasoning, action. What distinguishes the two programs is not agency but rather the level at which it is possible to characterize agency. The interpretive program implicitly assumes that there is no culturally neutral and nontrivial level at which to describe agency and personhood. The materialist program denies this, maintaining that a significant core of human agency is species specific but not culturally specific and that the content of this description permits, in many social circumstances, good social explanations of social patterns.

Causal Relations among Social Phenomena

The other chief element in common among most of the analyses considered in this study is causal explanations. Most simply, the investigator asserts that two states or conditions are linked, in that one leads through identifiable mechanisms to the second. Causal claims depend on two broad techniques of empirical investigation: study of regular association of factors and study of underlying causal mechanisms. We are confident that "smoking causes lung cancer" because statistical epidemiology establishes high levels of correlation between individual smoking and lung cancer. And we are confident that "lunar gravitation causes tides" because we have a good theoretical understanding of the mechanisms leading from the antecedent to the consequent.

Here are several examples of causal claims from the cases discussed above:

- The existence of a network of millenarian sects in the early nineteenth century caused the Eight Trigrams rebellion of 1815 (Naquin 1976)
- The social property arrangements of seventeenth-century England caused the economic revolution in agriculture in the following century (Brenner 1976)

- A rise in the real wage causes population growth (Malthus; Lee 1986)
- Offense to traditional subsistence rights causes rebelliousness (Scott 1976)

Two important questions arise. What does it mean to say that A causes B, in the context of social phenomena? And what sorts of empirical evidence are needed to evaluate causal assertions?

There are two broad types of interpretation of causal judgments: a "causation as regularity" view and a "causal mechanism" view. The regularity view, associated with Hume, holds that causal judgments are wholly parasitic on claims of regularities among classes of events. To say that "increase in sodium consumption causes increase in blood pressure" means only that there is a regular, predictable correlation between events of the first type and events of the second type. And to say that "John's high blood pressure today was caused by his consumption of salty pretzels yesterday" is to say only that these particular events are instances of a regular correlation among sets of events.[11]

The causal mechanism view accepts the strong link between regularities and causal relations but holds that a causal claim goes beyond a mere statement about regularities. It further postulates that there is some underlying mechanism or process that produces the regularity. On this approach, whenever we discover a true causal relation among events or types of events, we must ultimately be able to identify the process through which the relation is mediated from cause to effect. Knowledge of regularities is suggestive of causal relations, but the causal analysis is not complete until we discover the underlying processes. In the blood pressure case, therefore, a full causal analysis requires that we establish not only a correlation but the physiology: through what mechanisms salt consumption influences blood pressure.[12]

On this account, the Humean view of causation as regularities among classes of events is unsatisfactory in that it is often possible (and always desirable) to account for the processes or mechanisms that cause regularities. Much scientific research is directed at explaining observed regularities by discovering an underlying mechanism. Such discovery generally requires the identification of a set of laws (for example, a law of nature) that governs the behavior of the entities or processes which constitute the events in question. Thus Newton explained the empirical regularities identified by Kepler by formulating the laws of universal gravitation; these laws expressed the causal mechanism that governed planetary motion. A final stipulation is thus the requirement that it be possible to identify (at least approximately) the mechanism that links cause and effect.

For sake of illustration, consider an ordinary example of a causal sequence. Suppose a match is dropped into a pool of gasoline in normal atmospheric circumstances; the gasoline then ignites. Two related distinctions are useful in analyzing the idea of a causal relation.[13] We may distinguish first between necessary causal and sufficient causal conditions and second between standing and instigating conditions. Most fundamental is the distinction between necessary and sufficient conditions. A necessary causal condition for an event E is a condition C such that if C had not occurred E would not have occurred.[14] Both the presence of oxygen and the dropping of the match are necessary conditions for ignition. A sufficient causal condition is a condition such that if C occurs, E will necessarily occur. Our example lacks a sufficient condition; the match without the oxygen would not lead to the explosion, nor would the oxygen without the match. In a simple world, however, it is more promising to look for a set of jointly sufficient conditions: a set of conditions whose joint presence leads necessarily to the event.[15]

The other distinction is that between standing and instigating conditions. In our example the presence of oxygen is a standing condition. It is a condition whose parameters are relatively unchanging throughout the time leading up to the event. The dropped match, by contrast, is an instigating condition: it introduces a sudden change in the environment (rapid increase in temperature), which leads to the event. Both the presence of oxygen and the dropping of the match are causes of the fire, but for some purposes it is reasonable to identify only the instigating condition rather than the background conditions as the cause. Logically speaking, however, the two conditions are on the same level.[16]

In our example, then, we may make the following claims: The presence of oxygen, gasoline, and the dropped match are all necessary conditions. The set of these three conditions is jointly sufficient for the occurrence of the explosion. The former two conditions are standing conditions, whereas the dropped match is the instigating condition. The mechanism of this causal process is the chemistry of combustion: given the laws of chemistry and physics and the physical environment at the time of the dropped match, rapid oxidation necessarily occurs.[17]

This treatment permits us to construct the following analysis of causal explanation:

A causes B if and only if:
1. A is a necessary condition for the occurrence of B;
2. A belongs to a set of conditions C which are jointly sufficient to give rise to B; and
3. the mechanisms through which C gives rise to B include M, which rely on laws L_i.

This account of causation is neutral between social and natural phenomena. It does not require that the mechanisms connecting cause and effect be natural or mechanical or be determined by laws of nature; reference to rational-intentional factors is a legitimate link between factors.

In application to some of our cases, the method of correlation appears unpromising, with the partial exception of the Malthusian thesis. The first two claims concern relations between individual conditions or events, whereas the latter two concern relations between classes of events. In principle, the latter claims could be tested by sampling (as Lee 1986 attempts to do in connection with the Malthusian thesis). But in general, the number of instances available to examine supposed causal sequences is too small and the range of variation of events and circumstances too large to permit confident testing through inductive surveys.

More promising is Mill's method of difference: if the claim is that "in typical circumstances, tenure insecurity causes peasant militancy," it is enough to find a small number of cases that are arguably typical but that conjoin tenure insecurity with peasant passivity. The causal claim would stand refuted. Such an argument is inconclusive, of course, in that it is always debatable whether the circumstances are "typical," but the burden of proof passes to the defender of the causal claim to show how these exceptional cases are consistent with the causal assertion.[18]

The most convincing justification for a causal hypothesis is one that clearly accounts for the underlying causal mechanisms that establish the causal relation. Such an account invites evaluation of the theoretical analysis on which the causal claim depends. The chief justification of these causal hypotheses is a developed account of the causal processes underlying the phenomena in question and the derivation of a causal connection between the stipulated events. And, significantly, most of the causal arguments considered above devote much attention to discovering and analyzing the underlying causal mechanisms of rebellion, economic change, or change in social structures.

Here the salience of rational choice analysis again becomes evident. For the chief mechanism of social change that has emerged in the cases above is the deliberative agent making decisions within a particular social and natural environment. And the theory of practical rationality gives the social scientist a framework in terms of which to analyze individual behavior and to aggregate the effects of the decisions of many agents to explain macrolevel phenomena. Thus the regularities of human behavior deriving from the rationality and deliberativeness of the agents constitute the laws establishing causal relations among social phenomena.

Many of the causal explanations offered by the authors considered above, such as Chao, Lippit, and Skinner, refer to processes of social change that depend on what may be referred to as "structural causation." The general idea here is that a set of social institutions (structures) imposes a dynamic of development on a society or economy, given basic regularities describing human behavior and choice. The institutions—property relations, marketing system, kinship system—are embodied in the social practices of the persons involved, in the norms that govern their behavior, in the powers vested in political authorities at various levels of the state, and so forth. In Lippit's case the relevant social structure is the set of property relations through which economic activity proceeds. These property relations impose specific incentives, opportunities, and limitations on players; they constitute the institutional context within which individuals pursue their goals. In analyzing explanations of this sort we may distinguish between the structural feature of the social system, the social pattern that this structure is hypothesized to produce, and the mechanism through which this structure shapes individual conduct so as to lead to the pattern.

Examples of structural causation may be drawn from this and preceding chapters:

- The property relations of peasant farming and absentee landlordship cause agricultural stagnation
- The hierarchical structure of a traditional marketing system influences the spread of heterodox religious ideas
- The existential circumstances of peasant production engender a subsistence ethic

- Overpopulation within a traditional agricultural system produces involution rather than innovation

In each case a structural feature of society is identified as an important causal antecedent for some pattern of development within the society containing that feature, and in each case the mechanism of causal influence works through the individuals who are located within the context of those structural features. The investigator hypothesizes that the selected feature imposes distinctive incentives, powers, and limits on the individuals who act subject to its constraints and then shows how the resulting behaviors aggregate to the pattern to be explained (involution, stagnation, the spread of heterodox ideas, and so on).

Aside from the abstract nature of the causal factor in such an explanation, a structural-causal analysis conforms to fairly ordinary standards of causal reasoning. The two central requirements of causal judgment—that the investigator be prepared to identify the mechanism through which the influence between cause and effect is conveyed and that the cause should properly covary with its effect—are satisfied; so, for example, if we should find important examples of peasant economies characterized by absentee landlordism that are technologically dynamic or of heterodox ideas that spread through different channels than the local marketing hierarchy, then the corresponding causal hypothesis is cast into serious doubt.

One example of causal explanation is James Scott's treatment of the causal relations between the subsistence ethic and peasant rebellion (1976:chap. 5). Scott offers a fairly complex analysis of the field of causal factors pertinent to rebellion in Southeast Asia. The subsistence ethic, first, is a standing condition with causal consequences in peasant society. It is embodied in current moral psychologies of members of the group and in the existing institutions of moral training through which new members are brought to share these values. Through the workings of individual motivational psychology, individuals acquire certain dispositions to behave. The features and strengths of this system of values are relatively objective. In particular, the details of this ethic can be investigated through a variety of empirical means: interviews with participants, observation of individual behavior, or analysis of the content of the institutions of moral training. Call this ensemble of institutions and current moral psychologies the "embodied social morality" (ESM).

The framework of economic structures and practices surrounding the peasant is another standing condition in agrarian society. Land tenure, taxation, marketing, water control, and political institutions all constitute parts of this system. These institutions and practices are the object of inquiry of economic sociology.

The framework of economic structures interacts directly with the subsistence ethic. Changes in economic structures are *perceived* by peasants as influencing their subsistence security and cause either greater resentment and anger or more tolerance of the regime. Thus as tax policies or land tenure arrangements shift, they accord better or worse with the subsistence ethic and may trigger the individual's behavioral dispositions.

Inhibiting and accelerating causal factors are also present in Scott's account: those that retard the occurrence of rebellion (for example, the repressive powers of the state or the lack of effective political organization of the peasantry), on the one hand, and those that enhance the likelihood of rebellion (for example, forms of religious organization, kinship structures, and supernatural beliefs), on the other. Finally, Scott alludes to several instigating events: the crushing famines of the 1930s and the Japanese occupation of Indochina, the appearance of a charismatic religious or political leader, a sudden harshening of tax demands, and a sudden weakening of the state's repressive powers.

In line with the idea that the subsistence ethic is a standing causal condition, Scott notes that the effectiveness of shared values varies substantially over different peasant communities. "The social strength of this ethic . . . varied from village to village and from region to region. It was strongest in areas where traditional village forms were well developed and not shattered by colonialism—Tonkin, Annam, Java, Upper Burma—and weakest in more recently settled pioneer areas like Lower Burma and Cochinchina" (40). These variations, moreover, led to significant differences in the capacity of affected communities to achieve effective collective resistance. "Communitarian structures not only receive shocks more uniformly but they also have, due to their traditional solidarity, a greater capacity for collective action. . . . Thus, the argument runs, the more communal the village structure, the easier it is for a village to collectively defend its interests" (202).

We may now formulate Scott's causal thesis about rebellion fairly clearly. The embodied social morality is a standing condition within any society. This condition is causally related to collective dispositions to rebellion in support of the following judgments: (1) If the norms embodied in the ESM were suitably altered, the collective disposition to rebellion would be sharply diminished. (That is, the ESM is a necessary condition for rebellion in a suitable range of social situations.) (2) The presence of the ESM in conjunction with (a) suitable changes in the economic structure, (b) few inhibiting factors, and (c) appropriate stimulating conditions amount to a (virtually) sufficient condition for widespread rebellious behavior. (That is, the ESM is part of a set of jointly sufficient conditions for rebellion.) (3) It is possible to describe the causal mechanisms, and the social laws that underlie those mechanisms, through which the ESM influences rebellious dispositions. These mechanisms depend on (a) a model of individual motivation and action through which embodied norms influence individual behavior, and (b) a model of political processes through which individual behavioral dispositions aggregate to collective behavioral dispositions. (That is, the ESM is linked to its supposed causal consequences through appropriate mechanisms.)

Methodological Individualism and Microfoundations

Several cases described here purport to explain a social phenomenon—the occurrence of rebellion, the spatial distribution of cities and towns, or the stagnation of traditional farming systems—as the result of other social phenomena—millenarianism, a commercialized economic system, or the land tenure system. That is, one social pattern, structure, or entity is explained by reference to other social entities. This raises a much discussed issue in philosophy of social science: methodological individualism. Do macroexplanations of social phenomena require individualist foundations? Do social phenomena supervene upon individual actions? Social scientists and philosophers of science alike have argued that social science must be subject to the principle of methodological individualism. Thus in *The Open Society and Its Enemies*, Karl Popper writes, "All social phenomena, and especially the functioning of all social institutions, should always be understood as resulting from the decisions, actions, attitudes, etc. of human individuals, and . . . we should never be satisfied by an explanation in terms of so-called 'collectives'" (1947:98). Jon Elster puts the point in this way: "[Methodological individualism is] the doctrine that all social phenomena—their structure and their change—are in principle explicable in ways that only involve individuals—their properties, their goals, and their actions. Methodological individualism thus conceived is a form of reductionism" (1985b:22).

Virtually all the cases surveyed here conform to a weak requirement of individualism: explanations of macrophenomena must enable one to indicate, at least schematically, the mechanisms at the level of local individual behavior through which the aggregate phenomena emerge. Aggregative social explanations, that is, require microfoundations at the level of the processes of individual choice and action through which the social patterns and processes emerge.[19] The weak view is this: "All social processes, causal influences, systemic interactions, etc., are ultimately embodied in the actions of individual actors within a specific social and natural environment. Whenever a social explanation is offered according to which a social factor gives rise to any explanans, it must be possible in principle to indicate the mechanisms through which individual activity give rise to this outcome."

Do the cases studied here shed any light on the issue of methodological individualism? Can we extract reasons either to support or to reject individualism as a requirement of social explanation? The cases considered here illuminate this question in several ways. First, virtually all the explanations considered conform to this weak requirement of methodological individualism; these authors undertake to explain such diverse phenomena as technical innovation, peasant collective action, and the placement of towns and villages in terms of the actions of individual decision makers. When Perry analyzes the Nian rebellion in terms of the motives and interests of local leaders and followers, or when Lippit explains the persistence of peasant farming in terms of the interests, powers, and opportunities of landlords, each implicitly accepts the point that the aggregate phenomenon requires an explanation that derives from the circumstances of action of local actors. Second, a common way that explanations go awry among these cases is failure to consider the local environment—for example, when Robert Marks attempts to explain the appeal of revolutionary politics to the peasants of Haifeng on the basis of their objective collective interests rather than their particular local interests. Finally, several of these cases are specifically concerned with the problem of aggregation: the processes through which individual decision making aggregates into collective phenomena. These examples do shed light on connections that may exist between micro- and macrolevel descriptions of social processes.

Most of the explanations considered above, moreover, place a high value on analysis of the local mechanisms of social change—the processes at the level of the local community, marketing system, family, and so on through which social and environmental influences are translated into new trends of development. Popkin's analysis of village collective action is central to this; he emphasizes one local mechanism—the workings of individual rationality within the context of specific organizational forms. Perry offers a similar account— one in which individual strategies for survival have aggregate consequences for rebellion. Demographers who refer to family practices (nuptiality, infanticide) as the local causes of large-scale population trends offer a third. These cases support the requirements of methodological individualism in social science.

Some of the explanations considered in this book refer to social institutions and structures. How do these entities fare under the requirement of methodological individualism? There would appear to be no inconsistency between reference to such structures and adherence to methodological individualism. Social institutions exert their influence by structuring individual action. They do this, crudely, by providing incentives, by imposing coercive sanctions, and by influencing participants' goals, norms, and beliefs. The classical system of examinations in traditional China, for example, induced the sons of the elite to endure the lengthy, arduous process of classical teaching by offering successful examination takers the gains of office—prestige, power, and wealth. A land tenure system consists of both positive and negative incentives; it offers participants means to pursue material interests, and it embodies various official and private means of coercion to prevent people from violating the rules. And a religious culture—for example, the White Lotus sect—may influence its adherents through all these means. It may offer material incentives to potential followers; it may impose coercive sanctions on deviants; and, most strikingly, it may influence its followers' actions by inculcating in them shared beliefs about the causal properties of the world (the significance of the kalpa, for example), shared norms of behavior (the importance of deference to one's teacher), and shared expectations about the future (the coming of the Buddha Maitreya).

Consider the concept of a farming system (described in chapter 4, above). This is an abstract concept referring to a complex of social structures; yet this description is perfectly consistent with an appropriately modest methodological individualism. The "entity" identified here is a social entity (or a complex of social entities); but it is easy to show how this social entity is constituted by the individuals who fill positions within it. The farming system is ultimately constituted by the hundreds of millions of purposive individuals—farmers, landlords, merchants, tax collectors—who pursue their ends within specific institutional arrangements. And these institutional arrangements themselves are embodied in the persons who enforce, entice, or prohibit various kinds of action. So it is perfectly compatible with methodological individualism to employ concepts that refer to social entities or structures; individualism requires merely that it be possible to indicate how those entities or structures arise and reproduce through the actions of persons.

Structural explanation is fully compatible with a sensible methodological individualism. It postulates a set of structures that supervene upon the behaviors of many individuals and that in turn constrain and direct the behavior of individuals. Structural explanation offers a good example of an analysis that depends on "microfoundations" at the individual level; it draws force from the cogency of the analysis of the circumstances of choice of the persons who are located within these structures. A particular social-property system may accelerate or impede technical development, depending on the incentives and powers it confers on various participants in the local economy. These individuals will orient their actions to these incentives and powers, given their own purposes; and it may be that strong tendencies toward stagnation or change emerge as the aggregate of these local incentives, powers, and purposes. Thus social structures and practices do not autonomously affect social patterns and processes of change; rather, they unavoidably exert their influence through the behavior of the individuals whom they affect.

Chapter 8
Empirical Reasoning

Empirical Practices

Each debate discussed above contains, among other elements, an important range of *empirical* disagreements and arguments. Each author makes an empirical case for his or her conclusions, and much of each author's work involves gathering and assessing empirical data, critically assessing empirical findings of other researchers, and marshaling data through extended arguments to support a variety of conclusions. Let us analyze some of the empirical characteristics of these debates in an attempt to provide a more discriminating analysis of the use of empirical reasoning in social science than is typical in philosophy of social science today.[1]

We may begin with a brief, general treatment of empirical reasoning. Two central aims of research in social science are to arrive at true factual beliefs about social and historical phenomena and to arrive at sound explanations of these phenomena. These aims are pursued through empirical research: through a set of discipline-specific procedures for collecting, analyzing, and evaluating empirical data. Ideally, the empirical procedures of a discipline ought to be truth enhancing: they ought to lead the discipline over time to a more veridical set of beliefs about the phenomena.[2] They should permit investigators to assign a degree of credibility to factual assertions and explanatory claims. And they should allow the research community to attempt to resolve factual and explanatory disagreements on the basis of empirical evidence (as well as a number of other relevant factors—coherence, fit with other accepted results, and so on). Thus the empirical procedures of a discipline, and the body of empirical findings they engender, are crucial to the epistemic standing of the discipline.

The "received view" in much current philosophy of science holds that the central problem of empirical confirmation is to deploy observational evidence to corroborate or falsify theoretical beliefs. The central theory of confirmation offered by the received view is the hypothetico-deductive model (H-D). Scientific knowledge is held to consist of deductive systems composed of theoretical statements and observational statements. Theories refer to unobservable entities, mechanisms, and the like, and theoretical statements attribute diverse properties and relations to these unobservables. Theoretical systems are tested indirectly, by deriving observation sentences from them and evaluating these predictive consequences.[3] Schematically, Hempel describes the logic of confirmation in the following terms:

H (a theoretical hypothesis)
A_i (a set of auxiliary assumptions)
_____

O (an observational consequence derived from H and A_i)

A theoretical hypothesis H is formulated using theoretical terms, and a set of auxiliary assumptions (A_i) are proposed that employ both theoretical and observational terms. (These may describe an experimental procedure, for example.) Finally, an observational consequence O is derived from these premises. Since O is an observational sentence, its truth or falsity may be directly determined. If O is false, then the premises cannot be jointly true; if O is true, its truth is taken as some confirmation of the theoretical hypothesis. A hypothesis is taken to be confirmed if a number of observational consequences have been derived, tested, and found to be true.

Philosophers working within the tradition of logical positivism have thus tended to collapse the problems of empirical reasoning onto a highly abstract description of the relation between a range of data and a given hypothesis. Out of this domain emerged the hypothetico-deductive model of confirmation (Hempel 1965b), the doctrine of falsifiability (Popper 1968), the bootstraps method (Glymour 1980), and many other variants. And philosophers of social science working from an antipositivist perspective tend to downplay the importance of empirical evaluation of social theory altogether (Althusser 1970, Adorno 1969). I hold that empirical argumentation is critically important to social science—thus rejecting the various forms of skepticism raised by antipositivists—but that the logical positivists and their progeny have placed the focus of their discussion of empirical reasoning at too abstract a level. In the social sciences, the most vexing problems of empirical reasoning lie at the level of the low-level empirical study and the evaluation of fairly low-level causal hypotheses—not at the level of the evaluation of complete theories.

The central empirical problems in social science research arise in two general areas. First, a wide range of problems concern the discovery and evaluation of matters of *fact*. How are factual claims about the social world derived and corroborated? And second, there are more familiar problems having to do with the inferences that social scientists draw from a given range of empirical data. These problems may be grouped in several areas. First, there are problems of induction. What empirical research is needed to derive and evaluate generalizations in social science? Second, there are problems of causal reasoning. How are causal hypotheses to be evaluated in the social sciences and history? And finally, there are problems of theoretical models in explaining a range of social phenomena. How is empirical evidence used to evaluate theoretical explanations in social science? Such empirical questions are much more diverse than the hypothetico-deductive model of confirmation would suggest, and different sorts of philosophical work need to be done in relation to them.

Facts

A factual assertion is a singular statement that identifies one or more entities and attributes a property or relation to the entity or entities, with or without a reference to time. The logical form of such a statement may be represented as follows:

a has the property P at time t.

a bears the relation R to b at time t.

There is no a priori limit on what sorts of entities may be involved—in particular, no requirement of ontological individualism. It is possible, therefore, to make factual assertions about abstract or complex entities—General Motors as a business organization, the rate of unemployment in the English economy, and so on. (From this analysis it follows that a factual assertion may go wrong in two distinct ways; it may fail to refer to an existent entity, and it may attribute a property to a real entity that the entity does not possess.) An important type of factual assertion in social science is quantitative: a statement assigning a magnitude to some feature of economy or society (rate of profit, rate of unemployment, real wage).

The discovery of factual data is itself an important part of social scientific knowledge and research. Thus, establishing the techniques of irrigation in use in nineteenth-century Bali (Geertz 1980), the dowry arrangements practiced in nineteenth-century Hong Kong (Watson 1985), or the diffusion of new crops in seventeenth-century Oxfordshire (Havinden 1967) are significant tasks for empirical research, and the outcome of these researches will be the discovery of a set of empirical facts. These endeavors further our knowledge of the social organization of Bali, the lineage systems of Hong Kong, and the agriculture of England.

The results of these investigations are put forward as true statements about the social world; they are offered as *factual* descriptions. Typically, however, they cannot be directly confirmed or falsified. Instead, the investigator must engage in extensive empirical research to arrive at a credible factual judgment. The outcome will be an organized and logically structured argument that details a range of empirical data and shows why these data make the factual claim probable, plausible, or credible. This circumstance highlights an important feature of empirical reasoning. Many of the findings of social science research are factual claims ("the population of Beijing in 1853 was thus and so") that can, however, be empirically evaluated or supported only by weighing a range of other empirical evidence and that remain both approximate and contestable. Even at this level, moreover, disagreements arise over the facts and over appropriate techniques of data gathering and analysis.

How are factual claims derived and defended? Each discipline considered here possesses specialized research tools and techniques to investigate factual questions. A chief component of graduate training in these fields involves mastering the skills needed to apply these techniques—language skills, interviewing techniques, mathematical techniques employed in aggregating data, and so on. Historians, for example, use various primary sources—local county gazetteers, imperial tax and legal records, rebel confessions compiled by official investigators, Communist party documents, and the like. Anthropologists, by contrast, are less dependent on written records and more dependent on direct observation and conversation with members of the target community, and their training and specialized skills differ accordingly. The techniques to gather and assess data vary widely from discipline to discipline, depending on the exigencies of the subject, and few generalizations can characterize all these techniques. Yet virtually all the cases we have considered here provide convincing evidence of rigorous empirical investigation, and each gives good reason to suppose that the specialist's research results in reliable factual judgments (subject to the usual qualifications of imperfection, fallibility, and incompleteness).

A fundamental problem in research design for a given empirical program is the formulation of a scheme of concepts in terms of which to describe and aggregate data. (This problem is analogous to the problem of "operationalizing" an abstract concept in other areas of science.) This unavoidably introduces an element of arbitrariness into the process. The "standard of living" debate in English economic history is instructive in this context. The fundamental question is this: Did the working-class standard of living improve or decline during the first fifty years of industrialization (1750–1800)? This question cannot be directly evaluated, however, since the concept of the standard of living is vague. One line of thought in the debate thus uses the real wage of unskilled workers as a proxy for the standard of living. To estimate the real wage requires information about working-class consumption patterns (goods consumed), prices of these goods, and money wages during the period. With accurate information on these variables it is possible to compute the real wage. But each variable raises difficulties. The following questions must be answered:

- What portions of the working class are to be considered?
- Do we mean to include the conditions of the working poor in Ireland?
- Do we mean to include agricultural as well as industrial labor?
- Must we consider the welfare of different strata (regional, occupational) of the working class—with the possible result that some benefited and some lost ground?
- What does the expression "standard of living" refer to? Is the real wage an acceptable proxy?
- Is it desirable to give an account of the quality of life—deterioration of living conditions, conditions of work, health and sanitation conditions—in addition to purchasing power?
- If we are satisfied to consider only the real wage, how shall we arrive at a time series concerning this variable?

Different decisions on these questions lead to different ways of formulating the problem of measuring the real wage, and these variances sometimes lead to substantially altered answers to the most general question; on one formulation the real wage may be found to rise, whereas on an alternative formulation it is found to fall.

Can such a claim as "the real wage held constant during the eighteenth century" in principle be decided, given full access to historical data? At least these problems arise: The interpretation of real wage is inherently contestable; any given formulation is put forward as being plausible, but other interpreters may favor constructions that differ in important ways. This is true both at the level of providing a quantitative index (Crafts 1985) and at the level of debate over the "quality of life" as a component of the real wage. In addition, the data available are radically incomplete, so the researcher must make various assumptions—e.g., that a given price series for grain is representative of other agricultural products, or that a batch of wage data for several towns is representative of the region as a whole—in order to employ the data to support or criticize a given claim.

These points show that such factual claims as these can be interpreted only in the context of the larger framework of analysis in which they are put forward and that these issues cannot be decided in any strong sense. Instead, a conclusion on the behavior of the real wage is plausible or implausible, depending on (1) the plausibility of the research assumptions the investigator makes in formulating a representation of the real wage, and (2) the plausibility and comprehensiveness of the investigator's empirical argument, showing how the available data lead to a particular result within the conceptual framework.

Even highly factual research programs—projects aimed solely at uncovering the factual details of certain social or historical phenomena—depend on antecedent theoretical interests and assumptions. Concerning any particular domain of social phenomena there are indefinitely many factual questions the researcher could pose. In considering the rural history of medieval England one might ask: What were typical patterns of landholding? What patterns of domestic life were to be found? What demographic patterns were present— age of marriage, fertility rates, mortality rates? What types of crops and cultivation techniques were in use? How extensive was market activity? What were typical patterns of consumption? How widespread was literacy? What religious beliefs and institutions were to be found at the local level? What regional variations occurred for any of the above characteristics? And so on indefinitely. Each question can be investigated by studying available primary sources, but obviously no single study can pose all these questions. It is not possible, that is, to engage in a *comprehensive* factual inquiry into medieval England; the investigator must select a manageable number of factual problems and research those.

So selecting a small number of topics for extensive empirical research is itself a significant choice, guided, among other things, by a judgment of the relative explanatory importance of various factors. Historians within a Malthusian framework, for example, will be particularly interested in demographic variables and real income variables; Marxist historians may be more concerned with detailed information about land tenure, cultivation techniques, and class relations; contemporary social historians may pay more attention to whatever information is available about popular styles of living and domestic practices.[4]

A common antipositivist view about "facts" may be derived from these considerations: no facts are independent from a framework of theory, quantitative models, background assumptions, and the like. The facts and generalizations discussed here—for example, the concept of the real wage—are unavoidably enmeshed in assumptions and theoretical commitments. So it must be conceded that usually it is impossible to pose a factual inquiry except in the context of a developed system of specialized concepts and quantitative methods.

Yet this does not undercut the rational standing of empirical findings. Once this machinery has been established, the investigator can interrogate the available sources and arrive at justified conclusions (for example, about what the secular trends in the real wage were). The factual claim cannot be separated from its theoretical context, but taking this context into account, other researchers can use these data to develop and test their own hypotheses and claims.

In one factual controversy discussed above, Skinner holds that traditional China was structured into distinct macroregions, each of which had a core-periphery structure. Myers disagrees with the macroregions analysis itself; but, more fundamentally, he holds that in one macroregion (North China) the concentration of population and resources is just the reverse of that postulated by Skinner. This would appear to be a fairly concrete empirical disagreement, and one that can be resolved through closer analysis of available demographic data. Even here, though, we encounter a series of problems. First, the data themselves are sparse and unevenly distributed over time. Myers's arguments draw chiefly on data from the early Republican period (early twentieth century), whereas Skinner's data derive from an earlier time. Moreover, the data have been collected by researchers with their own theoretical and political biases, so the current researcher has to arrive at debatable judgments about the quality and consistency of the data. The Buck surveys for rural data in early twentieth-century North China, for example, have been faulted because Buck overrepresented larger farmers in his samples, whereas the Mantetsu surveys have been faulted because they were collected by the agents of a hostile military power (the Japanese army).[5] Second, substantive but empirically underdetermined decisions in how to organize the data must be made. Even as simple a concept as population density turns out to be contested; Skinner uses a measure of population per unit area, whereas Myers uses a measure of rural population per unit of *cultivated* area. Each has reasons for using either measure, but the claim that "core areas have higher population density than peripheral areas" cannot be resolved until we fix on one measure or the other.

In light of these problems of gathering and assessing empirical data, is it reasonable to suppose either that there is a fact of the matter or that more extensive research would definitively resolve the issue? The putative fact (for example, population density is higher in core areas than peripheral areas) must first be formulated more precisely than it stands presently; for as we have seen, one specification of population density confirms this fact, while another refutes it. This would suggest that there is no fact of the matter independent from a particular formulation of the putative fact. Once we have settled on a particular formulation—for example, total population per total land area—it is reasonable to say that the truth or falsity of the statement is in principle fixed by the circumstances on the ground at the relevant time. Even here, though, it is an open question whether it is feasible to acquire the data needed to determine truth or falsity— witness the high cost and variable precision of taking the census in large societies—and it may be flatly impossible to reconstruct the relevant census information for a century ago.[6]

Let us regroup. An empirical fact is an assertion about entities or processes that has been established through the accepted research procedures of a discipline at a given time. Factual beliefs may be assigned a range of levels of warrant within the research discipline, depending on the degree of confidence practitioners attribute to the belief on the basis of existing evidence. Thus the historian of China may attach a high level of warrant to the belief that a demographic shift from north to south occurred in the Ming dynasty, a middling level of warrant to the belief that the Qing bureaucracy was stretched thin by population growth in the nineteenth century, and a low level of warrant to the view that China's imperial longevity depends on its organizational form. What determines the level of warrant for a belief is the answer to this question: given the research available on the topic, how likely is it that the belief is nonetheless false? That is, to what extent do existing results within the discipline constrain the belief? (A low level of warrant for a belief does not imply that the belief is false but rather that the evidence is insufficient to allow us to determine the truth or falsity. Such thesis might be described as "speculative" in that it exceeds the current ability of the discipline to provide appropriate empirical evaluation.) In consideration of this range of levels of warrant, a fact is a singular statement with a high level of warrant, and a good empirical argument is one that depends on grounds with high warrant.

Generalizations

Social scientists make several categories of inferences from a range of data. Each author considered above offers generalizations about social phenomena that are constructed on the basis of a range of empirical data. These are statements of regularities among classes of events or entities. In the simplest case the regularity is exceptionless:

All F's are G.

More commonly, however, a generalization is a statement of a tendency or correlation of variables that may be represented as a probability or a statistical correlation:

Most F's are G.

A generalization, then, is a regularity, either universal or probabilistic, asserting a correlation between properties of events. Generalizations refer implicitly to individuals, a domain of individuals, and some selection of properties of individuals. Examples include "all swans are white," "spaniels are usually good-natured," and "doctors in the United States earn a high income." In the final case, the domain of individuals is "income earners in the United States"; F is the property "——— is a doctor"; and G is the property "——— earns high income."

Consider several examples of claims raised by the cases discussed above:

- Peasant farming systems are usually technically stagnant
- Rates of tenancy are inversely related to crop yields in different regions of China (Arrigo 1986)
- Peasant rebellions are usually conservative in their social goals (Scott 1976)

To evaluate any of these claims we must first identify the domain of individuals under consideration. In the first example the domain is "farming systems anywhere in the world"; F is the property "——— is a peasant farming system," and G is the property "——— is technically stagnant." In the third example the domain is "rebellions anywhere in the world"; F is the property "——— is largely composed of peasants"; and G is the property "——— is socially conservative." Before evaluating a generalization we must sufficiently precisely interpret the criteria of application of the properties in use. What definition of "peasant rebellion" shall we employ? How do we distinguish between peasant rebellions and urban rebellions that draw in large numbers of peasants? How will we distinguish between "social conservative" rebellions and "moderately progressive" rebellions? These points demonstrate that generalizations are unavoidably enmeshed in the investigator's framework of categories of analysis.

Once we have settled these problems, we may interpret the import of the generalization and suggest the sort of evidence needed to evaluate it. The rebellion claim, for example, may be amplified in these terms:

> Within the domain of all rebellions, those identified as "peasant rebellions" show a substantially higher incidence of "socially conservative goals" than is characteristic of the domain as a whole.

To test this claim, we would need to gather a representative sample of rebellions, suitably drawn from various regions and times, and to investigate the relevant conditional probabilities. In principle, then, generalizations may be tested by identifying the pertinent classes of events and determining whether the asserted regularities obtain.

Inductive generalizations are subject to several cautions that are well known from statistical theory and inductive logic: the requirement of statistical significance and the problem of avoiding accidental regularities. Both problems arise in cases where either the domain of events itself or the available sample is small. Significantly, many of the generalizations considered here suffer from one or both these problems. Perhaps several hundred major rebellions are documented in the historical literature—itself a small corpus—and none of the studies examined have considered more than a handful. Problems of statistical significance and accidental generalization appear as important obstacles in this area.

In addition to inductive generalizations in science, it is also possible to arrive at *theoretical* generalizations, which are derived from a theoretical representation of the causal processes at work in a given range of phenomena. Consider an example from evolutionary biology: "predator species tend to extinguish more quickly than prey species." This is evidently a true generalization. But to establish its truth it is not necessary to undertake the sort of inductive survey described above; rather, this regularity may be derived from the classical assumptions of evolutionary theory, along with a framework of analysis in which "predator" and "prey" are clearly defined. In this case, the generalization acquires some or all of its empirical warrant from that attaching to the higher-level theories from which it derives—not from an inductive survey of event classes.

Many generalizations encountered among the cases discussed above have an element of both inductive and theoretical support. Many begin life as informal perceptions of correlation by the researcher. Those that survive, however, are those for which the researcher is able to provide a theoretical account of the mechanisms at work among the phenomena, in the context of which the postulated correlation is a natural consequence. Both generalizations discussed in the previous paragraphs have this quality. Once the researcher spells out in greater detail what a "peasant farming system" is (as Chayanov does) and begins working out the economics and incentives of such a system, it becomes theoretically understandable that such systems will display a low rate of technical innovation, capital expenditure, and growth of output.

The empirical case for a generalization in social science may encounter many different criticisms. In some cases the debate is over what the data are. In principle, further empirical research should resolve the dispute, but it is often difficult or impossible to produce the right data. Obstacles to collecting the data include cost, the inaccessibility of the past, and ambiguity of the sources. We have seen disagreements of this sort in the macroregions theory and the moral economy debate. The macroregions thesis, for example, is in principle resolvable in part into a claim about price levels in different parts of China and volumes of trade between different areas. If these data were fully available, then much of the dispute between Myers and Skinner would evaporate. However, the data are only thinly available; so more indirect (and less conclusive) arguments are required.

A common empirical criticism of a proffered generalization has to do with the scope of evidence offered in support of the generalization. Thus Myers (1985) and other reviewers criticize Huang (1985) on the ground that his study is based on too slender and too selective a set of villages, whereas his conclusions extend to North China as a whole. Myers (1987) criticizes Kang Chao (1986) for the same reasons, and Wiens (1975) turns the same criticisms against Myers's (1970) own analysis. Likewise, the evidence offered for a generalization may be too narrowly drawn to constitute a secure ground for the generalization. The claim is sometimes made that, though the author has properly considered one available type of evidence, he has ignored other relevant sources.

Application of a Theoretical Construct

The most familiar empirical problem is the evaluation of a theoretical hypothesis. We have seen a variety of efforts to explain a range of social phenomena on the basis of a theoretical model of the underlying processes. The high-level equilibrium trap, the ideal type of a peasant farming system, the concept of the rational peasant—each is a theoretical construct put forth by the author to explain some feature of the social data. How are such explanations to be evaluated? What empirical data are relevant in deciding whether the hypothesized mechanism is embodied in the social phenomena?

Recall some of the theoretical constructs and explanations that have been surveyed here:

- Peasant farming in China leads to a state of self-exploitation (Chao 1986)
- Marketing hierarchies in traditional rural China conform to the forms predicted by central place theory (Skinner 1963–64)
- Millenarian religious values are conducive to rebellious behavior (Naquin 1976)

How are these theoretical claims evaluated? What data are relevant to their assessment? And to what extent is it credible that further empirical research might conclusively resolve disagreement over such theoretical assertions as these?

Consider the theoretical construct of a peasant farming organization in more detail. This construct is abstractive in that it singles out several salient elements and abstracts from all other elements. These include cultivation aimed exclusively at satisfying the subsistence needs of the family, exclusive use of family labor, small plots, and traditional agricultural techniques.[7] This model can be applied to farming systems throughout the world; but it is abstract, and no particular system exactly satisfies its assumptions. All farming systems, moreover, involve other elements that distinguish them from one another: cultural practices, kinship systems, religious values, levels of integration into a state system, levels of market activity, and so on.

The main purpose of a theoretical construct is to *explain* concrete historical phenomena. Thus Chao attempts to explain persistent stagnation of the traditional Chinese economy, in part at least, as the natural result of the dominance of peasant farm organization in the rural economy. That is, Chao asserts that the concept of the peasant farm fits the empirical data of the Chinese rural economy fairly well; that peasant farm organization in its ideal form leads to high land productivity through extremely low labor productivity; and as a result, it is more profitable for wealth-holders to collect rents than to manage capitalist farms. Peasant farmers, however, lack both the capital resources to introduce technical innovations into agriculture and the incentive to adopt labor-saving innovations, so the predictable result is that farm productivity remains stagnant.

This is a theoretical explanation. It is theoretical in that it offers an abstract model of the local organization of the rural economy, and it is explanatory in that it attempts to show that the observed economic characteristics may be derived from that model, using the tools of marginalist economic theory. The model, if accepted, is intended to show why the pattern of stagnation in the Chinese rural economy persisted over centuries.

How should such an explanatory hypothesis be evaluated empirically? It would appear that empirical evidence may be brought to bear on this explanatory claim from two points of view: the empirical status of its predictive consequences and the empirical status of the premises of the theoretical model itself. These complementary approaches may be illustrated using the example of the peasant farm organization. The Chayanov-Chao argument goes along these lines:

1   The traditional Chinese rural economy was dominated by peasant farm organization.
2   Peasant farmers aim at satisfying family subsistence needs.
3   Opportunity costs for family labor are low, since each family member must be fed whether he or she works or not.
4   Therefore it is rational for the peasant farmer to continue to expend family labor on cultivation so long as the marginal product of that labor is greater than zero.
5   Therefore peasant farming is labor intensive, low in labor productivity, and high in land productivity.
6   Managerial farming with hired labor and higher levels of capital investment cannot compete with the peasant farm.
7   Therefore the Chinese rural economy showed a secular tendency toward stagnation, small farm size, and low levels of capital investment.

The theoretical premises here are those defining a peasant farm organization, along with the hypothesis that the typical Chinese farm possessed those characteristics. The relevant portions of the model for this argument—the characteristics that lead to stagnation—are those described in (2), (3), and (4). The derived consequences are those represented by (5) and (6); these are the features that a pure peasant farm economy ought to display, assuming marginalist economic theory and the institutional assumptions built into the peasant farm model.

This theoretical explanation may be investigated, first, by investigating the empirical adequacy of its analytical premises. For farm organization is not hypothetical or unobservable in the way in which quarks and neutrinos may be. The concept of a peasant farm is an abstraction, but one whose main elements may fit the observed rural arrangements well or badly. The social historian can attempt to evaluate the accuracy of this model in application to rural China. Were most farms family operated? Did they employ wage labor? Were peasant farmers averse to risk? How extensively involved in commercial farming were most units? (This is just the sort of inquiry provided by Huang [1984], who concludes that the model is *not* empirically supported; instead, the rural economy of North China contained both managerial and peasant farms.)

It is also possible to investigate empirically the derived consequences of the model. Was labor productivity lower on peasant farms than on managerial farms? Did peasant farms tend to drive out managerial farms by inducing landowners to extract rents from tenants rather than profits from farming? Did levels of capital expenditure differ greatly between managerial farms and peasant farms? And were peasant farmers typically slow to introduce available innovations?

Through these investigations of both premises and consequences of the theoretical explanation both the truth of the theoretical claim (that the economy was dominated by peasant farming) and the adequacy of the explanation of technical stagnation can be judged.

Finally, there is an element involved in empirical justification of a theory that has to do with logic rather than empirical test; this is the logical adequacy of the mathematical and deductive arguments through which the findings are produced, and the arguments linking a range of empirical findings to the testing of a given hypothesis. For, as we have seen, any body of factual research findings rests on a complex set of assumptions, models, measurement processes, and the like, on whose adequacy the empirical argument crucially depends.

Such logical criticisms of an empirical argument may encompass some of the following points. First, the claim is sometimes made that a given range of data represents an artifact of research methodology. In principle, the rate of growth in output in seventeenth-century English agriculture ought to be an objective datum. However (as Crafts 1985 shows), to construct an estimate of this datum, it is necessary to make a series of assumptions about the behavior of other factors—e.g., the rate of population growth. And it is necessary to choose one out of a number of possible statistical techniques and weighting schemes. Different choices, however, lead to striking differences in estimates.

Second, it is often necessary to use some statistical procedure or mathematical model to analyze a data set and to use it to evaluate other claims. However, the choice of models and procedures is often controversial. In my discussion of Sands and Myers's empirical criticisms of Skinner's macroregions thesis, for example, I argued that the technique of discriminant analysis was inappropriate in that context; it did not establish the conclusions that Sands and Myers sought to reach.

Finally, it is sometimes alleged that a given author's hypothesis admits of empirical testing not at all, or only to a limited degree, because the hypothesis is formulated in vague concepts. On this line of criticism, the theoretical hypothesis has not been sufficiently articulated and spelled out. Sands and Myers (1986:721–22) apply this criticism against Skinner's concept of macroregions.

One example of theoretical disagreement is the debate over the moral economy of the peasant. Scott's moral economy theory holds that peasant communities are regulated by shared values, a subsistence ethic, which constrains individual behavior and village economic and political institutions. Popkin's rational peasant theory holds that peasants are rational decision makers who are concerned primarily with family welfare and security; that individual behavior largely follows from calculations of private interest; and that village economic institutions generally reflect the efforts of various agents to pursue their private interests. To what extent does this dispute admit of objective resolution on the basis of further empirical research? In particular, to what extent does the range of available or potential empirical data resolve the issue between Scott and Popkin?

In this case the vagueness and generality of the claims on both sides make resolution difficult. In chapter 2, I argued that the two theories are *not* as inconsistent with each other as advocates of each side believe them to be. However, suppose that we formulate the difference between the two positions in these terms: Scott holds that moral norms and a sense of justice are more important than calculations of individual interest in explaining important facts about peasant political behavior; Popkin denies this. Here we have a straightforward, logical inconsistency between the two positions.

There are possible data sets that could clearly discriminate between these two hypotheses. We might, for example, have access to village studies of a number of representative villages in the region that have collected data on the economic arrangements of the villages, the character of land tenure relations, the distribution of tax burdens; firsthand reports of participants' experience of various economic and political arrangements, and detailed records of acts of collective rural violence (riots, eat-ins, attacks on colonial offices). And it might turn out that these data are close to what we would expect on one theoretical model or the other. It might turn out, for example, that every village has effective institutions of redistribution of land and income and effective disaster insurance schemes; that land tenure relations are such that both patron and client acknowledge obligations to one another; and that riots and eat-ins are directed against agents known to flaunt traditional obligations. Yet it might turn out that virtually no effective redistribution occurs, that free rider problems are endemic, that landlords effectively maximize their incomes through carefully adjusting rent relations, and that acts of collective violence occur only when the participants have a fairly direct private interest in the outcome. The first data set would offer strong support for the moral economy view, whereas the second would support the political economy view.

However, it is also possible that the data are substantially ambiguous. Some economic institutions have a redistributive effect, along with other effects that favor elite interests. Some participants emphasize the importance of subsistence rights, whereas others emphasize the importance of individual economic striving. Some landlords make small loans in times of hardship to their tenants, whereas others do not. And some acts of collective violence seem to manifest a sense of moral outrage, whereas others seem to be directed toward narrow goals. In this case, it would appear that the data do not permit us to decide between the two theories; each can claim some support.

Let us suppose, however, that our local studies do strongly support the moral economy view. What implications does this have for the more general version of the moral economy theory? What would be needed to claim that the moral economy thesis has been empirically supported as an interpretation of all Vietnamese peasants, all Southeast Asian peasants, or all peasants everywhere? Does this local study confer some degree of empirical support for the moral economy theory against the rational peasant theory at the more general levels? To conclude that the moral economy theory accurately describes peasant behavior at a more general level, we would appear to need to provide some representative study of peasant behavior in the other cultures and regions contained in the more general version. When these data are collected, the same possibilities of ambiguity and incompleteness arise.

Contrast this empirical procedure with the data that Scott and Popkin offer in support of their views. The two authors draw their data from different regions of Indochina, so their cases have cultural and regional differences. Further, each offers fairly thin data; the data illustrate the theoretical view rather than severely test it.

These considerations suggest, first, that theories must be refined and limited before we arrive at a theoretical proposition that can be more or less directly evaluated, and second, that once this refinement has been performed and the resulting hypothesis evaluated, it will still be difficult to evaluate the more general thesis with which we began. This line of thought appears, then, to lead to the conclusion that the task of empirically resolving the moral economy debate through painstaking gathering of data is long and difficult. When we next consider, however, the range of data that are surveyed and advanced by either Scott or Popkin, it is difficult to hold that either view has been given a rigorous empirical evaluation. Instead, each author has argued for the plausibility of his own view by giving it a coherent theoretical formulation and by providing a sketchy survey of historical data that seems to support the case.

The Hypothetico-Deductive Model of Justification

The preceding discussion suggests that the hypothetico-deductive model of justification is unhelpful in application to much current social science because it postulates an overly simple logical relation between evidence and belief. This is true for a number of reasons. Most pertinent here is that this model abstracts altogether from the problem of assessing the truth value of factual claims (observations); instead, it is concerned with the relation between a given range of factual beliefs and the degree of corroboration that these confer on a theoretical hypothesis. However, many of the most difficult empirical problems in the social sciences arise at a lower level. As shown above, many empirical controversies in social science concern the adequacy of various ways to determine the facts in a given range of social phenomena—historical population data, econometric parameters, and the like. But the H-D model sheds little or no light on such problems.

Further, the model of scientific knowledge as a theoretical system in which theoretical axioms deductively entail a set of empirical observations is much less plausible in the social sciences than it is in at least some of the natural sciences. Many areas of social science are not deductive theoretical systems but rather a complex of empirical descriptions, generalizations, quantitative analysis, causal and functional explanations, and a plurality of explanatory models that are deployed for diverse explanatory purposes. A more accurate representation would hold, at least in many of the cases we have surveyed, that the body of knowledge in a given discipline consists of a range of empirical findings and an often eclectic set of causal hypotheses, quantitative models, *and* theoretical hypotheses. This diversity suggests that the results of a social science discipline are typically less tightly integrated around a small number of theoretical hypotheses than paradigm natural sciences—unlike, for example, the logical simplicity of Newton's laws of planetary motion and the infinite range of planetary observations they entail and explain. In general, the examples we have considered are much closer to the ground than are typical theories in the natural sciences.[8]

Third, the H-D model formulates the problem of justification in holistic terms—not hypothesis by hypothesis but theory by theory. As Duhem and Quine emphasized, the falsity of an observational test does not falsify a given premise of the argument; it only establishes that at least one premise is false. Thus the auxiliary hypotheses may be false, and the situation may be remedied by altering one or more of the auxiliary hypotheses. This holism implies that confirmation attaches only to theories as deductively unified wholes—not to individual hypotheses. However, much of the discussion above suggests that problems of empirical evaluation in social science are substantially less holistic than the received view would suggest. The hypotheses of a given area of social science can typically be investigated, tested, corroborated, and refined piecemeal. This contrasts sharply with the Duhemian holism that is attributed to natural science, according to which theoretical systems can be evaluated only as wholes.[9]

This defect derives from the hypothetico-deductive model's exclusive attention to the problem of corroboration of *theory*, as distinct from other types of empirical problem. A survey of the cases considered here shows that the diversity of empirical investigation and empirical controversy is much greater than this model would suggest; that the testing of theoretical assumptions through predictive consequences is a minor part of social science empirical practices; and that this model disregards altogether important problems of empirical inquiry—concerning, for example, the evaluation of low-level factual claims. Different disciplines confront substantially different problems arising out of empirical inquiry and embody substantially different procedures to evaluate and establish reliable data. Thus what counts as a fact, and what counts as a satisfactory demonstration of a fact, varies greatly from discipline to discipline. Historians, for example, are typically more concerned with such things as authenticity of archival materials, accuracy of translation, and exhaustiveness of archival study, than are political scientists concerned with the same domain of inquiry.

Unfortunately, such problems of empirical reasoning have not received adequate analysis in the philosophy of social science. Philosophers standing within enlightened logical positivism have by and large assumed that the H-D model is sufficient, whereas philosophers who reject positivist theory of science have largely denigrated or ignored problems of empirical reasoning and rigor.[10] The cases under consideration here cast doubt on both positions. Against the received view, I contend that the H-D method is of only limited use in social science, and against the antipositivists I contend that empirical methods have substantial grip on problems of social inquiry.

Objectivity in Social Science

A related but more abstract concern is the possibility of objective scientific knowledge of social phenomena. As we have remarked, a core aim of scientific research is to arrive at objective, true beliefs about the subject of the discipline: about what sorts of entities are to be found, what their properties are, and what causal relations obtain among them. Science aims at producing *knowledge* about natural and social phenomena. And this aim brings with it a concern for truth, a concern for rational standards of belief assessment, and a commitment to the notion that the standards of belief assessment are conducive to truth.

Are these aspirations borne out in social science? To what extent is there a fact of the matter in typical social science controversies? Do the standards of empirical reasoning—careful collection of pertinent data, reasoned analysis of data, and rigorous reasoning on the basis of available data—effectively constrain the inferences and conclusions reached in various debates? And are there standards of theoretical rigor—for example, conceptual precision, analytical care, and logical theory construction? If so, to what extent do these standards improve the veridicality of social science belief?

Against these aspirations toward objectivity are such skeptical concerns as: Scientific disputes are inherently underdetermined by the evidence. There are no pure facts, only facts as couched in one conceptual system or another. There are no pure observations, just observations couched in a theory-laden vocabulary. Theories bring with them their own empirical criteria, which favor the findings. The relations between observation and theory are hopelessly circular, with theories generating the observations that supposedly support them. Research projects are guided by antecedent assumptions about the structure of the phenomena that arbitrarily shape the eventual empirical findings. Scientific research communities are regulated by other criteria altogether (individual career advancement, political demands of funding agencies) rather than epistemic criteria (evidence, logical coherence).

Some skeptical claims are more directly pertinent to social science: Social phenomena are not objective in the first place but are defined by the fluid and changing intentions, meanings, and beliefs of the participants and observers. All observation in social science requires (1) the interpretation of behavior, so there are no brute facts at all (C. Taylor), (2) that the investigator constructs the world he or she observes (Berger), (3) or that all social observation depends on the perspective of the investigator, so that perspective-independent facts do not exist.

These points are intended to reduce the appeal of the claim of objectivity of empirical reasoning in social science. They contribute to a theory of science that, if accepted, would radically undermine the claims of objectivity, empirical control of belief, and rigor that science claims for itself, and they emphasize nonrational factors in the development of science. But the cases surveyed here do not support such a nonrational theory of science. Instead, they exhibit a clear set of empirical procedures that are well designed to collect and analyze empirical data. And they permit us to trace through the logical relations that obtain between the types of data collected and their more abstract or hypothetical claims. These findings suggest a level of objectivity and empirical rigor that is consistent with a sophisticated rationalist theory of science. Each case gives reason to affirm the elementary point that all significant empirical research is in an important sense inconclusive, producing findings that fall short of certainty. So if a sense of objectivity is to apply to social science, it must be consistent with fallibility and incompleteness.[11]

Yet these cases do not support currently fashionable forms of relativism and subjectivism in social science. For the limits on empirical determinacy that have emerged out of these cases do *not* derive from general philosophical considerations (the ultimate indeterminacy of social phenomena, for example) but from the humdrum limits of practical research: limited availability of data on contested questions, imperfections of available data, limits on research resources, and the like.

Two points stand out, and both support the possibility of objectivity. First, concerning any particular point of controversy social scientists can produce additional findings that will narrow the range of disagreement. Recall our discussion of the significance of inter-regional trade in the macroregions analysis. Skinner's initial theoretically based assumption was that interregional trade was little in comparison to intraregional trade. As this topic became controversial, however, additional empirical research shed new light on both the scope and the character of interregional commerce in China. As a result, the situation is now understood more clearly; there is little disagreement on the existence of such trade, and more narrow disagreement than previously over the scope and nature of that trade. This example represents perhaps a paradigm of progress within social science: a theoretically important controversy arises, further research ensues, and the controversy is narrowed or resolved.

This example underlines the importance of distinguishing between local and global perspectives in considering the rationality of science. In this case, on a particular empirical disagreement, we see that unmistakable progress has emerged. And it is probably true that most current empirical disagreements admit of eventual resolution through further research—if and insofar as the requisite research efforts are made. But a Malthusian twist lies here: controversies multiply geometrically, whereas research resources multiply only arithmetically. Many questions, though resolvable in principle, must remain unresolved; from a global perspective, then, much current social science belief remains controvertible.

The second point about objectivity that emerges from these cases has to do with the development of theoretical frameworks. Here, too, the subjectivist will hold that theoretical disagreements are ultimately unresolvable. But the cases we have considered suggest that this pessimism is misplaced (like its companion skepticism about the resolution of empirical disagreements). The sharpest theoretical disagreement we have surveyed here is the moral economy debate. Scott and Popkin offer apparently contradictory frameworks for understanding peasant motivation and social arrangements, and at first glance it may appear that the arguments of each are strong. But through careful consideration of the logic of the two cases, the conceptual work each does, the nature and limitations of the evidence that each offers, and so forth, both the relation between the two theories and the relation between each theory and the world can be assessed fairly credibly. Peasants are deliberative—thus bearing out part of Popkin's view—they also are subject to a wide range of other motivations, including moral ideas—thus bearing out part of Scott's view—and their communities embody features that derive from both aspects of their motivational systems.

This example appears to lead to the same conclusion concerning theoretical disputes that the previous example led to concerning empirical disagreements—namely, that any theoretical controversy can likely be resolved or at least narrowed through further empirical research and theoretical analysis. Once again, of course, the caution remains that though most disputes may have this character, not all disputes *will* be resolved in this way. For any research community, and any individual researcher, must select a few topics for intensive research, thus putting aside a vast range of unresolved potential topics.

Within a localist framework of justification, then, most of the cases surveyed here would appear to have the right empirical and logical credentials to make them plausible candidates as objective, empirically supported analyses of the phenomena they consider. Their findings may be contested on empirical and theoretical grounds, but this is precisely what makes them scientific. These researchers make a careful empirical case for the correctness of their claims, they explore the logic of these claims in extensive detail, and they offer their analyses to the larger scientific community for critical evaluation.

These cases show that, in major areas of social science, relativity arguments and problems concerning the interpretation of beliefs and values do *not* arise. These areas continue to have local problems of empirical indeterminacy, insufficiency of data, and so forth, but these problems yield to further research and debate. So it is worth emphasizing for philosophers that, in many areas of social science, the problems of objectivity and rationality are the humdrum ordinary problems of scientific research anywhere—*not* special and intractable problems arising from the specifics of social phenomena or social method.

These arguments supporting the possibility of objective, empirically controlled social inquiry should not be understood overly broadly. Plainly, some areas of social science are indeterminately vague, rhetorical, ideological, speculative, and indifferent to empirical controls. My claim is that social science *can* achieve great rigor and empirical warrant and that it should aspire to such standards.

Notes

Chapter 1: Preliminaries

1. For full-scale introductions to the philosophy of social science, see: Braybrooke 1987, Rosenberg 1988, and Miller 1987. Ernest Nagel 1961 provides a thoughtful interpretation of social science from the point of view of logical positivism.

2. This approach was most apparent in the early formulations of logical positivism within the Vienna Circle and in the writings of such authors as Carnap, Schlick, and Neurath.

3. Hempel writes, "The defining characteristic of an empirical statement is its capability of being tested by a confrontation with experiential findings, *i.e.* with the results of suitable experiments or focused observations" (1965a:3). Of course, some recent philosophy of science, including particularly writings of Paul Feyerabend, rejects the idea of strong testability.

4. Newton-Smith 1981 offers substantial description of the epistemic importance of the institutional structure of science. Merton 1973 provides a classic collection of empirical studies of the institutional structure of science.

5. Popper 1965 offers criteria of these sorts as a "demarcation criterion" on the basis of which to distinguish between science and pseudo-science.

6. Consider, for example, efforts to use Quine's (1960) indeterminacy of translation thesis to shed light on problems of interpretation of action and meaning (Hookway and Pettit 1978; Hollis and Lukes 1982; Roth 1987).

7. Consider, for example, Kuhn 1970, Lakatos 1970, Friedman 1982, Sober 1984, Fodor 1975, and Flanagan 1984.

8. For accessible exposition and discussion of the main ideas of rational choice theory applied to social science, see Barry 1978, Becker 1976, Elster 1986, and Frohlich and Oppenheimer 1978. Good introductions to social choice theory and collective action theory include Hardin 1982, Bonner 1986, and MacKay 1980. Rapoport 1966 provides an accessible introduction to two-person game theory, and Shubik 1982 provides a more technical presentation of the applications of game theory to social science. Schelling 1978 provides examples of aggregative explanations based on analysis of individual intentions.

9. See Dalton 1969 for a careful, though partisan, review of this literature.

10. "Economic theory (roughly equivalent to the political economy approach) is a method of analysis: the postulation of a number of actors with certain ends and a deductive attempt to work out how persons will act in situations which present certain alternatives, 'on the assumption that they pursue their goals rationally'" (Popkin 1979:30–31).

11. Particularly important contributions to this literature include Olson 1965, Barry 1978, Samuelson 1955, and Hardin 1982.

12. Historical materialism has been a central topic of discussion within recent "analytical Marxism." For important expositions and critical developments of the central ideas of materialism within this approach, see G. A. Cohen 1978, Shaw 1984, and Elster 1985b. See also Roemer 1986, and Ball and Farr 1984.

13. See also Sabel and Zeitlin 1985 on artisanal production versus factory production.

14. *Determine* in this context does not mean *uniquely determine* but rather *constrain* or *influence*. It is of course true that social processes are multicausal and nondeterministic. For discussion of this issue within analytic Marxism, see McMurtry 1977, Cohen 1978, and Little 1986.

15. The chief sources for Marx's theory of historical materialism are *The German Ideology*, "Preface to a Contribution to a Critique of Political Economy," and scattered comments throughout *Capital*. For a pivotal contemporary exposition of Marx's theory of historical materialism, see G. A. Cohen 1978. The extensive literature that has developed on this topic is surveyed in Little 1986:chap. 2.

16. See Przeworski's (1985a) important discussion of these issues.

17. See Miliband (1969, 1977) for discussion of both mechanisms.

18. This latter is perhaps the least plausible of these assertions, since it presupposes the effectiveness of existing property relations in enhancing the growth of the forces of production.

Chapter 2: The Moral Economy Debate

1. It should be noted that this debate does not originate with Scott and Popkin; rather, it reflects a longstanding disagreement between "substantivists" and "formalists" involved in studies of peasant societies and agrarian relations. In European studies, the moral economy theory has been extensively developed by E. P. Thompson 1963 and 1971. Dalton 1969 and Nash 1966 provide clear statements of the debate from contending sides. For a brief review of the history of this debate in application to China, see Huang 1985:3–14. The substantivist school includes Geertz 1963, Polanyi 1957, and

E. Wolf 1969; important examples of the formalist school include Schultz 1964, Myers 1970, and Becker 1976. The Scott-Popkin debate is the subject of a special issue of the *Journal of Asian Studies* (Keyes 1983).

2. Moore (1978) provides a detailed treatment of several different historical cases that illustrate this point: "This is a book about why people so often put up with being victims of their societies and why at other times they become very angry and try with passion and forcefulness to do something about their situation. . . . What are their notions of injustice and thereby of justice, and where do these ideas come from?" (xiii). Rawls (1971) provides a philosopher's account of the sense of justice, writing, "Let us assume that each person beyond a certain age and possessed of the requisite intellectual capacity develops a sense of justice under normal social circumstances. We acquire a skill in judging things to be just and unjust, and supporting these judgments by reasons" (46).

3. The subsistence ethic obviously works differently from a Marxian notion of exploitation. It is not the absolute level of exploitation that is crucial, on this approach, but the pattern of peaks and troughs of income, grain, and so on, available to the peasant household.

4. It is important to note that this aspect of the moral economy theory has a strongly functionalist tone. For it to be credible that village institutions work to level out subsistence crises, we must have some idea of the social processes that shape and stabilize such institutions. We will return to this concern below.

5. Scott 1985 brings this story into the late twentieth century; here Scott examines the effects of the green revolution on rural Malaysian society.

6. The passage quotes Barry 1978:5.

7. "By applying theories of individual decision making to villages we can begin to develop a deductive understanding of peasant institutions and move the analysis back one step to the level of the individual. By using the concepts of individual choice and decision making, we can discuss how and why groups of individuals decide to adopt some sets of norms while rejecting others" (18). The public choice paradigm is an application of the concept of economic rationality and the tools of economic analysis to problems of political behavior. These tools include applied decision theory and game theory; the theory of public goods and collective action; the theory of social decision rules; and formal social welfare theory. See Mueller 1976 for a review of the literature.

8. "Many collective projects—such as law and order, fire-fighting, slaying marauding tigers—benefit an individual whether he contributes or not. I assume that the individual weighs his decision about participation in the supply of these public goods" (24). For a good overview of the public choice literature, see Mueller 1976. Olson 1965 and Hardin 1982 provide pivotal discussions of the collective action problem.

9. "I shall argue that village institutions work less well than [moral economists] maintain, in large part because of conflicts between individual and group interests, and that far more attention must be paid to motivations for personal gain among the peasantry. I shall argue that village procedures reinforce, not level, differences and that both village procedures and the relations between peasants and lords are sources of stratification within the peasantry" (17).

10. "The only groups commonly granted tax relief, for example, are the aged, widowed, and orphaned, whose conditions can be easily verified. . . . In Vietnam, . . . peasants typically were expected by fellow villagers to pay their own taxes even if it meant selling or mortgaging land, entering into debt-slavery, or breaking up the family" (1979:41).

11. He writes: "problems of coordination and investment invariably tend to break down communal rotation systems where they have existed. As agricultural techniques develop and intensify, greater investment in the land is required. To receive maximum benefits from irrigation, for example, countless hours of fine grading of the land is required" (68).

12. In light of this skepticism about the effectiveness of moral constraints on patron-client relations, it may be noted that Bianco (1971) describes the relation between landlord and tenant in late Qing China in strikingly similar terms: "The other new feature of the prerevolutionary period lay in the domain of social relations, specifically relations between members of the landed upper class and their tenants. Under the Empire, in part because of Confucianism, these relations were what might be called paternalistic. In hard times, for example, land rent was waived or deferred and grain was distributed to the starving. In the twentieth century [these relations] became more distant, less human" (105–6).

13. "The inconsistencies and conflicts among norms suggest that norms cannot directly and simply determine actions, that decision making is involved in assessing need, and that the principles for making such comparative decisions are not easily arrived at or maintained. It is extremely difficult to rank-order norms—that is, to develop a single, stable, universally accepted social welfare function" (22).

14. See, for example, Popkin's discussion (1979:139ff.) of the changes wrought in the social arrangements of village society in Annam in the face of commercialization and colonialism.

15. Buchanan 1979 provides a developed application of this line of thought to the problem of proletarian revolution within classical Marxism. Buchanan's arguments are rebutted by Shaw 1984. Related issues are raised by Elster 1985a and 1985b.

16. Hue-Tam Ho Tai 1983 is a detailed study of the Hoa Hao sect and the rebellion it mounted in the twentieth century. Like Popkin, Tai emphasizes organizational resources as the primary factor in explaining the success of

this movement, but she pays closer attention than does Popkin to the details of the millenarian ideology that lay at the core of this movement.

17. The concept of the political entrepreneur is developed most extensively in Frohlich, Oppenheimer, and Young 1971.

18. Geertz 1980, Bloch 1966, and Migdal 1974 provide extensive detail on these village societies.

19. This method of analysis has much in common with Weber's theory of ideal types, but it also conforms to the spirit of the public choice paradigm. It is an effort to construct an abstract model of a decision-making environment to deduce the features of rational action in such circumstances. The main difference between this treatment and Popkin's is its level of detail. Popkin thinks it sufficient to refer chiefly to material interests in the context of a thin description of local institutions, whereas this model attempts to incorporate a more detailed account of the institutional and normative context within which individual action occurs.

20. See, for example, Nash 1966, Wolf 1966, and Migdal 1974.

21. It might be noted that this observation directly contradicts Skinner's analysis of Chinese marketing systems, according to which the lowest-level social unit was the standard marketing system (encompassing as many as thirty villages) rather than the village itself (1964:65). This model is discussed in chapter 3.

22. Other examples may be identified in widely different peasant communities. Thus Bloch (1966) writes, "Rich and poor alike were bound by the custom of the whole group, which helped to preserve some kind of balance between these social classes and the different ways of exploiting the soil" (47–48). And Hue-Tam Ho Tai (1983) writes, "The smooth functioning of the Vietnamese social and political order depended on a strong tradition of village institutions which catered to the emotional as well as the material needs of the villagers" (10).

23. Many authors have documented the existence of patterns of reciprocity in the rural Chinese economy: labor sharing, draft animal and tool sharing, house building. Myers 1975 surveys some of the forms of traditional cooperation. And Pasternak 1978 describes the forms of cooperation found in mid-size water management systems in Taiwan.

24. In analyzing reciprocity, Taylor writes, "Each individual act in a system of reciprocity is *usually* characterised by a combination of what one might call short-term altruism and long-term self-interest: I help you out now in the (possibly vague, uncertain and uncalculating) expectation that you will help me out in the future" (28–29).

25. Note that this practice illustrates Axelrod's TIT FOR TAT strategy.

26. Huang (1985) points out that the scale and success of collective irrigation projects in Chinese village society depends directly on the forms of community solidarity available to coordinate collective works. "The North

China plain differed sharply from the lower Yangzi delta or the Pearl River delta, where networks of canals channeled river and lake water for irrigation. . . . There . . . lineage organizations were in fact highly developed and powerful, more so than in the North China plain; the scale of the organizing capacities of lineages was thus relatively well matched to the scale of irrigation works" (56–57).

27. David Lewis (1969) describes coordination problems in these terms: "Suppose you and I both want to meet each other. We will meet if and only if we go to the same place. It matters little to either of us where (within limits) he goes if he meets the other there; and it matters little to either of us where he goes if he fails to meet the other there. We must each choose where to go. The best place for me to go is the place where you will go, so I try to figure out where you will go and to go there myself. You do the same. Each chooses according to his expectation of the other's choices" (5).

28. "Suppose we have been given a coordination problem, and we have reached some fairly good coordination equilibrium. Given exactly the same problem again, perhaps each of us will repeat what he did before. If so, we will reach the same solution. . . . Coordination by precedent [is this:] achievement of coordination by means of shared acquaintance with a *regularity* governing the achievement of coordination in a class of past cases which bear some conspicuous analogy to one another and to our present coordination problem" (Lewis 1969:40–41).

29. Elster (1982, 1985a) discusses conditional altruism and its contribution to collective action problems. This issue is also closely related to the idea of an assurance game: one in which cooperation is the best strategy if and only if one is confident that sufficient other players will cooperate as well.

30. Axelrod (1984:120–24) makes a similar point in discussing alternative strategies of conditional cooperation. He holds that it is important to choose a strategy which is simple enough that other players will be able to recognize it and act accordingly. TIT FOR TAT is a successful strategy in part because it is extremely simple to understand and to coordinate with.

31. Perry (1980a) indirectly describes this effect when she argues that large landowners had a rational incentive lacking for the village poor to lead collective defense organizations against bandits in nineteenth-century China. See also Perdue 1987 for a detailed discussion of collective action problems arising in the context of water management associations in Hunan.

32. See Duara's (1988) analysis of the functioning of temple associations in the organization of water resources in North China.

33. "These modest but critical redistributive mechanisms [communal lands, obligatory charity] nonetheless do provide a minimal subsistence insurance for villagers" (Scott 1976:5).

34. One possible prudential consideration might lead to redistribution in these circumstances: elite fears of local unrest might lead them to contribute

to charity and redistributive institutions so as to keep pressures from the poor at a manageable level. Scott seems to allude to this sort of consideration at various points.

35. Huang (1985:259–74) notes that villages in North China differed in their capacity to absorb such stresses: more solidary villages were capable of organizing for collective defense against bandits, drought, or a predatory state, whereas more atomized villages collapsed. "The combined effects of population pressure, commercialization, natural disasters, and urban employment produced a considerably higher degree of social stratification and semiproletarianization in this village than in Houxiazhai or Lengshuigou" (264).

36. Migdal (1974:14—22) emphasizes this point in his study of Mexican village life.

37. Consider Geertz's description (1971:142—69) of a failed Javanese funeral ritual: "The complex of beliefs and rituals which had for generations brought countless Javanese safely through the difficult postmortem period suddenly failed to work with its accustomed effectiveness" (146). Geertz's central point is that traditional religious beliefs and practices had effectively organized Javanese village life but that "population growth, urbanization, monetization, occupational differentiation, and the like, have combined to weaken the traditional ties of peasant social structure. . . . The rise of nationalism, Marxism, and Islamic reform as ideologies . . . has affected not only the large cities . . . but has had a heavy impact on the smaller towns and villages as well" (148).

38. This position brings Scott close to Geertz's interpretation-theory model. Geertz's central point is that action is the complex product of cultural values and individual deliberation (see chapter 7).

39. This line of thought concerning the character of social action has much in common with the interpretation-theory model of anthropology (see chapter 7): to understand social behavior the meanings that participants assign to various actions and institutions must be interpreted. Here Geertz 1973, 1983, is a central contributor.

40. Significantly, *Weapons of the Weak* (1985) shifts its focus to the interpretation-theory dimension of analysis; there Scott expends great effort attempting to reconstruct the meanings of elements of village life for the participants.

41. This is an effect identified in Axelrod's analysis of cooperation.

42. For extensive discussion of the need for microfoundations for social explanations within Marxism, see Roemer 1982a, b, Elster 1982, Van Parijs 1983, and Little 1986.

43. See Elster 1985b for extensive argument in favor of the requirement of microfoundations for social explanations.

44. Human Relations Area File no. 130 (Paris: Augustin Clallamel, 1894).

Chapter 3: Regional Systems in Traditional China

1. Paul Cohen (1984:164–66) offers a survey and appraisal of this generation of China historians and of Skinner's contributions.

2. For exponents of this view, see Dalton 1969, 1971, and Polanyi 1957. Geertz's (1984) criticisms of "economism" in anthropology are also relevant.

3. Recent researchers have emphasized the importance of other forms of functional organization across the traditional Chinese landscape. Particularly important are the institutions of water management—flood control and irrigation—which often diverged from both administrative and marketing hierarchies. See Pasternak 1978 and Perdue 1987 for recent treatments of this type of organization. And Duara (1988) argues that religious temple hierarchies and political hierarchies below the county level in North China conformed neither to the marketing nor to the administrative hierarchy.

4. This is an analytical distinction and does not imply that the two systems are distinct on the ground.

5. Skinner offers these examples of diagnostic goods for distinguishing intermediate market towns from standard towns: hardware and tools, caps, wine, and religious supplies; and as diagnostic artisan services at this same level he lists coffin makers, blacksmiths, tailors, and noodle makers (351).

6. Rozman (1973:14) offers a seven-level hierarchical framework for the central places in China that differs in some important details from Skinner's account. Rozman's scheme relies on administrative features at the higher levels and marketing features in the bottom two levels. See Skinner's stringent criticisms of Rozman's criteria in his review of *Urban Networks in Ch'ing China and Tokugawa Japan* (1975).

7. Walter Christaller, *Die zentralen Orte in Süddeutschland;* August Lösch, *Die räumliche Ordnung der Wirtschaft* [*The Economics of Location*].

8. This framework of analysis owes much to August Thünen's treatment of the isolated city (1826)—which Skinner refers to in "The Population Geography of Agrarian Societies" (n.d.).

9. Rozman (1973) offers data that suggest, however, that market-village ratios varied substantially. "Skinner has suggested a fluctuating ratio gravitating around one standard marketing settlement for each eighteen villages in China. Checking data in local gazetteers, I have found a somewhat higher ratio of villages to markets prevailing throughout the Ch'ing period. Variations were marked; some hsien contained a market for each 10 villages and other hsien contained a market for 50 or more villages" (100). Part of this variation may reflect the different effects of "top-down" and "bottom-up" marketing-system formation.

10. The most prominent exceptions to this point include settlements established by the central authorities to satisfy defensive needs, colonize a frontier area, or establish a center for regional government.

11. This problem has been discussed extensively within current analytical Marxism. See, for example, Elster's critique of functional explanation (1983:chap. 2). Also pertinent are G. Cohen 1978, 1982, Elster 1982, Roemer 1982, and Van Parijs 1982.

12. "It will be noted that the level of transport is a crucial variable no matter how one accounts for the periodicity of traditional markets. It is the 'friction of distance' which limits both the demand area of the firm and the dependent area of a market. Thus the periodicity of markets in traditional agrarian societies is, in the last analysis, a function of the relatively primitive state of transport" (Skinner 1964–65:11).

13. Crissman (1972:242–43) argues that the geometrical regularity of central-place theory is distorted by the fact that consumers may favor one marketing place over another for noneconomic reasons—its entertainment value, for example. Crissman suggests that nonmarket factors thus have an important role as well in determining whether a given place develops into a higher-level place.

14. Huang (1985) argues against Skinner's view of the standard marketing system as the basis for community in North China. He holds that social life was quite different in the North China plain than in the Chengdu plain (the region studied by Skinner); villagers rarely had any contact with members from nearby villages (220ff.). Huang argues that villages in his region were highly isolated from social contact (as well as economic contact) with the society around them. "Villagers had minimal social intercourse with outsiders, and village affairs were governed largely by endogenous leaders" (220). Insularity was greatest for middle peasants (222).

15. Consider Elizabeth Perry's analysis of the mechanisms of the spread of Nian political and religious ideas in Perry (1980a).

16. Important recent works that have incorporated Skinner's analysis of marketing hierarchies include Naquin 1981, Marks 1984, Kuhn 1980, and Perdue 1987.

17. "Fairly early in my research on Chinese cities it became clear that in late imperial times they formed not a single integrated urban system but several regional systems, each only tenuously connected with its neighbors. In tracing out the overlapping hinterlands of the cities in each one of these regional systems, I came to the realization that the region they jointly defined coincided with minor exceptions to a physiographic unit. In short, it appears that each system of cities developed within a physiographic region" (1977b:211). Gilbert Rozman (1982:15–17) agrees with Skinner that the province is too large a unit of study; county and prefecture are possible, and village studies would be optimal. Rozman criticizes Skinner, however, for paying insufficient attention to the need for local-level studies to establish the fine structure of the patterns of spatial organization that Skinner emphasizes. Rozman describes his own approach as "inductive" and "micro-

regional" (1982:25, 126): it is designed to work from the local statistics upward, to discern whatever patterns of population and marketing are to be found.

18. Schoppa (1982:16–22) employs this internal differentiation of regions into homogeneous zones—extended by distinguishing between inner and outer core and inner and outer periphery—as a basis for his analysis of elite politics in Zhejiang.

19. "As applied to China, this involves plotting county-level population densities, from which contours are derived showing density gradients" (1977a:282).

20. Skinner identifies nine macroregions, including Manchuria, but excludes Manchuria from his comments because of its late and abnormal economic development (1977b:213). In later writings he separates part of the Middle Yangzi region to form a small new macroregion, Gan Yangzi (1985:273).

21. Consider, for example, Skinner's application of the framework to the system of imperial administration. "The chief argument of the paper is that the formal administrative attributes of capital cities stemmed in large part from their place in the relevant regional system of economic central places. A secondary thesis is that the size and strength of informal political systems varied inversely with the intensity of bureaucratic government—a covariation that expressed the structure of 'natural' economic regions at least as much as the arrangement of provinces" (Skinner, ed. 1977:254).

22. Skinner also cites the drain of resources from periphery to core that accompanies the flow of lumber, firewood, and silt from the hinterlands to the urban core.

23. They write, "This essay argues that although Skinner's concepts [macroregions, cores, and peripheries] are intuitively appealing, some are too vague to be tested, while others are not supported by the economic and demographic facts they claim to represent" (1986:721). And they conclude "the following: his concepts are difficult to test, they are seriously flawed, and they lack real explanatory power" (737). There appears to be some confusion here concerning the logic of empirical confirmation—in particular, as to whether *concepts* or *hypotheses* are subject to test.

24. The arguments of the following two sections have benefited from collaboration with Joseph Esherick on a joint critique of Sands and Myers (Little and Esherick 1989).

25. Curiously, however, they do not provide evidence that there was grain trade into the Southeast Coast or Middle Yangzi regions; they refer to trade along the Grand Canal to Peking and northern capitals and imports into lower Yangzi coastal provinces (1986:724)—a region that, according to their data, was self-sufficient in the early twentieth century.

26. Sands and Myers also hold that the mobility of scholar-officials importantly reduced the isolation of macroregions. Rowe (1984:213–51) makes a

similar point about the diffusion of regional merchant groups throughout the empire.

27. Perdue 1988, Lee 1988. These are conference papers prepared for the American Council of Learned Societies/Social Science Research Council conference on Economic Methods for Chinese Historical Research, January 1988, in Oracle, Ariz.

28. See also Naquin 1981 for thoughtful consideration of the significance of Skinner's spatial constructs for the understanding of the unfolding of the White Lotus rebellion in North China. Lavely (1988) shows that female literacy rates in the early twentieth century show a marked core-periphery variation.

29. Skinner himself places little weight on this model, offering it as a rough first-order analysis rather than as a conclusive demonstration of the respective causal roles of the factors he analyzes.

30. This analysis illustrates the element of arbitrary choice involved in constructing estimates of demographic data (in this case, what criteria should define an urban place). And it focuses attention on the need for accurate data to produce reliable estimates.

31. "A qualitative discussion of these variables plus recourse to some approximate weighting can at least demonstrate that in all likelihood these are the most important factors affecting the level of urbanization in late imperial China" (1977b:232).

22. This problem would be amenable to treatment by regression analysis, discriminant analysis, or other statistical correlation techniques—*if* Skinner were working with a larger data set. If the data set included several hundred individuals (macroregions) and associated measures of the urbanization rate and the several factors, then statistical techniques could determine which if any of these factors correlate with the urbanization rate. However, since he is working only with data describing eight individuals (macroregions), Skinner cannot use these statistical techniques.

33. Skinner explicitly denies that the factors are independent; however, his aggregation rule (summing the factors) presupposes the contrary.

34. MacKay (1980) provides an extensive discussion of the problem of scales of measure, aggregation of independent scales, and the requirement of independence of irrelevant alternatives.

35. Skinner (1977b) appears to acknowledge this point: "Since only two of the six dimensions were 'scored blind,' as it were, it must be admitted that the numerical model as a whole is rigged. Nothing is demonstrated other than the plausibility of the arguments made in qualitative terms" (714n).

36. The aggregation function constructed here is the same in logical form as the discriminant function described by Sands and Myers. *If* there were sufficient macroregions, it would be possible to use discriminant analysis to assign values to the coefficients of the aggregation function. Since there are only eight macroregions, however, this is not possible.

37. This problem is directly analogous to the problem of interpersonal comparisons of utility. MacKay 1980, Sen 1982, and Bonner 1986 provide good discussions of this problem.

38. We could avoid many of these problems of measurement and aggregation by abandoning the quantitative information provided by the six measurement scales and considering only the rank orderings they impose on the macroregions for each factor. Each factor imposes a rank ordering on macroregions which may be construed as a "voter preference" in which macroregions are candidates and the six factors are voters. Now instead of aggregating factors by mathematical addition, we aggregate by a pairwise voting scheme. This data imposes a transitive ranking on the regions: LY > L > SC > MY > NWC > NC > UY > YG. This ranking corresponds to the ranking of regions by urbanization rates with one exception: the latter ranking places NWC ahead of MY by a small margin. It should also be remarked that it is the fact that each region generally dominates the next in almost every factor which assures that there is a consistent ranking. If factors were more variously distributed over regions, considerations derived from the voters' paradox would make it likely that no consistent ranking can be formed by aggregating individual rankings. See MacKay 1980 for a readable discussion of this problem. Arrow 1963 and Sen 1970 represent the classical discussions.

Chapter 4: The Breakthrough Debate

1. Although I do not discuss this material in detail, European economic historians currently debate the rate of growth of the English economy in the eighteenth century. Against earlier interpretations, it is now claimed that the growth rate was more continuous over an extended period than the term *industrial revolution* would suggest. For a careful review of the current literature on this topic, see Crafts 1985. "The general impression to be obtained is that in much of the British economy productivity growth was slow at least until the second quarter of the nineteenth century. Whilst in Chapter 3 a case was made for stressing rapid structural change in the use of the labour force, and that this justified the conventional use of the term 'Industrial Revolution', this chapter has indicated that the term should *not* be taken to imply a widespread, rapid growth of productivity in manufacturing" (Crafts 1985:86).

2. For brief synopses of the distributional and technological schools, see Riskin 1975:56–64, Myers 1970, and Huang 1985:18–21. See also Joshua Fogel's (1984) survey of Japanese historiography on the Qing economy, which suggests that Japanese scholars have strongly emphasized the distributional model—production relations, surplus extraction, and class.

3. In addition to the works cited here, Rawski 1972 and Myers 1970 are also major studies of traditional Chinese agriculture.

4. Elvin (1973:235) dates the disappearance of the manorial economy to the mid-Qing (eighteenth century).

5. Huang (1985) seconds this judgment for North China: "This crops-only agrarian economy is distinctive for its very high land productivity and very low labor productivity. Kawachi Juzo, working with John Lossing Buck's data, has shown that Chinese agriculture in the 1930's in fact attained a much higher crop yield per unit of cultivated area than the much more modernized American agriculture of the day" (15).

6. Schultz (1964) offers an early and classic formulation of a formalist analysis of traditional agriculture and problems of development, arguing that "there are comparably few significant inefficiencies in the allocation of the factors of production in traditional agriculture" (37). Significant improvement in agricultural output, therefore, can be achieved only through application of scientific and technical knowledge to farm production and public investment in the knowledge and skills available to the farmer.

7. The explanation considered shares much with several other important contributions to the study of peasant societies: Geertz's analysis of agricultural involution in Java (1963), Elvin's analysis of the "high-level equilibrium trap" in traditional China (1972, 1973), and Chayanov's analysis of the "self-exploitation" endemic within the Russian peasant economy (1924).

8. For a good, brief account of modern Malthusian doctrine, see Schofield 1986. In European studies a comparable line of analysis is to be found in the work of M. M. Postan and Emmanuel Le Roy Ladurie.

9. "The Chinese traditional family system functioned quite differently, for two important reasons. One was the drive for family perpetuation, the obsession with having male heirs to carry on the family lineage. Marriage was a decision not dependent on one's economic condition, but on one's deepest obligation to one's whole family as well as to one's ancestors. The second was the strength of family feeling, the family as institution often became a multi-worker business entity, provider of employment and basis for intrafamily income distribution. Consequently, instead of functioning as an automatic regulator, the Chinese family system tolerated overpopulation" (1986:8–9).

10. Schofield (1983) draws a similar contrast between traditional northern European cultures and the developing world: "In the latter, marriage takes place at an early and customary age (usually in the late teens) and almost everyone marries, often living initially in their parents' household. Consequently, fertility in these societies is high and unvarying" (68). A more complex analysis may be found in Hanley and Wolf 1985, who offer a model according to which universal marriage is accompanied by customs that depress marital fertility.

11. This conclusion seems inconsistent with Chao's (1986:89) own data, however, where Chao accepts an estimate of 200 million for the year 1592 and of 70.2 million for 1657. The latter figure is derived from *ting* data collected by the early Qing dynasty (39–41) and represents a catastrophic popu-

lation drop following the Qing conquest. However, these data themselves are suspect; the earlier figure appears to be too high, and the later figure too low. Wakeman (1985:1054n) accepts a figure of 150 million for the sixteenth century and 76 to 92 million for 1661, representing a 40–50 percent drop.

12. For a detailed treatment of the process of land reclamation in Hunan and its effects on the ecology, see Perdue 1987.

13. "The data point overwhelmingly to the fact that ancient China was an atomistic market economy; indeed, it continued to be so until the 1950's. By atomistic I mean made up primarily of countless small production units making independent decisions. Such units were frequently described as 'households with five persons tilling 100 *mou* of land.' These freeholders or tenants of the large landlords that figured in every period were themselves independent decision-making units" (Chao 1986:5).

14. For further description of the smallholding and leaseholding peasant economy, see Perkins 1969 and Eastman 1988.

15. "After overpopulation reduced the marginal product of labor to below the subsistence level, subsistence cost constituted a wage floor for both latifundia and handicraft factories. Just like tenant farming, rural subsidiary production by household members had no such cost rigidity" (Chao 1986:224).

16. However, Huang (1985:155–68) offers data to suggest that no such inequality exists between the marginal product of labor in peasant and managerial farms in North China.

17. "The predictable result of such a situation would be a gradual shift from owner cultivation of land to tenant farming" (Chao 1986:12). Chao holds that the same result also attaches to rural subsidiary handicraft production: a handicraft factory employing wage labor creates a lower return than the same amount of capital expended on putting-out production (12–13). This conclusion runs contrary to Huang's (1985) findings on this subject in his major study of the rural economy of North China: "Managerial farming brought better returns than leasing landlordism. This was in part because most managerial farmer households did some farm labor themselves, whereas those who leased out their land did not. But it was also in part because the managerial farmers were able to use labor much more effectively compared with the small tenant family farms on which leasing landlordism was based" (72).

18. "The other profound impact of overpopulation was on the technological preference of producers. . . . The primary direction of Chinese agricultural development after the twelfth century was towards intensified farming" (Chao 1986:224–25).

19. Chao's analysis closely parallels the "proto-industrialization" framework in European studies. The central discussions of this concept may be found in Mendels 1972, Kriedte 1983, and Kriedte, Medick, and Schlumbohm 1981.

20. Chao does estimate real wages between 50 B.C. and A.D. 1818 (218–19),

which he summarizes as showing a trend downward from the twelfth century. This data is based on wage rates for unskilled workers, which were then converted into units of grain, using contemporary grain prices. This data set shows such wild variation, however, that it is difficult to interpret meaningfully. Thus in Shaanxi in 1742 a farmer's wage is 400 wen, whereas in the same province in 1749 it is 1,200 wen. At opposite ends of the time frame, Chao finds a draft worker's wage (grain equivalent) in Kaifeng in 1080 to be 800 sheng, whereas in Yunnan in 1805 a farmer's (grain equivalent) wage is 3.7—a range of roughly 250 to 1. Given the range of findings here, and given that Chao provides no information about the grain price data he uses, it is difficult to attach much significance to these data.

21. Liu Ts'ui-jung's work (1985) with genealogies in Zhejiang is exemplary in this regard. See also Harrell 1985 and Rozman 1982.

22. Consider, by way of contrast, the highly detailed demographic arguments offered by Wrigley and Schofield 1981. Their work is based on an extremely large data set drawn from several centuries of English parish registers and permits credible testing of a variety of demographic hypotheses—including the Malthusian thesis.

23. See also Pasternak's (1985) treatment of uxorical marriage customs in Taiwan, where once again he finds family arrangements highly sensitive to economic circumstances.

24. A different flaw in this analysis arises because the land–man ratios in this table are computed on the basis of population estimates and land estimates from different years: 976 and 961, 1072 and 1109, 1581 and 1592, and so forth. If we normalize the population data to the year for corresponding land data by assuming a growth rate of 1 percent per year (a reasonable assumption for short periods of time and an unreasonable one for several decades), we find that the results change substantially; for example, the ratio for 976 falls to 6.86 and that for 1072 rises to 7.98—reversing the direction of change for this period! This suggests that the land–man ratios computed here are unreliable.

25. "Because of resilient economic institutions, overpopulation did not express itself in the form of open unemployment and high population pressure can be detected only indirectly" (222).

26. Myers (1987) makes a similar point in his review of Chao.

27. Myers (1970) refers to models of this sort as "distribution" theories: "The distribution theory is that such a large portion of income was taken from the peasants in rent, high interest charges, taxes, and unfair terms of price exchange that they were left with little surplus to improve or enlarge their farms" (14). Myers argues that this interpretation is incorrect in application to North China in the nineteenth century, but his arguments have not persuaded other observers; see Wiens 1975, Riskin 1972, and Huang 1985. John Lossing Buck (1937) describes the distributionalist approach in these terms: "Some reformers assign most of the Chinese agricultural ills to a

faulty agrarian situation comprising such problems as farm tenancy, injustice in the settlement of legal questions and disputes, usury, exorbitant profits of middlemen and the like" (1). Buck doubts the priority of these factors, however.

28. For a general overview of this model in application to economic development, see Brenner 1986.

29. The term *microclass* rather than *class* is appropriate here because Brenner emphasizes that local class alignments, not regional or national alliances, constitute the point of change within an agrarian system.

30. "Changes in relative factor scarcities consequent upon demographic changes exerted an effect on the distribution of income in medieval Europe only as they were, so to speak, refracted through the prism of changing social-property relations and fluctuating balances of class forces" (Brenner 1982:21).

31. "Indeed, the central question we must ask is why, given the substantial investment potential indicated by the size of the surplus, so little investment, modernization, and technical progress actually took place" (1987:72).

32. "There was one dominant class, the gentry in late imperial China, drawing its income from the surplus produced by the peasants, artisans, and workers above their own subsistence requirements. Landowning, moneylending, mercantile activity, official position, and so forth were different means of garnering this surplus, not the demarcations of distinct classes" (1987:78).

33. Lippit draws these data from Chung-li Chang's *Income of the Chinese Gentry* (1962).

34. "About one-third of China's farmland was owned by landlords, and while precise quantification is difficult, it appears that about three-fourths of this was owned by members of the gentry" (1987:80–81). Perkins (1969) provides a similar estimate.

35. The Gini coefficient is the ratio of the area enclosed between the straight line and the curved line to the area of the lower triangle; it is a measure of the degree of stratification of wealth holding in a society. A perfectly egalitarian distribution produces a coefficient of 0.00, whereas the opposite extreme, in which one person owns all land, produces a coefficient of 1.00. The Gini coefficient of wealth inequality in the United States today is approximately 0.35. The inequalities found in Huang's data, then, are substantially greater than those in the United States or Western Europe today. My estimate of the Gini coefficient implied by Huang's data is corroborated by Kang Chao's calculation of a Gini coefficient of 0.66 for North China, based on the land studies of the 1930s (125).

36. Perkins (1969) provides extensive information about the pattern of tenancy in late Qing China. He finds that tenancy rates varied greatly by region from a high of 56 percent (Sichuan) to a low of 12 percent (Shandong). The areas of highest tenancy are in Southwest China, Southeast China, Central China, and East China. North China shows consistently lower rates of

tenancy—mostly below 20 percent, with a few areas between 20 and 29 percent.

37. "The uses of the surplus included primarily luxury consumption (including conspicuous consumption), the purchase of land, ceremonial expenditures, the military expenditures necessary to defend the empire against the foreigners and against the Chinese, and expenditures on classical education" (1987:90–91).

38. "Thus in both industry and agriculture, the production relations of late imperial China were marked by a fairly complete separation between large-scale owners and production processes. The path to profit was not the improvement of production but command over the social processes whereby the direct producers were relieved of the surplus they produced" (1987:84).

39. Elvin (1973) quotes a Ming observer, Keng Chu, in terms that strikingly confirm this observation: "There are one-fold profits in agriculture and it needs very great labour. Fools do it. There are two-fold profits in manufacture and it needs great labour. Those who have skilful fingers do it. There are three-fold profits in trading, and little labour is needed. Those who are prudent and thoughtful do it. There are five-fold profits in the [illegal] sale of salt, and labour is not necessary. Bad and powerful people do it" (248).

40. There is some countervailing evidence on this point; some authors do find evidence of production-oriented wealth holders. Perdue's (1987) analysis of Hunan, for instance, provides many examples of elite investments in irrigation, land clearing, and other forms of productivity-enhancing infrastructure.

41. Rowe (1984:160–61) provides some data on native banks in South China. See also Eastman (1988:112–14) for a description of native banking and remittance banking.

42. Anderson (1986) describes the problem of moving from raw data to estimates of economic variables in these terms. "Later, in the data analysis stage, we have a further problem: to find ways of modeling with our data the social or economic relationships or processes that we wish to explore. Most of the debate which has surrounded recent cliometrics stems either from questions about the validity of the indicators employed, or from the over-simplified models that are used to build equations which can be solved with the data and computational techniques available" (39). Anderson implicitly distinguishes between raw data, mathematical models used to summarize the data, summary representations of the data as time series, interpretation of the data, and causal hypotheses concerning variations among the data.

43. Crafts 1985 provides a more extensive discussion of this point.

44. Schofield (1986) offers this assessment of the role of assumptions in economic history, in the context of a discussion of problems of English demography. "The level of uncertainty in historical discussion is often high, and the scope for disagreement is correspondingly large. Accordingly, an investigation of the sensitivity of results to alternative assumptions about

the evidence can often play a valuable role by indicating the bounds of the area of dispute and so keep the argument focused within manageable limits" (25).

45. "The general conception of explanation by deductive subsumption under general laws or theoretical principles . . . will be called the deductive-nomological-model, or the D-N model of explanation" (Hempel 1965a:345).

46. The following are drawn from Marx's own writings on materialism, including his preface to *A Contribution to the Critique of Political Economy*, *The German Ideology*, and *Capital*. For more extensive discussion, see Little 1986:chap. 2, G. Cohen 1978, and Miller 1984.

47. This stance is further developed in my *Scientific Marx* (1986:65–67).

Chapter 5: Theories of Peasant Rebellion

1. Besides the books discussed in this chapter, see Feuerwerker 1975 and Chesneaux 1973 for an overview of the main contours of this aspect of Chinese history. For accounts of the development of the Communist movement in China, see Lucien Bianco 1986, Chalmers Johnson 1962, Mark Selden 1971, Ralph Thaxton 1983, and Yung-fa Chen 1986.

2. Bianco (1975, 1986) argues that this tendency toward political rather than social goals persisted even into the twentieth century; he surveys a large number of peasant disturbances outside of Communist areas in the 1920s and 1930s and holds that attacks on landlords, moneylenders, and the like were rare in comparison to tax and conscription riots. Bianco also emphasizes the localism of most peasant disturbances in China.

3. For an important account of the military and institutional arrangements through which the Taiping rebellion was repressed, see P. Kuhn 1980.

4. See Hardin 1982 for an extensive discussion of collective action problems.

5. The idea of a collective goal, I emphasize, refers to a goal shared by many or all participants and playing a significant role in explaining their behavior. This formulation does not commit the error of supposing that groups have goals over and above the goals of the individuals who constitute the group.

6. This account oversimplifies, of course, by assuming that one shared goal underlies the collective action. More commonly, however, a political movement or collective action is motivated by overlapping—even contradictory—goals shared by various groups within the coalition.

7. In Hardin's words, the goal of collective action theory is "to decompose group action into individual actions in order to explain collective outcomes in terms of individual motivations" (1982:2).

8. Hobsbawm 1959.

9. Soboul (1975:230–32) describes the political organization and program of the radical middle class.

10. Hobsbawm (1959) presents Judeo-Christian messianism as the chief example of such a chiliastic ideology. Ironically, Hobsbawm specifically doubts that Buddhism or Hinduism contain the seeds of a millenarian sect (58).

11. Naquin 1976, 1981, 1985. See also Tai 1983 for an account of millenarian movements in nineteenth- and twentieth-century Vietnam, and Adas 1979 for a comparative discussion of several non-European millenarian movements.

12. Naquin emphasizes, however, that White Lotus sects were only loosely linked through a common tradition and that sects varied significantly in doctrine. This account is taken from Naquin 1976:9–18. Naquin 1985 contains a somewhat more detailed account.

13. "Sect members believed it their responsibility to 'respond to the kalpa' by mobilizing their sects and, as the agents of the Eternal Mother and the avant-garde of the millennium, to speed the destruction of the existing order and its replacement by a better system. Sect members called this 'making known the Way' and in this response to the kalpa were transformed from secret believers into openly and publicly committed followers of the Eternal Mother" (1976:17).

14. Naquin (1985) suggests that the ordinary followers of the White Lotus sects were typically rural people on the fringes of more orthodox institutions: "Men and women who were elderly or without families, monks without temples, migrant laborers and other itinerant workers, urban immigrants, peasants whose village and temple organizations were dominated by others, and so forth" (257).

15. Naquin (1976) also refers to negative incentives addressed toward defectors from sects during the planning process: "It was not unusual for warnings and the threat of death to accompany requests [for contributions]. Sect members believed that when the kalpa did come, all nonbelievers would be killed" (51).

16. "His takeover and subsequent efforts to reach out and contact other sect groups may not have been motivated by anything beyond a desire to ride the wave of power and respect as far as it would take him" (78). Lin's behavior in the event seems to further support this interpretation of his motives; he remained at home and did not accompany his group of rebels in their attack on the Forbidden City. (He was arrested in his home and executed after the rebellion failed.)

17. Skinner's analysis of marketing systems is relevant in this context, since the transportation and communication resources that facilitate marketing are also available for the diffusion of heterodox religious ideas, through the travels of itinerant magicians, martial arts instructors, and the like.

18. Recall Durkheim's distinction between mechanical and organic solidarity in this context; the organizational structure identified here is mechan-

ical in that it involves little hierarchical articulation. Rather, several bands are simply linked, with no effective hierarchy among leaders of the diverse groups.

19. Naquin offers a brief account of the military institutions of the Qing state: the deployment of forces in the region and the fragmented command system the empire adopted as a hedge against excessive concentration of military power. She notes that this system was adequate for small disturbances but could not respond quickly enough to a rebellion that rapidly gained in size. Thus it was possible for a local disturbance to leapfrog the capacity of local military forces to repress it. Philip Kuhn (1980) describes the military organization of regular army forces (the Green Standard) in similar terms.

20. But contrast this more rationalist approach with the reality of politico-religious movements of fundamentalist Islam, for example, Iran. Is it plausible to suppose that this system works through a calculus of individual interests? Adas (1979) draws this connection in the Foreword to the second edition of his book.

21. Eric Wolf's writings provide an important example of this approach to peasant rebellions. See E. Wolf 1969 for an ambitious effort to analyze rebellions and revolutions in Russia, China, Cuba, Mexico, Algeria, and Vietnam. A useful collection on this subject is Lewis 1974. Paige 1975, Chesneaux 1973, and Migdal 1974 are also relevant contributions from this point of view.

22. Hilton's (1973) account of the English rising of 1381 may serve as a paradigm of such an account. He writes, "I aim to demonstrate that peasant society in medieval Europe, from the Dark Ages to the end of the fifteenth century, like peasant societies at all times and in all places, contained social tensions which had their outcome in social movements, some on a small and some on a large scale, some peaceful and some violent. Those which resulted from the very nature of the peasant economy are considered first. . . . I have attempted to describe the growing complexity of peasant movements" (19). See also Vlastos 1986 for an application of the class-conflict model to peasant movements in Tokugawa Japan.

23. Brenner's analysis (1976, 1982) of class and local power relations in early modern France represents an important neo-Marxist application of this view to agrarian politics.

24. Haifeng county, however, was more subject to the effects of Western economic intervention than other areas of China because of its proximity to coastal cities. This again raises the problem of generalizability and regional differentiation.

25. Myers's views are advanced in many articles and books; particularly important are Myers 1970 and 1986.

26. In his review of Myers's book, Wiens (1975) raises a different sort of

objection to Myers's "no-exploitation" view: "The author asserts that 'there is little evidence that merchants, absentee landlords, and moneylenders blocked rural improvement and caused peasant misery' [Myers 1970:127]. The fact is that such evidence is not sought or analyzed: Where is his analysis of interest rates and the burden of debt relative to net incomes? Of rent levels relative to net incomes of tenants or the proportion of production expenses they bore? Of the degree to which wealth bred further wealth, and poverty led to deeper poverty?" (285).

27. In this vein Watson (1985) writes of the New Territories in the seventeenth century, "These markets were not free and open trading centers; they were, in fact, monopolies of the large lineages. They were controlled by certain individuals, or later by ancestral estates. In the end one lineage dominated each market, controlling access to it, claiming a percentage of sales, and charging a 'protection fee' to shopkeepers. This control was backed up by the lineage's self-defense corps" (25).

28. Of course, class relations varied extensively among regions. In some areas of China (for example, North China) the primary form of land tenure was private smallholding, not tenancy. These areas had no landlord-tenant relations, though indebtedness was a chronic feature of rural life (Arrigo 1986). This form of variation implies that a class-conflict model of political behavior must identify different property relations in different regions; it also leaves open the possibility that natural and ecological crisis, not exploitation, is the primary cause of peasant misery—as appears to be the case in the rebellions Perry considers in North China.

29. Watson's (1985) ethnographic study of the New Territories of Hong Kong details the interacting cultural systems constituted by lineage and property stratification.

30. "Peasant collective action in the eighteenth and nineteenth centuries had led to a considerable amount of rural social violence in Haifeng, but these disruptions could hardly be described as class conflict. Most of the conflict for which we have documentation occurred between lineages or the Red and Black Flags, vertically aligned social groupings, or between state and society, as in the food riots" (Marks 1984:96).

31. Chen Yung-fa (1986:173–91) details the extensive efforts that the CCP was forced to make to bring local class conflict to the surface in its mobilization efforts. See also Watson 1985 for extensive discussion of the tensions between class and lineage in the New Territories (Hong Kong).

32. The Taiping rebellion represents something of an exception to this point.

33. See Chen Yung-fa's (1986) important analysis of Communist mobilization efforts in the base areas during the Japanese occupation. Chen demonstrates that the CCP skillfully manipulated class fissures in its efforts to advance its program of social revolution in the countryside.

34. Joshua Fogel's biography of Ai Siqi (1987b) provides a useful description of the intellectual origins of the communist movement in China. See also Fairbank 1986: chap. 12.

35. Winston Hsieh (1974) notes, on a related theme, that unemployed boatmen, displaced by steam boats on the Lower Yangzi, were critical to the spread of revolutionary ideas in the Canton area; and Tai (1983) writes that bus drivers, with their mobility and their independence from village society, were critical for the same function in Vietnam.

36. Other scholars of China whose work falls into this area include P. Kuhn 1980 and Lucien Bianco 1975, 1986.

37. This account is derived from Feuerwerker's description of the Nian rebellion (1975:38–42).

38. This is one of the regions of China where Tawney's celebrated remark applies most vividly: when the peasant is standing up to his neck in water, even a ripple will drown him.

39. Perry describes hers as an ecological approach. It would be more accurate, though, to see it as a rational collective action approach, given the centrality of the "strategies of survival" framework.

40. Perry writes, "The origins of the uprising lie not in anti-Manchu millenarianism, but rather in a highly pragmatic effort by vast numbers of Huaipei inhabitants to seize and sustain a livelihood" (1980a:97). Bianco (1975) emphasizes this localism of peasant protest in his analysis of spontaneous peasant disturbances during the Nationalist period: "Indeed, a fourth characteristic of these peasant uprisings not led by Communists was their *overriding concern with local interests*. Rioting peasants would be pacified once their rebellious attitude had persuaded the authorities to transfer a troublesome military unit to the neighbouring *hsien*, where it could freely squeeze and terrify other helpless villagers" (320).

41. Recall in this context the criticisms by Sen and others of the concept of narrow economic rationality.

42. Important discussions on the free rider problem in connection with revolution include Buchanan 1979, Shaw 1984, and Popkin 1979.

43. See chapters 2 and 3; conditional altruism is one possible model of rationality to handle this problem.

44. Chalmers Johnson (1962) emphasizes the latter, whereas Mark Selden emphasizes the former. Selden (1972:35) considers whether rural "modernization"—commercialization and advances in transportation—can account for the success of the CCP's mobilization efforts and concludes that these factors play a minor role in Shaanxi.

45. Chen (1986) provides a detailed and informative analysis of this process, based on secret party documents, in Central China during the Sino-Japanese war.

46. Moore (1978) places the particulars of the political culture of an op-

pressed group at the core of his account of the political behavior of the group. Moore contends that the historically specific sense of justice possessed by an exploited group is crucial to understanding its political behavior.

47. Consider Ralph Thaxton's efforts to connect religious and folk political values in China with the program of revolutionary change in twentieth century China; Thaxton (1983) holds that the presence of this "little tradition," and the CCP's effort to capitalize on it, accounts for much of the success of that movement. Perry, by contrast, holds that indigenous political culture was more of an impediment because of its localism.

48. Marx's treatment of this process falls under the heading of "class consciousness": the process through which a group forges its own awareness of its identity as a group and the nature of its collective interests. In the *Communist Manifesto*, he writes, "This organization of the proletarians into a class, and consequently into a political party, is continually being upset again by the competition between the workers themselves. But it ever rises up again, stronger, firmer, mightier" (Marx and Engels [1848] 1974:76).

49. Esherick (1987) analyzes the origins of the Boxer uprising with particular sensitivity to the salience of local political culture. His account is more satisfactory than any of those considered above in its attempt to incorporate features of the class conflict model, the local politics model, and the importance of local political culture in explaining collective action.

Chapter 6: Generalization and Theory

1. Tilly (1964) provides an admirable example of an area study that combines theoretical analysis with close empirical investigation. Tilly attempts to explain the counterrevolution of 1793 (the Vendée) in terms of the material and social wellsprings of political attitudes and behavior in Western France.

2. "I have argued that (1) state organizations susceptible to administrative and military collapse when subjected to intensified pressures from more developed countries abroad and (2) agrarian sociopolitical structures that facilitated widespread peasant revolts against landlords were, taken together, the sufficient distinctive causes of social-revolutionary situations commencing in France, 1789, Russia, 1917, and China, 1911" (154).

3. The very decision to select these occurrences as elements of a single complex historical event or process—even before deciding what sort of process it is—involves the construction of a conceptual space.

4. This is not to suggest that the concept of class is uncontroversial—even among those investigators who accept the framework. One central line of controversy concerns the role of class consciousness in the definition of class; see Thompson 1963 for the most important contribution to this issue. Another important controversy is the explanatory significance of this defini-

tion of class; it might be held, for example, that analysis along class lines sheds no light whatsoever on economic or political behavior. There are also, of course, non-Marxian theories of class; these typically depend on subjective criteria of classification. However, the Marxian concept of class is the most fully developed.

5. We might ask, however, whether there are natural kinds that do *not* possess identical internal structure—for example, the noble gases. This type refers to a family of gases with similar chemical properties and similar internal structures, but each gas has a distinct atomic structure. This sort of example is more analogous to social types because the individuals within the class are not identical; they merely have some important structural elements in common that give rise to similar causal properties.

6. For an extensive treatment of this issue, see Putnam 1975e, f.

7. The most prominent counterexample in natural science is quantum mechanics.

8. This position bears obvious similarities to Merton's (1963) classic views on the role of "theories of the middle-range" in social research.

9. A similar analysis of comparative politics is provided by Rudolph 1987. She cautions against simply applying concepts of the state that were developed for Western Europe (732). "What we need to do is begin with more manageable comparisons, with a considerable degree of historical concreteness, sensitive to variation in comparable functions or processes, sensitive to how wholes differ. At this stage we need fragile theoretical templates, made of soft clay rather than hard steel, that adapt to the variety of evidence and break when they do not fit" (738).

10. Thus Chen (1986) summarizes his approach to the CCP's base areas in Central China: "This brief review of our current understanding of wartime Chinese communism suggests the need to study the Party's actual interaction with peasants in village settings and the changing power contexts in which this interaction occurred. I will study peasant motivation from the perspective of both its facilitating and inhibiting factors, giving equal weight to the CCP's positive appeals and its removal of negative constraints" (8).

11. "I was interested—in connection with long-term tendencies—in the major variables susceptible to lasting inflections and to secular fluctuations; that is to say, population, the different sectors of productions and the regional gross product, nominal as well as metallic prices, aggregate income (both nominal and real), revenues, and exactions of various sorts (land rent, tithes, taxes, interest, farm profits, or income, money wages, . . .)" (Ladurie 1974:7).

12. An example of a local study that has just this virtue is Watson 1985, an anthropological field study of the New Territories (Hong Kong), and the relations between kinship and economy in this small handful of villages. But Watson plainly hopes to shed light on the relations between these cultural forms in other regions of China as well.

Chapter 7: Explanation

1. Mann (1986) offers an extensive analysis of the history of the institutions of power in Western society that explores these sorts of organizational forms in detail.

2. It is noteworthy also that none of these explanations depends crucially on statistical generalizations or inferences.

3. Harré and Madden (1975) explore the ontological assumptions built into this strong (and decidedly anti-Humean) conception of causal necessity.

4. Of course, these cases do *not* represent all kinds of social science, and the model described here does not apply to all areas of social science. The most prominent exception is interpretation sociology; interpreting the meaning of a social practice differs fundamentally from identifying causal conditions and practices. But other exceptions are apparent as well; narrowly inductive social research (for example, voter attitude studies) avoids assumptions about causal mechanisms and processes. One of the chief findings of this study, however, is that social inquiry is widely and fundamentally diverse and that there is little reason to expect there to be valid generalizations about the whole of social science—beyond truisms about rigor of analysis, the use of empirical data, and the institutionalized character of science.

5. G. A. Cohen (1978:15–60) employs similar assumptions in his reconstruction of Marx's theory of historical materialism to motivate the general Marxian view of the primacy of the forces of production over the relations of production (technological determinism).

6. Rawls's (1971) account of primary goods is relevant in this context. Shue (1980) offers an account of basic rights that singles out income, security, and basic political liberties.

7. The classic application of microeconomics to traditional agriculture is Schultz 1964. See Myers 1970 and Chao 1986 for applications of such a model to traditional Chinese agriculture.

8. Geertz (1973) offers an extensive discussion of the existence of cross-cultural universals of human nature.

9. "Only the recontextualisation of Javanese and Indonesian economic processes within Javanese and Indonesian life as concretely enacted, the de-externalisation of culture, can reduce this indeterminacy, however slightly, and deliver answers we can have some faith in, however modest. It is not economic analysis itself that is the problem, any more than it is quantification. It is economism: the notion . . . that a determinate picture of social change can be obtained in the absence of an understanding of the passions and imaginings that provoke and inform it. Such understanding is inevitably limited. . . . But without it there is nothing but polemic, schematicism and endless measurement of amorphous magnitudes: history without temper, sociology without tone" (Geertz 1984:523). Geertz's arguments here and E. P.

Thompson's (1978) arguments against structuralist Marxism are strikingly similar.

10. In addition to the authors considered here, see Donald Davidson's writings on the subject of agency, especially 1980:43–61.

11. John Mackie (1976) provides an extensive and useful explication of the regularity view.

12. Salmon's reconstruction of causal reasoning represents a robust defense of this approach. He holds that the notion of a *causal process* is essential to causal explanation: a postulated mechanism or process leading from the event identified as cause to that identified as effect. "Causal processes are the means by which structure and order are propagated or transmitted from one space-time region of the universe to other times and places" (1984:179).

13. The following analysis relies on Mackie's (1976) treatment of causation.

14. This sentence is a counterfactual conditional (or a subjunctive conditional). Logicians and philosophers have shown that serious problems arise in assigning truth value and meaning to such sentences. The most promising line of thought on this problem relies on the idea of natural necessity, or causal necessity: To say that if A had not occurred B would not have occurred is to say that: If A had not occurred in circumstances C subject to laws of nature L, B would not appear in the causal chains that follow from C minus A. The problem with this analysis for our purposes is that it depends upon the idea of causation, whereas we are using counterfactuals to define causation. For further discussion of this problem, see Elster 1983:34–41.

15. Our world, however, is not simple, in at least two respects. First, usually an indefinite number of conditions are necessary background conditions; so it is impossible to specify a complete set of jointly sufficient conditions. Causal laws therefore typically take the form of ceteris paribus laws, laws that assume "normal" background conditions (Mackie 1976). Second, causal relations are often more complex than this account suggests in that there may be no individually necessary conditions. An event may be causally overdetermined (for example, both an electric spark and a dropped match are present).

16. This distinction is generally described as pragmatic: one based on interest-relativity rather than the logic of explanation. When the police officer asks for the cause of the accident, he or she is not interested in the information that the car had mass; the officer wants to know whether the car was traveling too fast in the circumstances. See Scriven 1962 and Garfinkel 1981 on the pragmatics of explanation, and Mackie 1976 on the pragmatics of causal judgment.

17. Philosophical literature on the concept of natural necessity is extensive. The most reasonable interpretation of this idea is this: An event is naturally necessary in a set of circumstances if and only if full knowledge of

the laws of nature would permit us to derive a statement of the occurrence of the event from a description of the circumstances at the time.

18. Brenner makes just this sort of argument against Postan and Ladurie in his analysis of the causes of agrarian change in England and France. The neo-Malthusians maintain that a process of population increase in Europe led to agricultural revolution. But, Brenner replies, "The obvious difficulty with this whole massive structure [the demographic interpretation] is that it simply breaks down in the face of comparative analysis. Different outcomes proceeded from similar demographic trends at different times and in different areas of Europe. Thus we may ask if demographic change can be legitimately treated as a 'cause', let alone the key variable" (1976:39).

19. The issue of methodological individualism has received substantial new attention within analytical Marxism, where Elster 1982, 1985b, Roemer 1982b, and Van Parijs 1983 argue that Marxist explanations require microfoundations at the level of individual behavior.

Chapter 8: Empirical Reasoning

1. Important recent contributions to the philosophy of social science have largely neglected this issue. Thus Braybrooke (1987) devotes only a few pages to empirical problems in social science (25–26), as does Rosenberg (1988). Miller (1987) provides an extensive analysis of confirmation in science (chaps. 4–7). On Miller's account, "a hypothesis is confirmed just in case its approximate truth, and the basic falsehood of its rivals, is entailed by the best causal account of the history of data-gathering and theorizing out of which the data arose" (155), and Miller devotes several chapters to explicating this theory. However, Miller's account does not give attention to empirical problems specific to the social sciences, and it begins at the point of an existing data set in relation to a given hypothesis. However, as will emerge in the following, some of the hardest problems arise before this stage.

2. This feature is similar to Newton-Smith's concept of verisimilitude (1981:chap. 8).

3. Hempel (1966:19–32) provides a simple description of the logic of confirmation in science; this view of confirmation is developed in greater detail in Hempel 1965. Ernest Nagel (1961) provides a similar account, with more extensive application to social science. Suppe (1970) provides an extensive description and critical evaluation of this set of doctrines. Glymour (1980) offers a sophisticated discussion and defense of the model in reply to various criticisms.

4. Research programs may also be guided by nontheoretical interests—for example, concern for economic development in the less-developed world today has given direction to much research in economic history of England.

5. The Mantetsu surveys were a collection of field surveys in the North China plain in the 1930s performed by research teams of the Japanese South Manchurian Railway Company. Huang (1985) and Myers (1970) both rely on these data for their assessments of North China's rural economy. Huang (1985:4–43) offers a careful evaluation of the survey material. Fogel (1987b) offers a somewhat different assessment.

6. See Morgenstern 1963 for a careful discussion of this sort of low-level empirical problem.

7. This account is drawn from Chayanov's (1925) analysis of traditional Russian farming systems; it is also representative of Chao's (1986) analysis of traditional Chinese farm organization.

8. Merton's concept of "theories of the middle range" captures much the same point that I emphasize here. He defines this concept in these terms: "Theories that lie between the minor but necessary working hypotheses that evolve in abundance during day-to-day research and the all inclusive systematic efforts to develop a unified theory that will explain all the observed uniformities of social behavior, social organization and social change" (1967:39). Merton maintains, as I do, that hypotheses at this level can be empirically investigated more or less independently from the larger theoretical systems (Marxism, social behaviorism, functionalism) within which they may be lodged (43). In *The Scientific Marx* (1986), I argue that Marx's analysis of capitalism is eclectic in just this sense (chap. 1).

9. Quine (1960) extends Duhem's theoretical holism; the general point is that theoretical systems only confront the tribunal of experience as wholes, and it is not possible to parcel out empirical support to various parts of the theoretical system. This holism does not appear persuasive in connection with the social science controversies we have considered, however.

10. Rudner (1966:chap. 3) briefly considers justification and offers a version of the H-D model. Friedman (1953) takes an unabashedly positivist stance: "The ultimate goal of a positive science is the development of a 'theory' or 'hypothesis' that yields valid and meaningful predictions about phenomena not yet observed" (7). Thomas (1979) barely discusses the question of empirical justification. Taylor has virtually nothing to say about empirical methods; nor do most contributors to the rationality literature and the *verstehen* literature. And recent discussions of the "rhetoric of economics" (McCloskey 1985; Klamer 1983) suggest that empirical arguments are polemical rather than rational in their force.

11. But this is equally true of any significant program of research in the natural sciences as well.

References

Adas, Michael. 1979. *Prophets of rebellion: Millenarian protest movements against the European colonial order.* Chapel Hill: University of North Carolina Press.

Adorno, Theodor W. 1969. Sociology and empirical research. In *The positivist dispute in German sociology,* ed. Theodor W. Adorno et al. New York: Harper and Row.

Althusser, Louis, and Etienne Balibar. 1970. *Reading Capital.* London: New Left Books.

Anderson, Michael. 1986. Historical demography after *The population history of England.* In *Population and economy: Population and history from the traditional to the modern world,* ed. Robert I. Rotberg and Theodore K. Rabb. Cambridge: Cambridge University Press.

Arrigo, Linda Gail. 1986. Landownership concentration in China: The Buck survey revisited. *Modern China* 12:259–360.

Arrow, Kenneth. 1963. *Social choice and individual values.* New York: Wiley.

Arrow, Kenneth, and F. H. Hahn. 1971. General competitive analysis. San Francisco.

Aston, T. H., and C. H. E. Philpin, eds. 1985. *The Brenner debate: Agrarian class structure and economic development in pre-industrial Europe.* Cambridge: Cambridge University Press.

Axelrod, Robert. 1984. *The evolution of cooperation.* New York: Basic.

Barclay, George W., et al. 1976. A reassessment of the demography of traditional rural China. *Population Index* 42:606–35.

Barry, Brian. 1978. *Sociologists, economists, and democracy.* Chicago: University of Chicago Press.

Becker, Gary. 1976. *The economic approach to human behavior.* Chicago: University of Chicago Press.

Bendix, Reinhard, and Seymour Martin Lipset, eds. 1966. *Class, status, and power,* 2d ed. New York: Free Press.

Bianco, Lucien. 1971. *Origins of the Chinese revolution, 1915–1949.* Stanford: Stanford University Press.

———. 1975. Peasants and revolution: The case of China. *Journal of Peasant Studies* 2:313–35.

———. 1986. Peasant movements. In *The Cambridge History of China.* Vol. 13: *Republican China, 1912–1949, Part 2. See* Fairbank and Feuerwerker 1986.

Blalock, H. M., Jr. 1972. *Social statistics,* 2d ed. New York: McGraw-Hill.

———. 1982. *Conceptualization and measurement in the social sciences.* Beverly Hills, Calif.: Sage Publications.

Blalock, H. M., Jr., ed. 1971. *Causal models in the social sciences.* Chicago: Aldine-Atherton.

Bloch, Marc. 1966. *French rural history.* Berkeley: University of California Press.

Bonner, John. 1986. *Introduction to the theory of social choice.* Baltimore: Johns Hopkins University Press.

Brandt, Loren. 1987. Review of Philip C. C. Huang, *The peasant economy and social change in North China. Economic Development and Cultural Change* 35:670–82.

Braverman, Harry. 1974. *Labor and monopoly capital.* New York: Monthly Review.

Braybrooke, David. 1987. *Philosophy of social science.* Englewood Cliffs, N.J.: Prentice-Hall.

Brenner, Robert. 1976. Agrarian class structure and economic development in pre-industrial Europe. *Past and Present* 70:30–75.

———. 1982. The agrarian roots of European capitalism. *Past and Present* 97:16–113.

———. 1986. The social basis of economic development. In *Analytic Marxism. See* Roemer 1986.

Brown, Harold I. 1979. *Perception, commitment, and theory.* Chicago: University of Chicago Press.

———. 1987. *Observation and objectivity.* Oxford: Oxford University Press.

Buchanan, Allen. 1979. Revolutionary motivation and rationality. *Philosophy and Public Affairs* 9:59–82.

———. 1982. *Marx and justice.* Totowa, N.J.: Littlefield, Adams.

Buck, John Lossing. 1937. *Land utilization in China.* Chicago: University of Chicago Press.

Chang, Chung-li. 1962. *The income of the Chinese gentry.* Introduction by Franz Michael. Seattle: University of Washington Press.

Chao, Kang. 1975. The growth of a modern cotton textile industry and the competition with handicrafts. In *China's modern economy in historical perspective. See* Perkins 1975b.

———. 1986. *Man and land in Chinese history: An economic analysis.* Stanford: Stanford University Press.

Chayanov, A. V. 1924. On the theory of non-capitalist economic systems. In *The theory of peasant economy,* ed. D. Thorner, B. Kerblay, and R. E. F. Smith. Madison: University of Wisconsin Press, 1986.

———. 1925. Peasant farm organization. In *The theory of peasant economy,* ed. D. Thorner, B. Kerblay, and R. E. F. Smith. Madison: University of Wisconsin Press, 1986.

Chen, Fu-Mei C., and Ramon H. Myers. 1985. Rural production and distribution in late imperial China. *Chinese Studies* 3:657–704.

Chen, Yung-fa. 1986. *Making revolution: The Communist movement in eastern and central China, 1937–1945.* Berkeley: University of California Press.

Chesneaux, Jean. 1971. *Secret societies in China in the nineteenth and twentieth centuries,* trans. Gillian Nettle. Ann Arbor: University of Michigan Press.

————. 1973. *Peasant revolts in China, 1840–1949*. New York: Norton.

Chesneaux, Jean, ed. 1972. *Popular movements and secret societies in China, 1840–1950*. Stanford: Stanford University Press.

Chesneaux, Jean, Marianne Bastid, and Marie-Claire Bergere. 1976. *China from the Opium Wars to the 1911 Revolution*. Trans. Anne Destenay. New York: Random House.

Cohen, G. A. 1978. *Karl Marx's theory of history: A defence*. Princeton: Princeton University Press.

————. 1982. Functional explanation, consequence explanation, and Marxism. *Inquiry* 25:27–56.

Cohen, Paul. 1984. *Discovering history in China*. New York: Columbia University Press.

Crafts, N. F. R. 1981. The eighteenth century: A survey. In *The economic history of Britain since 1700*, Vol. 1: *1700–1860*, ed. Roderick Floud and Donald McCloskey. Cambridge: Cambridge University Press.

————. 1985. *British economic growth during the industrial revolution*. Oxford: Oxford University Press.

Crissman, Lawrence, W. 1972. Marketing on the Changhua plain, Taiwan. In *Economic organization in Chinese society. See* Willmott 1972.

Dalton, George. 1969. Theoretical issues in economic anthropology. *Current Anthropology* 10:63–102.

————. 1971. *Economic anthropology and development*. New York: Basic.

Davidson, Donald. 1980. *Essays on actions and events*. Oxford: Oxford University Press.

Deane, Phyllis. 1979. *The first industrial revolution*, 2d ed. Cambridge: Cambridge University Press.

Deane, Phyllis, and W. A. Cole. 1967. *British economic growth, 1688–1959: Trends and structure*, 2d ed. Cambridge: Cambridge University Press.

Duara, Prasenjit. 1987. State involution: A study of local finances in North China, 1911–1935. *Comparative Studies in Society and History* 29:132–61.

————. 1988. *Culture, power, and the state: Rural North China, 1900–1942*. Stanford: Stanford University Press.

Eastman, Lloyd E. 1988. *Family, fields, and ancestors: Constancy and change in China's social and economic history, 1550–1949*. New York: Oxford University Press.

Elster, Jon. 1978. *Logic and society*. Chichester, Eng.: Wiley.

————. 1979. *Ulysses and the sirens*. Cambridge: Cambridge University Press.

————. 1982. Marxism, functionalism, and game theory. *Theory and Society* 11:453–82.

————. 1983. *Explaining technical change*. Cambridge: Cambridge University Press.

————. 1985a. Rationality, morality, and collective action. *Ethics* 96:136–55.

————. 1985b. *Making sense of Marx*. Cambridge: Cambridge University Press.

Elvin, Mark. 1972. The high-level equilibrium trap: The causes of the decline of invention in the traditional Chinese textile industries. In *Economic organization in Chinese society. See* Willmott 1972.

———. 1973. *The pattern of the Chinese past.* Stanford: Stanford University Press.

———. 1975. Skills and resources in late traditional China. In *China's modern economy in historical perspective. See* Perkins 1975b.

———. 1982. The technology of farming in late-traditional China. In *The Chinese agricultural economy,* ed. Randolph Barker and Radha Sinha. Boulder, Colo.: Westview Press.

Elvin, Mark, and G. William Skinner, eds. 1974. *The Chinese city between two worlds.* Stanford: Stanford University Press.

Esherick, Joseph W. 1976. *Reform and revolution in China: The 1911 Revolution in Hunan and Hubei.* Berkeley: University of California Press.

———. 1981. Number games: A note on land distribution in prerevolutionary China. *Modern China* 7:387–411.

———. 1987. *The origins of the Boxer uprising.* Berkeley: University of California.

Evans-Pritchard, E. E. 1934. Levy-Bruhl's theory of primitive mentality. *Bulletin of the Faculty of the Arts.*

Fairbank, John King. 1986. *The great Chinese revolution, 1800–1985.* New York: Harper and Row.

Fairbank, John King, and Albert Feuerwerker, eds. 1986. *The Cambridge History of China.* Vol. 13: *Republican China, 1912–1949, Part 2.* Cambridge: Cambridge University Press.

Feigl, Herbert, and Grover Maxwell, eds. 1962. *Minnesota studies in the philosophy of science.* Vol. 3. Minneapolis: University of Minnesota Press.

Feuerwerker, Albert. 1975. *Rebellion in nineteenth-century China.* Ann Arbor: Center for Chinese Studies, University of Michigan.

Feyerabend, Paul. 1975. *Against method.* London: New Left Books.

Fodor, Jerry. 1980. Special sciences, or the disunity of science as a working hypothesis. In *Readings in philosophy of psychology.* Vol. 1. Ed. Ned Block. Cambridge, Mass.: MIT Press.

Fogel, Joshua. 1987a. Liberals and collaborators: The research department of the South Manchurian Railway Company. Conference paper, Association for Asian Studies.

———. 1987b. *Ai Ssu-ch'i's contribution to the development of Chinese Marxism.* Cambridge, Mass.: Council on East Asian Studies/Harvard University: Distributed by the Harvard University Press.

Fogel, Joshua, ed. and trans. 1984. *Recent studies of modern Chinese history.* Armonk, N.Y.: M. E. Sharpe.

Frohlich, Norman, and Joe A. Oppenheimer. 1974. The carrot and the stick: Optimal program mixes for entrepreneurial political leaders. *Public Choice* 19:43–61.

———. 1978. *Modern political economy.* Englewood Cliffs, N.J.: Prentice-Hall.

Frohlich, Norman, et al. 1975. Individual contributions to collective goods: Alternative models. *Journal of Conflict Resolution* 19:310–29.

Frohlich, Norman, Joe Oppenheimer, and Oran R. Young. 1971. *Political leadership and collective goods.* Princeton: Princeton University Press.

Galbiati, Fernando. 1985. *P'eng P'ai and the Lu-Feng Soviet.* Stanford: Stanford University Press.

Garfinkel, Alan. 1981. *Forms of explanation: Rethinking the questions of social theory.* New Haven and London: Yale University Press.

Geertz, Clifford. 1963. *Agricultural involution: The process of ecological change in Indonesia.* Berkeley: University of California Press.

————. 1968. *Islam observed.* New Haven and London: Yale University Press.

————. 1971a. *The interpretation of cultures.* New York: Basic.

————. 1971b. Religion as a cultural system. In *The interpretation of cultures. See* Geertz 1971a.

————. 1980. *Negara: The theatre state in nineteenth-century Bali.* Princeton: Princeton University Press.

————. 1983. *Local knowledge.* New York: Basic.

————. 1984. Culture and social change: The Indonesian case. *Man* 19:513–32.

Glymour, Clark. 1980. *Theory and evidence.* Princeton: Princeton University Press.

Hahn, Frank, and Martin Hollis, eds. 1979. *Philosophy and economic theory.* Oxford: Oxford University Press.

Hamilton, W. D. 1971. Geometry for the selfish herd. *Journal of Theoretical Biology* 31:295–311.

Hanley, Susan B. 1985. Family and fertility in four Tokugawa villages. In *Family and population in East Asian history,* ed. Susan B. Hanley and Arthur Wolf. Stanford: Stanford University Press.

Hardin, Russell. 1982. *Collective action.* Baltimore: Johns Hopkins University Press.

Harré, Rom. 1970. *Principles of scientific thinking.* Chicago: University of Chicago Press.

Harré, Rom, and P. F. Secord. 1973. *The explanation of social behaviour.* Totowa, N.J.: Littlefield, Adams.

Harré, Rom, and E. H. Madden. 1975. *A theory of natural necessity.* Oxford: Basil Blackwell.

Harrell, Stevan. 1985. The rich get children: Segmentation, stratification, and population in three Chekiang lineages, 1550–1850. In *Family and population in East Asian history,* ed. Susan B. Hanley and Arthur Wolf. Stanford: Stanford University Press.

Harsanyi, John C. 1976. *Essays on ethics, social behavior, and scientific explanation.* Dordrecht: D. Reidel.

————. 1977. *Rational behavior and bargaining equilibrium in games and social situations.* Cambridge: Cambridge University Press.

Hart, Gillian. 1988. Agrarian structure and the state in Java and Bangladesh. *Journal of Asian Studies* 47:248–67.

Havinden, M. A. 1967. Agricultural progress in open-field Oxfordshire. In *Agriculture and economic growth in England, 1650–1815,* ed. E. L. Jones. London: Methuen.

Hempel, Carl. 1965a. *Aspects of scientific explanation.* New York: Free Press.

——. 1965b. Confirmation, induction, and rational belief. In *Aspects of scientific explanation. See* Hempel 1965a.

——. 1965c. The function of general laws in history. In *Aspects of scientific explanation. See* Hempel 1965a.

——. 1966. *Philosophy of natural science.* Englewood Cliffs, N.J.: Prentice-Hall.

Hilton, Rodney. 1973. *Bondmen made free.* London: Maurice Temple Smith.

Hobsbawm, E. J. 1959. *Primitive rebels: Studies in archaic forms of social movement in the nineteenth and twentieth centuries.* New York: Praeger.

Hollis, Martin, and Steven Lukes, eds. 1982. *Rationality and relativism.* Cambridge, Mass.: MIT Press.

Hookway, Christopher, and Philip Pettit, eds. 1978. *Action and interpretation studies in the philosophy of the social sciences.* Cambridge: Cambridge University Press.

Hsieh, Winston. 1974. Peasant insurrection and the marketing hierarchy in the Canton delta, 1911. In *The Chinese city between two worlds. See* Elvin and Skinner 1974.

Huang, Philip C. C. 1985. *The peasant economy and social change in North China.* Stanford: Stanford University Press.

Hull, David. 1974. *Philosophy of biological science.* Englewood Cliffs, N.J.: Prentice-Hall.

Johnson, Chalmers A. 1962. *Peasant nationalism and communist power: The emergence of revolutionary China, 1937–1945.* Stanford: Stanford University Press.

Jones, Susan Mann, and Philip A. Kuhn. 1978. Dynastic decline and the roots of rebellion. In *The Cambridge History of China.* Vol. 10. *See* Twitchett and Fairbank 1978.

Keat, Russell, and John Urry. 1975. *Social theory as science.* London: Routledge and Kegan Paul.

Keyes, Charles, et al. 1983. *Peasant strategies in Asian societies: Moral and rational economic approaches—a symposium. Journal of Asian Studies* 42:753–868.

Kriedte, Peter. 1981. The origins, the agrarian context, and the conditions in the world market. In *Industrialization before industrialization. See* Kriedte, Medick, and Schlumbohm 1981.

——. 1983. *Peasants, landlords and merchant capitalists in Europe and the world economy, 1500–1800.* Cambridge: Cambridge University Press.

Kriedte, Peter, Hans Medick, and Jurgen Schlumbohm. 1981. *Industrialization before industrialization: Rural industry in the genesis of capitalism.* Trans. Beate Schempp. Cambridge: Cambridge University Press.

Kuhn, Philip A. 1977. Origins of the Taiping vision: Cross-cultural dimensions of a Chinese rebellion. *Comparative Studies in Society and History* 19:350–66.

——. 1978. The Taiping rebellion. In *The Cambridge History of China.* Vol. 10. *See* Twitchett and Fairbank 1978.

——. 1980. *Rebellion and its enemies in late imperial China: Militariza-*

tion and social structure, 1796–1864. Cambridge: Harvard University Press. Reprint; orig. publ. 1970.

Kuhn, Thomas. 1970. *The structure of scientific revolutions,* 2d ed. Chicago: University of Chicago Press.

Lakatos, Imre. 1978. *The methodology of scientific research programmes: Philosophical papers.* Vol. 1. Cambridge: Cambridge University Press.

Lakatos, Imre, and Alan Musgrave, eds. 1970. *Criticism and the growth of knowledge.* Cambridge: Cambridge University Press.

Laudan, Larry. 1977. *Progress and its problems.* Berkeley: University of California.

Lavely, William R. 1988. The spatial approach to Chinese history: A critique of Sands and Myers. Manuscript.

Le Roy Ladurie, Emmanuel. 1974. *The peasants of Languedoc.* Urbana: University of Illinois Press.

Lee, James Z. n.d. A century of mortality in rural Liaoning, 1774–1873. Manuscript.

Lee, James Z., and Fu Kedong. 1987. The Eight Banner registration system. Manuscript.

Lee, James Z., Cameron Campbell, and Guofu Tan. 1988. Price and population history in rural Fengtian, 1772–1873. Paper for conference on Economic Methods for Chinese Historical Research, January 1988, Oracle, Ariz.

Lee, R. D., and R. S. Schofield. 1981. British population in the eighteenth century. In *The economic history of Britain since 1700,* Vol. 1: *1700–1860,* ed. Roderick Floud and Donald McCloskey. Cambridge: Cambridge University Press.

Levine, Andrew. 1986. Review of Jon Elster, *Making sense of Marx. Journal of Philosophy* 83:721–28.

Lewis, David K. 1969. *Convention.* Cambridge, Mass.: Harvard University Press.

Lewis, John Wilson, ed. 1974. *Peasant rebellion and communist revolution in Asia.* Stanford: Stanford University Press.

Li, Lillian M. 1981. *China's silk trade: Traditional industry in the modern world, 1842–1937.* Cambridge, Mass.: Harvard University Press.

Lippit, Victor D. 1974. *Land reform and economic development in China: A study of institutional change and development finance.* White Plains, N.Y.: International Arts and Sciences Press.

———. 1978. The development of underdevelopment in China. *Modern China* 4:251–328.

———. 1987. *The economic development of China.* Armonk, N.Y.: Sharpe.

Little, Daniel E. 1986. *The scientific Marx.* Minneapolis: University of Minnesota Press.

Little, Daniel, and Joseph Esherick. 1989. Testing the testers: A reply to Barbara Sands and Ramon Myers' critique of G. William Skinner's regional systems approach to China. *Journal of Asian Studies* 48.

Liu, Kwang-Ching. 1978. The Ch'ing restoration. In *The Cambridge History of China.* Vol. 10. *See* Twitchett and Fairbank 1978.

Liu, Ts'ui-jung. 1985. The demography of two Chinese clans in Hsiao-shan,

Chekiang, 1650–1850. In *Family and population in East Asian history*, ed. Susan B. Hanley and Arthur Wolf. Stanford: Stanford University Press.

Luce, R. D., and Howard Raiffa. 1958. *Games and decisions*. New York: Wiley.

Lukes, Steven. 1973. Methodological individualism reconsidered. In *The philosophy of social explanation. See* Ryan 1973.

———. 1982. Relativism in its place. In *Rationality and relativism. See* Hollis Lukes 1982.

MacIntyre, Alasdair. 1973. Is a science of comparative politics possible? In *The philosophy of social explanation. See* Ryan 1973.

———. 1984. *After virtue*, 2d ed. Notre Dame, Ind.: University of Notre Dame Press.

MacKay, Alfred. 1980. *Arrow's theorem: The paradox of social choice*. New Haven and London: Yale University Press.

Mackie, J. L. 1976. *Cement of the universe*. London: Oxford University Press.

McMurtry, John. 1977. *The structure of Marx's world-view*. Princeton: Princeton University Press.

Malinowski, Bronislaw. 1922. *Argonauts of the western Pacific*. New York: E. P. Dutton, 1961.

Mann, Michael. 1986. *The sources of social power*. Vol. 1: *A history of power from the beginning to A.D. 1760*. Cambridge: Cambridge University Press.

Mann, Susan. 1986. Review of Huang, *The peasant economy. Journal of Asian Studies* 45:572–74.

Margolis, Howard. 1982. *Selfishness, rationality, and altruism: A theory of social choice*. Chicago: University of Chicago Press.

Marks, Robert. 1984. *Rural revolution in South China: Peasants and the making of history in Haifeng county, 1570–1930*. Madison: University of Wisconsin Press.

Marx, Karl. [1867] 1977. *Capital*. Vol. 1. New York: Vintage.

Marx, Karl, and Frederick Engels. [1845–46] 1970. *The German ideology*. New York: International Publishers.

———. [1848] 1974. *The Communist Manifesto*. In *The Revolutions of 1848: Political Writings*. Vol. 1. Ed. David Fernbach. New York: Vintage.

Medick, Hans. 1981. The proto-industrial family economy. In *Industrialization before industrialization. See* Kriedte, Medick, and Schlumbohm 1981.

Mendels, Franklin F. 1981. Agriculture and peasant industry in eighteenth-century Flanders. In *Industrialization before industrialization. See* Kriedte, Medick and Schlumbohm 1981.

Merton, Robert K. 1963. *Social theory and social structure*. New York: Free Press.

———. 1967. *On theoretical sociology*. New York: Free Press.

———. 1973. *The sociology of science: Theoretical and empirical investigations*. Chicago: University of Chicago Press.

Migdal, Joel. 1974. *Peasants, politics, and revolution*. Princeton: Princeton University Press.

Miliband, Ralph. 1969. *The state in capitalist society*. New York: Basic.

———. 1977. *Marxism and politics*. Oxford: Oxford University Press.

Miller, Richard. 1978. Methodological individualism and social explanation. *Philosophy of Science* 45:387–414.

———. 1984. *Analyzing Marx*. Princeton: Princeton University Press.

———. 1987. *Fact and method*. Princeton: Princeton University Press.

Moore Jr., Barrington. 1966. *Social origins of dictatorship and democracy*. Boston: Beacon.

———. 1978. *Injustice: The social bases of obedience and revolt*. White Plains, N.Y.: Sharpe.

Morgenstern, Oskar. 1963. *On the accuracy of economic observations*, 2d ed. Princeton: Princeton University Press.

Mueller, Dennis C. 1976. Public choice: A survey. *Journal of Economic Literature* 14, 2:395–433.

Myers, Ramon H. 1970. *The Chinese peasant economy*. Cambridge, Mass.: Harvard University Press.

———. 1975. Cooperation in traditional agriculture and its implications for team farming in the People's Republic of China. In *China's modern economy in historical perspective*. *See* Perkins 1975b.

———. 1980. North China villages during the Republican period: Socio-economic relationships. *Modern China* 6:243–66.

———. 1986. The agrarian system. In *The Cambridge History of China*. Vol. 13. *See* Fairbank and Feuerwerker 1986.

Nagel, Ernest. 1961. *The structure of science*. New York: Harcourt, Brace and World.

Nagel, Thomas. 1970. *The possibility of altruism*. Oxford: Oxford University Press.

Naquin, Susan. 1976. *Millenarian rebellion in China: The Eight Trigrams uprising of 1813*. New Haven and London: Yale University Press.

———. 1981. *Shantung rebellion: The Wang Lun uprising of 1774*. New Haven and London: Yale University Press.

———. 1985. The transmission of White Lotus sectarianism in late Imperial China. In *Popular culture in late imperial China*, ed. David Johnson, Andrew J. Nathan, and Evelyn S. Rawski. Berkeley: University of California Press.

Nash, Manning. 1965. *The golden road to modernity: Village life in contemporary Burma*. New York: Wiley.

———. 1966. *Primitive and peasant economic systems*. San Francisco: Chandler.

Newton-Smith, W. H. 1981. *The rationality of science*. Boston: Routledge and Kegan Paul.

North, Douglas C., and Robert Paul Thomas. 1973. *The rise of the Western world: A new economic history*. Cambridge: Cambridge University Press.

Olson, Mancur. 1965. *The logic of collective action: Public goods and the theory of groups*. Cambridge, Mass.: Harvard University Press.

Outhwaite, William. 1975. *Understanding social life: The method called Verstehen*. London: George Allen and Unwin.

Paige, Jeffrey. 1975. *Agrarian revolution*. New York: Free Press.

Pasternak, Burton. 1978. The sociology of irrigation: Two Taiwanese villages. In *Studies in Chinese society*. *See* A. Wolf 1978.

Perdue, Peter. 1986. Insiders and outsiders: The Xiangtan riot of 1819 and collective action in Hunan. *Modern China* 12:166–201.

———. 1987. *Exhausting the earth: State and peasant in Hunan, 1500–1850.* Cambridge, Mass.: Harvard University Press.

———. 1988. The Qing state and the Gansu grain market, 1739–1864. Paper for conference on Economic Methods for Chinese Historical Research, January 1988, Oracle, Ariz.

Perkins, Dwight H. 1969. *Agricultural development in China.* Chicago: Aldine.

———. 1975a. Growth and changing structure of China's twentieth-century economy. In *China's modern economy in historical perspective. See* Perkins 1975b.

Perkins, Dwight H., ed. 1975b. *China's modern economy in historical perspective.* Stanford: Stanford University Press.

Perry, Elizabeth. 1976. Worshippers and warriors: White Lotus influence on the Nian rebellion. *Modern China* 2:4–22.

———. 1980a. *Rebels and revolutionaries in North China 1845–1945.* Stanford: Stanford University Press.

———. 1980b. When peasants speak: Sources for the study of Chinese rebellions. *Modern China* 6:72–85.

Perry, Elizabeth, and Tom Chang. 1980. The mystery of yellow cliff: A controversial "rebellion" in the late Qing. *Modern China* 6:123–60.

Phelps Brown, E. Henry, and Sheila V. Hopkins. 1956. Seven centuries of the prices of consumables compared with builders' wage rates. *Economica* 23:296–314.

Polachek, James M. 1983. The moral economy of the Kiangsi Soviet (1928–34). *Journal of Asian Studies* 42:805–30.

Polanyi, Karl. 1957. *The great transformation.* Boston: Beacon Press.

Popkin, Samuel L. 1979. *The rational peasant.* Berkeley: University of California Press.

———. 1981. Public choice and rural development: Free riders, lemons, and institutional design. In *Public choice and rural development. See* Russell and Nicholson 1981.

Popper, Karl. 1947. *The open society and its enemies.* Vol. 2. London: Routledge.

———. 1961. *The poverty of historicism.* London: Routledge and Kegan Paul.

———. 1965. *Conjectures and refutations: The growth of scientific knowledge.* New York: Basic Books.

Postan, M. M. 1975. *The medieval economy and society.* Harmondsworth: Penguin Books.

Przeworski, Adam. 1985a. *Capitalism and social democracy.* Cambridge: Cambridge University Press.

———. 1985b. Marxism and rational choice. *Politics and Society* 14:379–409.

Putnam, Hilary. 1975a. *Mathematics, matter and method.* Cambridge: Cambridge University Press.

————. 1975b. *Mind, language, and reality.* Cambridge: Cambridge University Press.

————. 1975c. The analytic and the synthetic. In *Mind, language, and reality. See* Putnam 1975b.

————. 1975d. Is semantics possible? In *Mind, language, and reality. See* Putnam 1975b.

————. 1975e. Explanation and reference. In *Mind, language, and reality. See* Putnam 1975b.

————. 1975f. The meaning of "meaning." In *Mind, language, and reality. See* Putnam 1975b.

————. 1975g. The "corroboration" of theories. In *Mathematics, matter and method. See* Putnam 1975a.

Rankin, Mary. 1986. *Elite activism and political transformation in China: Zhejiang province, 1865–1911.* Stanford: Stanford University Press.

Rapoport, Anatol. 1966. *Two-person game theory.* Ann Arbor: University of Michigan.

Rapoport, Anatol, and A. M. Chammah. 1965. *Prisoners' dilemma: A study in conflict and cooperation.* Ann Arbor: University of Michigan.

Rawls, John. 1971. *A theory of justice.* Cambridge, Mass.: Harvard University Press, 1971.

Rawski, Evelyn Sakakida. 1972. *Agricultural change and the peasant economy of South China.* Cambridge, Mass.: Harvard University Press.

Riskin, Carl. 1975. Surplus and stagnation in modern China. In *China's modern economy in historical perspective. See* Perkins 1975b.

Roemer, John. 1981. *Analytical foundations of Marxism.* New York: Cambridge University Press.

————. 1982a. *A general theory of exploitation and class.* Cambridge, Mass.: Harvard University Press.

————. 1982b. Methodological individualism and deductive Marxism. *Theory and Society* 11:513–20.

Roemer, John, ed. 1986. *Analytical Marxism.* Cambridge: Cambridge University Press.

Rosenberg, Alexander. 1988. *Philosophy of social science.* Boulder, Colo.: Westview.

Rotberg, Robert I., and Theodore K. Rabb, eds. 1986. *Population and economy: Population and history from the traditional to the modern world.* Cambridge: Cambridge University Press.

Roth, David. 1987. *Meanings and methods: A case for methodological pluralism in the social sciences.* Ithaca: Cornell University Press.

Rowe, William T. 1984. *Hankow: Commerce and society in a Chinese city, 1796–1889.* Stanford: Stanford University Press.

Rozman, Gilbert. 1973. *Urban networks in Ch'ing China and Tokugawa Japan.* Princeton: Princeton University Press.

————. 1977–78. China's traditional cities: A review article. *Pacific Affairs* 50:65–91.

————. 1982. *Population and marketing settlements in Ch'ing China.* Cambridge: Cambridge University Press.

Rudner, Richard. 1966. *Philosophy of social science.* Englewood Cliffs, N.J.: Prentice-Hall.

Rudolph, Susanne Hoeber. 1987. State formation in Asia. *Journal of Asian Studies* 46:731–46.

Russell, Clifford S., ed. 1979. *Collective decision making.* Baltimore: Johns Hopkins University Press.

Russell, Clifford S., and Norman K. Nicholson, eds. 1981. *Public choice and rural development.* Washington, D.C.: Resources for the Future.

Ryan, Alan, ed. 1973. *The philosophy of social explanation.* Oxford: Oxford University Press.

Sabel, Charles, and Jonathan Zeitlin. 1985. Historical alternatives to mass production: Politics, markets and technology in nineteenth-century industrialization. *Past and Present* 108:133–76.

Sahlins, Marshall. 1972. *Stone age economics.* New York: Aldine.

———. 1976. *Culture and practical reason.* Chicago: University of Chicago Press.

Salmon, Wesley C. 1984. *Scientific explanation and the causal structure of the world.* Princeton: Princeton University Press.

Samuelson, Paul. 1955. Diagrammatic exposition of a theory of public expenditure. *Review of Economics and Statistics* 37:350–56.

Sands, Barbara, and Ramon H. Myers. 1986. The spatial approach to Chinese history: A test. *Journal of Asian Studies* 45:721–43.

Schelling, Thomas C. 1978. *Micromotives and macrobehavior.* New York: Norton.

Schlumbohm, Jurgen. 1981. Relations of production—productive forces—crises in proto-industrialization. In *Industrialization before industrialization. See* Kriedte, Medick, and Schlumbohm 1981.

Schofield, Roger S. 1986. Through a glass darkly: *The population history of England* as an experiment in history. In *Population and economy. See* Rotberg and Rabb 1986.

Schoppa, R. Keith. 1982. *Chinese elites and political change: Zhejiang province in the early twentieth century.* Cambridge, Mass.: Harvard University Press.

Schultz, Theodore W. 1964. *Transforming traditional agriculture.* New Haven and London: Yale University Press.

Scott, James C. 1976. *The moral economy of the peasant.* New Haven and London: Yale University Press.

———. 1977a. Hegemony and the peasantry. *Politics and Society* 7:267–96.

———. 1977b. Protest and profanation: Agrarian revolt and the little tradition. *Theory and Society* 4:1–38, 211–46.

———. 1979. Revolution in the revolution: Peasants and commissars. *Theory and Society* 7:97–134.

———. 1985. *Weapons of the weak: Everyday forms of peasant resistance.* New Haven and London: Yale University Press.

Scriven, Michael. 1962. Explanations, predictions, and laws. In *Minnesota studies in the philosophy of science.* Vol. 3. *See* Feigl and Maxwell 1962.

Selden, Mark. 1971. *The Yenan way in revolutionary China.* Cambridge, Mass.: Harvard University Press.

Sen, A. K. 1970. *Collective choice and social welfare.* San Francisco: Holden-Day.

———. 1979. Rational fools. In *Philosophy and economic theory. See* Hahn and Hollis 1979.

———. 1982. *Choice, welfare, and measurement.* Cambridge, Mass.: MIT Press.

———. 1987. *On ethics and economics.* New York: Basil Blackwell.

Shanin, Teodor. 1985. *The roots of otherness: Russia's turn of century.* Vol. 1: *Russia as a Developing Society.* New Haven and London: Yale University Press.

Shaw, William. 1978. *Marx's theory of history.* Stanford: Stanford University Press.

———. 1984. Marxism, revolution and rationality. In *After Marx,* ed. Terence Ball and James Farr. Cambridge: Cambridge University Press.

Shubik, Martin. 1982. *Game theory in the social sciences: Concepts and solutions.* Cambridge, Mass.: MIT Press.

Shue, Henry. 1980. *Basic rights.* Princeton: Princeton University Press.

Shue, Vivienne. 1980. *Peasant China in transition: The dynamics of development toward socialism, 1949–1956.* Berkeley: University of California Press.

Simon, Herbert. 1971. Spurious correlation: A causal interpretation. In *Causal models in the social sciences. See* Blalock 1971.

———. 1979. From substantive to procedural rationality. In *Philosophy and economic theory,* ed. Frank Hahn and Martin Hollis. Oxford: Oxford University Press.

Sivin, Nathan. 1978. Imperial China: Has its present past a future? *Harvard Journal of Asiatic Studies* 38:449–80.

Skinner, G. William. 1964–65. Marketing and social structure in rural China. 3 parts. *Journal of Asian Studies* 24:3–43, 195–228, 363–99.

———. 1971. Chinese peasants and the closed community: An open and shut case. *Comparative Studies in Society and History* 13:270–81.

———. 1975. Review of Gilbert Rozman, *Urban networks in Ch'ing China and Tokugawa Japan. Journal of Asian Studies* 35:1.

———. 1977a. Cities and the hierarchy of local systems. In *The city in late imperial China. See* Skinner, ed. 1977.

———. 1977b. Regional urbanization in nineteenth-century China. In *The city in late imperial China. See* Skinner, ed. 1977.

———. 1985. Presidential address: The structure of Chinese history. *Journal of Asian Studies* 44:271–92.

———. 1987. Sichuan's population in the nineteenth century. *Late imperial China* 7:1–79.

———. n.d. The population geography of agrarian societies. Manuscript.

Skinner, G. William, ed. 1977. *The city in late imperial China.* Stanford: Stanford University Press.

Skocpol, Theda. 1979. *States and social revolutions.* Cambridge: Cambridge University Press.

Sober, Elliott. 1984. *The nature of selection.* Cambridge, Mass.: MIT Press.

Soboul, Albert. 1975. *The French Revolution, 1787–1799: From the storming of the Bastille to Napoleon.* New York: Vintage.

Ste. Croix, G. E. M. de. 1981. *The class struggle in the ancient Greek world: From the archaic age to the Arab conquests.* Ithaca: Cornell University Press.

———. 1984. Class in Marx's conception of history. *New Left Review* 146.

Stinchcombe, Arthur L. 1966. Agricultural enterprise and rural class relations. In *Class, status, and power. See* Bendix and Lipset 1966.

———. 1978. *Theoretical methods in social history.* New York: Academic Press.

Tai, Hue-Tam Ho. 1983. *Millenarianism and peasant politics in Vietnam.* Cambridge, Mass.: Harvard University Press.

Tawney, R. H. 1966. *Land and labor in China.* Boston: Beacon.

Taylor, Charles. 1985a. *Philosophy and the human sciences: Philosophical papers 2.* Cambridge: Cambridge University Press.

———. 1985b. Interpretation and the sciences of man. In *Philosophy and the human sciences. See* C. Taylor 1985a.

———. 1985c. Neutrality in political science. In *Philosophy and the human sciences. See* C. Taylor 1985a.

Taylor, Michael. 1976. *Anarchy and cooperation.* London: Wiley.

———. 1982. *Community, anarchy and liberty.* Cambridge: Cambridge University Press.

Thaxton, Ralph. 1983. *China turned rightside up: Revolutionary legitimacy in the peasant world.* New Haven and London: Yale University Press.

Thomas, David. 1979. *Naturalism and social science.* Cambridge: Cambridge University Press.

Thompson, E. P. 1963. *The making of th English working class.* New York: Vintage.

———. 1971. The moral economy of the English crowd in the eighteenth century. *Past and Present* 50:71–136.

———. 1975. The crime of anonymity. In *Albion's fatal tree: Crime and society in eighteenth-century England,* ed. Douglas Hay, Peter Linebaugh, and John Rule. New York: Pantheon.

———. 1978. *The poverty of theory and other essays.* New York: Monthly Review.

Tilly, Charles. 1964. *The Vendée.* Cambridge, Mass.: Harvard University Press.

———. 1984. *Big structures, large processes, huge comparisons.* New York: Russell Sage Foundation.

Tilly, Charles, Louise Tilly, and Richard Tilly. 1975. *The rebellious century, 1830–1930.* Cambridge, Mass.: Harvard University Press.

Twitchett, Denis, and John K. Fairbank, eds. 1978. *The Cambridge History of China.* Vol. 10: *Late Ch'ing, 1800–1911, Part 1.* Cambridge: Cambridge University Press.

Van Parijs, Philippe. 1981. *Evolutionary explanation in the social sciences.* Totowa, N.J.: Rowman and Littlefield.

———. 1983. Why Marxist economics needs microfoundations. *Review of Radical Political Economics* 15:111–24.

————. 1984. Marxism's central puzzle. In *After Marx*, ed. Terence Ball and James Farr. Cambridge: Cambridge University Press.

Vlastos, Stephen. 1986. *Peasant protests and uprisings in Tokugawa Japan.* Berkeley: University of California Press.

Von Wright, Georg Henrik. 1971. *Explanation and understanding.* Ithaca: Cornell University Press.

Wagner, Rudolf G. 1982. *Reenacting the heavenly vision: The role of religion in the Taiping rebellion.* Berkeley: Institute of East Asian Studies, University of California.

Wakeman, Frederick, Jr. 1985. *The great enterprise: The Manchu reconstruction of imperial order in seventeenth-century China.* 2 vols. Berkeley: University of California Press.

Watkins, J. W. N. 1968. Methodological individualism and social tendencies. In *Readings in the philosophy of the social sciences*, ed. May Brodbeck. New York: Macmillan.

Watson, Ruby. 1985. *Inequality among brothers.* Cambridge: Cambridge University Press.

Weber, Max. 1949. *The methodology of the social sciences.* Trans. and ed. E. Shils and H. A. Finch. New York: Free Press.

Wiens, Thomas B. 1975. Review of Ramon H. Myers, *The Chinese peasant economy. Modern Asian Studies* 9:279–88.

Willmott, W. E., ed. 1972. *Economic organization in Chinese society.* Stanford: Stanford University Press.

Wilson, Bryan R., ed. 1970. *Rationality.* Oxford: Blackwell.

Wittgenstein, Ludwig. 1953. *Philosophical investigations.* New York: Macmillan.

Wolf, Arthur P. 1985. Fertility in prerevolutionary rural China. In *Family and population in East Asian history*, ed. Susan B. Hanley and Arthur Wolf. Stanford: Stanford University Press.

Wolf, Arthur P., ed. 1978. *Studies in Chinese society.* Stanford: Stanford University Press.

Wolf, Eric. 1966. *Peasants.* Englewood Cliffs, N.J.: Prentice Hall.

————. 1969. *Peasant wars of the twentieth century.* New York: Harper and Row.

————. 1986. The vicissitudes of the closed corporate peasant community. *American Ethnologist* 13:325–29.

Wong, David. 1984. *Moral relativity.* Berkeley: University of California Press.

Wrigley, E. Anthony, and Roger S. Schofield. 1981. *The population history of England, 1541–1871: A reconstruction.* Cambridge, Mass.: Harvard University Press.

Index